# EGYPTIAN CIVILIZATION ITS SUMERIAN ORIGIN & REAL CHRONOLOGY
## AND SUMERIAN ORIGIN OF EGYPTIAN HIEROGLYPHS

BY

## L. A. WADDELL
LL.D., C.B., C.I.E.

AUTHOR OF "THE MAKERS OF CIVILIZATION IN RACE AND HISTORY,"
"A SUMER-ARYAN DICTIONARY," "THE ARYAN ORIGIN OF THE ALPHABET"
"THE BRITISH EDDA," ETC., ETC., ETC.

*WITH 21 PLATES, 97 TEXT ILLUSTRATIONS & 2 MAPS*

# PREFACE

> "What were the People by whom it (Egyptian Civilization) was developed, the Country whence they came, the Race to which they belonged, is to-day unknown."
> —Sir G. MASPERO, *Dawn of Civilization,* 1922, 45.
>
> "In dealing with Egyptian Chronology it must always be remembered that, comparatively speaking, little is known about it."—Sir WALLIS BUDGE, *The Book of Kings of Egypt,* I, xlii.

IN spite of the advances in our knowledge of Ancient Egypt which decipherment of many of the monuments of the old Pharaohs has made possible, two basic questions of the first magnitude still remain outstanding in as great uncertainty as in the days of Herodotus. These are the question of the Origin of the Civilization of the Country, and the question of the Dates of its Kings and Dynasties.

As regards the former, opinions differ as to whether civilization was indigenous or imposed from without. And, although on the whole the tendency is towards belief that the Egyptians, like so many other races both ancient and modern, owed their culture to conquest by more advanced and intrusive peoples, yet who the conquerors were and when the invasions took place has remained unknown owing to lack of evidence on which to base a judgment. And a like absence of evidence as regards chronology has made the dating of the early and most of the later Pharaohs an affair of guesswork, and led equally able and conscientious inquirers to fix the period of Menes and his First Dynasty at dates differing from one another by as much as over two millenniums of years.

In my recently published *Makers of Civilization*, I showed incidentally the bearing upon Egyptian problems of my collation of the Mesopotamian inscriptions and official King-Lists of the Sumerians (the oldest known civilized people) with the official King-Lists of the Early Aryans of the "Caucasian race" in the Indian Purānas. And in the present work I have sought to meet the requirements and

## viii EGYPTIAN CIVILIZATION OF SUMER ORIGIN

expressed wishes of Egyptologists by supplying them with a statement in full of the new evidence as to the real date and origin of the Nile Valley Civilization and the historical personalities and origin and real dates of its unknown introducers and early developers, disengaged from the extraneous matters with which the subject was necessarily mixed up in the larger treatise. For all the latest excavations in Mesopotamia and the Indus Valley, further confirm those discoveries.

What put me on the track of the new evidence was the discovery that a great deal in the ancient Indian Epics and Vedas regarding the Early Aryans, hitherto considered fabulous is historic. Comparing the King-Lists of the Early Aryans in the Purānas with the records of the Sumerian Mesopotamian kings on their inscribed monuments and in the official Mesopotamian King-Lists, I observed that the two records, Early Aryan and Sumerian, are in entire agreement from the First Dynasty, Aryan and Sumerian, down through the long period of over two thousand years to the opening of the classic Greek epoch in Europe ; and that the identity was complete not only in the names, titles, order of succession and exploits of the kings, but extended to such minute details as the names of their consorts and sons, and to the culture, language, writing, religion, symbolism, arts and industries of the peoples over whom they ruled.

The official King-Lists, Indian and Mesopotamian, show Menes and his predecessors and successors in his First Dynasty in the same chronological order and position, with the names and titles they bear in the Egyptian records. The Sumerian Mesopotamian and Indus Valley script of those kings is the same as that used by the pre-dynastic and First Dynasty Pharaohs in their monumental inscriptions. The Egyptian Hieroglyphs are discovered to be a slightly modified conventional form of the Sumerian diagrammatic picture-writing which came into use gradually during the rule of Menes and his immediate successors, and to have the same phonetic values as their parent picture-signs in the Sumerian. And the radical words in Ancient Egyptian are of Sumerian origin, though later they became adapted to a large extent to the Semitic speech and idioms of the aborigines.

The above discoveries enable us to explain and definitely

date for the first time Egyptian Civilization from the conquest of the country by the pre-dynastic Pharaohs, now shown to have been Sumerian emperors, about the year 2780 B.C. How the culture thus introduced into Egypt acquired a local conventional complexion disguising its exotic source and affinities; how the Sumerian rulers of Egypt came to be called pre-dynastic Pharaohs; how Menes, Sumerian crown-prince, and governor of the Sumerian Indus Valley colony, erected Egypt into an independent kingdom and preserved its independence within the Mesopotamian empire when he succeeded eventually to the throne after his father's death; how, as the Min or Minos sea-emperor of Greek legend, he annexed and civilized Crete and extended his rule westwards to the Pillars of Hercules and Britain, all this as well as the hitherto wholly unknown ancestry and real dates of Menes and his dynastic successors is duly disclosed by the new evidence.

The accounts of Menes or "Manj-the-Warrior" in the Egyptian monuments and King-Lists and of "Manis-the-Warrior" in the Sumerian monuments and King-Lists are identical to a degree that precludes all doubt as to their being actually records of the same personalities and events. Menes, his emperor-father, and two of his successors in the First Egyptian Dynasty boast in their Egyptian monuments of being descendants of the first king of the First Sumerian Dynasty; and the name given to this common ancestor in the Egyptian inscriptions is the same as that given him in the Sumerian Kish Chronicle. And in the Indian Epics Manja (or Menes), as well as his father and descendants are expressly stated to have been lineal descendants of the first Aryan king of corresponding name to the Sumerian.

The unity as regards type and source of the ancient civilizations of Sumerian Mesopotamia, India and Egypt is in keeping with the physique of the ruling people in all three countries, which is shown by their portraits, sculptures and skeletal remains to have been of the long-headed, fair, grey or blue-eyed type recognized by moderns as marking the Aryan section of the Caucasian race.

The "Caucasian" type of the early Sumerian skeletal remains exhumed from the graves at Ur has been duly attested anthropologically by Sir Arthur Keith; and the

# x EGYPTIAN CIVILIZATION OF SUMER ORIGIN

same type is also found in the tombs and portraits of the early dynastic ruling race in Egypt, apart from the evidence of their positively established Aryan genealogies.

Unfortunately however, the terminology for this racial type, to which the Sumerians belong as well as the Early Aryans, classic Greeks and Romans and many of the modern people of Europe, is in a very confused state through anthropologists including "Mediterraneans" amongst the "Caucasians," and using both terms ambiguously. "Mediterranean Race" is at present used to include two totally distinct racial types, namely the *narrow*-browed dark long-heads, the type of the Iberian, S. Italian, Corsican and Aegean aborigines, *i.e.* the Mediterranean Race proper ; and secondly the *broad*-browed fairer long-heads comprising the classic Greeks and Romans, Achaians, Ionians, Phœnicians, Berbers and Hamites on the south coast of the Mediterranean, whose head-forms are essentially of the type of the Sumerians, Indo-Aryans (and thus inferentially of the Early Aryans) and the type of the Goths, Anglo-Saxons and Nordics, and also as we shall find of Menes and his dynasty and his ancestral Pharaohs who brought civilization into Egypt. In the absence of any better name for the broad-browed long-headed type, I have called it "Aryan," after its most characteristic group. In any case, the term "Nordic Race" is quite inapplicable as a synonym for "Aryan Race," as the Norse are only a late specialized branch of one section of the Aryans. In former works, following the current fashion, I was led or misled into using that term occasionally in such synonymous sense, though usually under protest as "the so-called Nordic race." But that term should now be wholly discarded in this connexion, if we would avoid needless confusion and anachronism. And after all, the question of the racial affinity of the Sumerians is wholly secondary to that of their historical identity with the race of Menes and his dynasty in Egypt, now discovered and established.

Lastly, the newly found real date for the accession of Menes to the throne in Egypt at about 2704 B.C., is in full agreement with the form of the culture of his dynasty, which is distinctively of the Sumerian type of that period.

L. A. WADDELL.

*September 1st,* 1930.

# CONTENTS

| | PAGE |
|---|---|
| PREFACE . . . . . . . | vii |
| ABBREVIATIONS FOR CHIEF REFERENCES . . | xix |

CHAP.

I. MENES' HISTORICITY DISCOVERED WITH ANCESTORS AS PREDYNASTIC PHARAOHS:

Disclosing Menes as son of the world-emperor " Sargon-the-Great " of Mesopotamia and his Date, about 2704 B.C. . . . .  1–10

II. " SARGON - THE - GREAT " AND HIS FATHER AND GRANDFATHER AS PREDYNASTIC PHARAOHS:

Disclosing his Annexation or Reconquest of Egypt, *c.* 2714 B.C. His Egyptian Tomb Inscriptions in Sumerian deciphered. His titles " Pharaoh," Kad (" Ka "), Ukus, " Goth " and Aryan Race. And his Father and Grandfather as Predynastic Pharaohs " Ro " and " Khetm " with their real Dates, about 2765 and 2780 B.C. respectively . . 11–31

III. MENES' LOST HISTORY AND ACHIEVEMENTS IN EGYPT RECOVERED:

Disclosing his identity with Manis of Mesopotamia. His Sumerian Governorship of Elam and Indus Valley. His Seizure of Egypt from his Father-emperor. His establishment of First Egyptian Dynasty, *c.* 2704 B.C., with a fully-fledged Sumerian Civilization. His Sea- and World-Empire, Sun-worship and Aryan Race  32–59

IV. MENES' TRAGIC DEATH ON SEA-EXPLORATION IN ATLANTIC ISLAND, *c.* 2641 B.C.:

With Decipherment of Sumerian Inscriptions on Ebony Labels in his tomb in Egypt . 60–70

xii EGYPTIAN CIVILIZATION OF SUMER ORIGIN

CHAP. PAGE
V. MENES OR MIN AS KING MINOS OF CRETE AND REAL DATE OF MINOAN CIVILIZATION, *c.* 2700 B.C. . . . . . . 71–75

VI. MENES' OR MANJ'S FIRST DYNASTY OF EGYPT IDENTICAL WITH MANIS-TUSU'S DYNASTY IN MESOPOTAMIA :

Also identity in Indo-Aryan King-Lists and Chronicles . . . . . . 76–82

VII. SECOND KING OF FIRST DYNASTY, NARMAR, IDENTICAL WITH NARAM, SECOND KING OF MANIS' DYNASTY IN MESOPOTAMIA, *c.* 2640 B.C. :

Disclosing his Sonship to Menes. His prehistory and achievements. His Sumerian Inscriptions in Egypt and Indus Valley deciphered and his title " Goth " . . 83–100

VIII. THIRD KING OF FIRST DYNASTY, GANI, GUNI OR " KHENT " IDENTICAL WITH GANI, GUNI OR GAN-ERI, THIRD KING OF MANIS' DYNASTY IN MESOPOTAMIA, *c.* 2584 B.C. :

With his Sumerian Inscriptions in Egypt and Indus Valley deciphered . . . . 101–105

IX. FOURTH KING OF FIRST DYNASTY, BAGID OR " ZET," ALSO SUMER EMPEROR, *c.* 2560 B.C. :

With his Sumerian Inscriptions in Egypt deciphered . . . . . . 106–107

X. FIFTH KING OF FIRST DYNASTY, DUDU, DAN OR " DEN," IDENTICAL WITH DUDU OF MANIS' DYNASTY IN MESOPOTAMIA, *c.* 2557 B.C. :

With his Sumerian Inscriptions in Egypt and Indus Valley deciphered. His title of " Usaphaidos." His invocation of the Sun-archangel Tasia or Tascio as in Sumerian, Asia Minor, Indus Valley and Ancient Briton Inscriptions. And his Aryan titles of " Ukus " and " Goth " . . . . . . 108–121

## CONTENTS

CHAP.
XI. SIXTH AND SEVENTH KINGS OF FIRST DYNASTY, BIDI OR " MIE-BIDOS " AND " SAMPATI " AS TRIBUTARY LOCAL KINGS OF EGYPT . 122–123

XII. EIGHTH OR LAST KING OF FIRST DYNASTY, SHUDUR KIB, " QA " OR " QEBH," IDENTICAL WITH SHUDUR KIB, LAST KING OF MANIS' DYNASTY IN MESOPOTAMIA, c. 2536–2527 B.C. :

With his Sumerian Inscriptions in Egypt and Indus Valley deciphered. And his Aryan titles of " Ukush " and " Goth " . . . 124–129

XIII. COMPLETE IDENTITY OF MENES' DYNASTY IN EGYPT WITH MANIS' IMPERIAL DYNASTY IN MESOPOTAMIA AND IN INDO-ARYAN KING-LISTS, AND SUMERIAN OR ARYAN ORIGIN OF EGYPTIAN CIVILIZATION . 130–131

XIV. SECOND EGYPTIAN DYNASTY WITH RISE OF INDEPENDENT KINGDOM OF EGYPT . 132–138

XV. REAL CHRONOLOGY OF EARLY EGYPT AND ITS CIVILIZATION AND KINGS RECOVERED :

With fixed Dates for Predynastic and First Dynasty Kings and basic Date of Menes as c. 2704 B.C. . . . . . . 139–158

XVI. SUMERIAN ORIGIN OF EGYPTIAN HIEROGLYPHS AND OF RADICAL, CULTURAL AND OFFICIAL WORDS IN THE EGYPTIAN LANGUAGE . . . . . . 159–162

XVII. MYTHOLOGY OF EARLY DYNASTIC EGYPT ESSENTIALLY IDENTICAL WITH SUMERIAN, ARYAN AND GOTHIC . . . . 163–166

XVIII. DIFFUSION OF SUMERIAN CULTURE BY SEA-FARING ARYAN PHŒNICIANS, SO-CALLED HAMITES v. EGYPTIANS . . 167–173

XIX. HISTORICAL EFFECTS OF THE DISCOVERIES 174–178

## APPENDICES

                                                                       PAGE

I. Sanskrit Text of Mahā-Bhārata Epic *re* Menes and his Dynasty in Egypt . 179

II. Indus Valley Seals of Sargon and his father with titles of " Pharaoh " and " Goth " and mentioning Egypt deciphered . . 179–184

III. Indus Valley Sumerian Seals of Menes with titles of " Governor," " Pharaoh " and " Goth " deciphered . . . . 184–188

IV. Great Ebony Label from Menes' Tomb at Abydos with Sumerian Inscription deciphered . . . . . . 188–195

V. Indus Valley Sumerian Seals of First Egyptian Dynasty Kings with titles of " Governor," " Pharaoh," " Goth," etc., and giving genealogies, etc. . . . 196–210

INDEX . . . . . . . . 211–223

# LIST OF ILLUSTRATIONS

## PLATES

PLATE  
                                                                                               FACING PAGE

I. Contemporary alabaster inscribed statue of King Menes, Founder of First Dynasty of Egypt, as King Manis-the-Warrior, Sumerian world-emperor, c. 2655 B.C. Found at Susa in Elam. Now in the Louvre. (After D.P. x. Pl. I) . . . . . . . . FRONTISPIECE

II. Sumerian Origin of Egyptian Hieroglyphs (Pl. A) . . 8

III. General plan of Tombs of Predynastic and First Dynasty Pharaohs at Abydos showing Sargon's Tomb. (After Petrie) 20

IV. Indus Valley Seals of Sargon and his Father as " Pharaohs." (From photos after Sir J. Marshall) . . . . 30

V. Indus Valley Seals of Pharaoh Menes and his son Narmar. (From photos after Sir J. Marshall) . . . . 42

VI. Lesser Labels from Menes' Tomb. (After Sir F. Petrie) . 58

VII. Great Ebony Label from Menes' Tomb at Abydos. (After Sir Flinders Petrie.) For decipherment, see App. IV. . 62

VIII. Decipherment of Menes' Tomb Lesser Labels . . . 70

IX. Naram Enzu's Victory Stele (in Louvre), about 2620 B.C. . 84

X. Naram Enzu in bas-relief, c. 2600 B.C. . . . . 86

XI. Indus Valley Seals of Pharaohs Ner-Mar, Ganeri (or Dudu Dan, Bagid, Shem and Shudur-Kib or Qa. From photos after Sir J. Marshall) . . . . . . . 88

XII. Narmar's Slate Palette of Victory from Egypt, about 2630 B.C. (After J. E. Quibell and Sir F. Petrie) . . . 92

XIII. Plan of Dudu's Tomb in Egypt. (After Petrie) . . 114

XIV. King Dudu's (Den-Setui) Ebony Labels from Tomb at Abydos, about 2540 B.C. (After Sir Flinders Petrie) . 116

XV. Indus Valley Seals of Pharaoh Shudur-Kib or Qa and of Uri-Mush. (From photos after Sir J. Marshall) . . 124

XVI. Plan of Shudur-Kib's Tomb at Abydos . . . . 126

XVII. Shudur-Kib's (Qa-Sen) Ivory Labels from Tomb at Abydos, about 2520 B.C. (After Sir Flinders Petrie) . . . 127

XVIII. Sumerian Origin of Egyptian Hieroglyphs (Pl. B) . . 158

XIX. Sumerian Origin of Egyptian Hieroglyphs (Pl. C) . . 160

XX. Sumerian Origin of Egyptian Hieroglyphs (Pl. D) . . 160

XXI. Sumerian Origin of Egyptian Hieroglyphs (Pl. E) . . 162

## xvi EGYPTIAN CIVILIZATION OF SUMER ORIGIN

### TEXT ILLUSTRATIONS

| FIG. | | PAGE |
|---|---|---|
| 1. | King " Ro's " Name from his Tomb at Abydos | 15 |
| 2. | Name of Predynastic Pharaoh " Ro " deciphered as BAU or BAKU or PURU-GIN | 16 |
| 3. | King " Khetm's " Name deciphered as *Tukh, Dukhu or Tekhi* | 18 |
| 4. | Sargon's Sumerian Inscription as Pharaoh at Abydos, on a Jar, about 2670 B.C. (After Sir F. Petrie) | 19 |
| 5. | Sargon's Inscription on Tomb of his Queen " The Lady Ash " at Abydos, on a Jar, about 2700 B.C. (After Sir F. Petrie) | 19 |
| 6. | Sargon's Tomb Inscription as " *Gin* or *Sha-Gin* the Ukussi " at Abydos deciphered | 23 |
| 7. | Sargon's Queen's Tomb Inscription at Abydos deciphered | 25 |
| 8. | Sealing of King Gin or " Sargon " at Abydos. (After Petrie) | 26 |
| 9. | King Gin's or " Sargon's " Abydos Sealing deciphered | 26 |
| 10. | Statue of Manis-Tusu (or Menes) in alabaster. From Susa in Elam. (After D.P. x. Pl. I) | 39 |
| 11. | Menes' Title of *Aha* or *Akha* in Egypt. (After Sir F. Petrie) | 57 |
| 12. | Menes' Title of Tusu-Menna on Egyptian Label Inscription deciphered | 58 |
| 13. | Menes' Great Ebony Label Tomb Inscription | 62 |
| 14. | The Fatal Fly on Menes' Tomb Label as a Wasp or Hornet | 64 |
| 15. | Narmar or Narâm or " The Strong Wild Bull " son of Menes or Manis as Mino's son Mino-Taur. From slate palette | 72 |
| 16. | Naram's Name in Egypt as " Narmar " | 85 |
| 17. | Sealing of Narmar. (After Petrie) | 85 |
| 18. | Narmar's Slate Palette, Reverse | 91 |
| 19. | Narmar's Palette Inscription over enemy dead deciphered | 93 |
| 20. | Narmar's Palette Standard Inscriptions, Nos. 1 and 2 | 94 |
| 21. | Narmar's Standards, Nos. 3 and 4 | 95 |
| 22. | Inscription on Narmar's Standard No. 1 deciphered | 95 |
| 23. | Inscription on Narmar's Standard No. 2 deciphered | 96 |
| 24. | Narmar's Standard Inscriptions, Nos. 3 and 4, deciphered | 97 |
| 25. | Ivory Label of Third King of Menes' or First Dynasty of Egypt. (After Sir F. Petrie) | 103 |
| 26. | Sealing of Third King of First Dynasty of Egypt. (After Petrie) | 103 |
| 27. | Third King's Name on Ivory Label deciphered | 104 |
| 28. | Third King's Name on Sealing deciphered | 105 |
| 29. | Stele of 4th King of Menes' Dynasty. (After Sir F. Petrie) | 106 |
| 30. | Seal of Fourth King " Zet " in Egypt. (After Sir F. Petrie) | 106 |
| 31. | Seal of Fourth King of Menes' Dynasty deciphered | 107 |
| 32. | King Dudu or " Den's " Portrait on a label from Abydos | 109 |
| 33. | Personal Name of Dudu or Dundu in Fifth King's Inscriptions in Egypt. (After Sir F. Petrie) | 110 |
| 34. | The Sumerian Mound-sign in Egyptian=*Du* or *Dun* as in Sumerian | 111 |
| 35. | Inscription of Dudu or Dundu from lid of a seal box. (After Sir F. Petrie) | 113 |
| 36. | Inscription of Dundu with title *Busahap* on seal-box deciphered | 113 |
| 37. | Line 1 of Col. 1 of Dudu's Tomb Ebony Label No. 1 deciphered | 116 |
| 38. | Line 2 of Col. 1 of Dudu's Tomb Ebony Label No. 1 deciphered | 117 |
| 39. | Line 2 continued of Dudu's Tomb Ebony Label No. 1 deciphered | 118 |
| 40. | Line 3 of Col. 1 of Dudu's Tomb Label No. 1 deciphered | 119 |

# LIST OF ILLUSTRATIONS xvii

| FIG. | | PAGE |
|---|---|---|
| 41. | Line 1 of Col. 2 of Dudu's Label No. 1 deciphered . . . | 119 |
| 42. | Line 2 of Col. 2 of Dudu's Label No. 1 deciphered . . . | 120 |
| 42A. | Tasia or Reshef or "Tascio," the Resurrecting Archangel . | 121 |
| 43. | Clay Sealing of Sixth King of First Dynasty of Egypt. (After Sir F. Petrie) . . . . . . . . . . | 122 |
| 44. | Name of Sixth King of First Dynasty of Egypt deciphered . | 123 |
| 45. | Name of last King of Menes' Dynasty Shudur Kib on Ivory Label A deciphered . . . . . . . . . | 127 |
| 46. | Inscription of Shudur Kib on Ivory Label B., Cols. 4 and 5, deciphered . . . . . . . . . . | 128 |
| 47. | Clay Sealings of King Shudur Kib in Egypt. (After Sir F. Petrie) | 128 |
| 48. | Name on Sealings A deciphered . . . . . . . | 129 |
| 49. | Captive on Ivory gaming-reed of King Shudur Kib or Qa's period. (After Petrie) . . . . . . . | 131 |
| 50. | Egyptian Cross Button Amulets of Sumerian type . . | 138 |
| 51. | Seal of "Sargon "-the-Great as Sag, The Seer, the Kad, the One Overlord, the *Gut*, deciphered . . . . . . | 180 |
| 52. | Sargon's Father's Seal as Puru Gina, of Mushir (Egypt) and Magan, deciphered . . . . . . . . | 181 |
| 53. | Sargon's Father's Seal as The Overlord Puru Par-Gin at Uridu Land deciphered . . . . . . . . . | 181 |
| 54. | Sargon's Seal as Sharu-Gin of Uriki (Akkad) Land deciphered . | 182 |
| 55. | Sargon's Seal as Shar-Gin, the Great Khāti deciphered . . | 182 |
| 56. | Sargon's Seal as Sharum-Gin, The *Gut*, at Agdu Land deciphered | 183 |
| 57. | Sargon's Seal as Gan the Pur (Pharaoh) of Khamaesshi Land (Egypt) at Agdu Land deciphered . . . . . | 183 |
| 58. | Sargon's Seal as Gan, the Pur, the Paru *Gut* at Uridu Land, deciphered . . . . . . . . . . | 183 |
| 59. | Menes' Seal as Overlord-Companion Aha, the son of Sha-Gani the Bara (or Pharaoh) at Edin Land, deciphered. . . | 185 |
| 60. | Menes' Seal as Under-King Companion Mānshu the Bara (Pharaoh) at Agdu deciphered . . . . . . | 185 |
| 61. | Menes' Seal as Overlord-Companion Aha-Men deciphered . | 186 |
| 62. | Menes' Seal as Under-King Companion Aha-Men, The *Gut*, at Agdu Land deciphered . . . . . . . | 186 |
| 63. | Menes' Seal as The One Overlord Aha, The Son of the *Gut* Gin, at Agdu Land deciphered . . . . . . . | 186 |
| 64. | Menes' Seal as The Overlord-Companion Aha-Man (or -Min), the son of Azu-Esh-tar Gin deciphered, compare Fig. 51 . | 187 |
| 65. | Menes' Seal as Aha, The Overthrower of King Mush, deciphered | 187 |
| 66. | Menes' Seal as Under-King Companion Aha of Ma-esh-gan and Mush(-sir ?) [Egypt], deciphered . . . . . | 187 |
| 67. | Seal of Aha-Mena at Agdu Land deciphered . . . . | 188 |
| 68. | Abydos Tomb Great Ebony Label of Menes as King Minas, The Pharaoh of Mushsir Land (Egypt) of the Two Crowns, Line 1 deciphered . . . . . . . . | 189 |
| 69. | Menes' Tomb Great Ebony Label Line 1 concluded decipherment | 190 |
| 70. | Menes' Tomb Great Ebony Label Line 2 deciphered . . | 191 |
| 71. | Menes' Tomb Great Ebony Label Line 2 concluded decipherment | 192 |
| 72. | Menes' Tomb Great Ebony Label Line 3 deciphered . . | 192 |
| 73. | Menes' Tomb Great Ebony Label Line 4 deciphered . . | 194 |
| 74. | Menes' Tomb Great Ebony Label Line 4 concluded decipherment | 195 |
| 75. | Narmar's Seal as Under-King Companion Mar-Neru, The *Gut*, at Elephant Land deciphered . . . . . . | 198 |

## xviii EGYPTIAN CIVILIZATION OF SUMER ORIGIN

| FIG. | | PAGE |
|---|---|---|
| 76. | Narmar's Seal as The *Gut* of the Lower Land, Nera, the *Gut* at Agdu Land, deciphered . . . . . . | 199 |
| 77. | Seal of Under-King Companion Marrū, son of The Lofty *Gut* of the Deep Waters, the Ruler, deciphered . . . . | 199 |
| 78. | Seal of Under-King Companion (son ?) of the Heavenly Pharaoh, Nerau of Agdu Land, deciphered . . . . | 200 |
| 79. | Sha-Gin (II) or Gan-Eri's Seal as Ganeri son of The Land, The Overlord Ruler at Agdu Land, deciphered . . . . | 201 |
| 80. | Sha-Gin's (II) Seal as Under-King Companion Sha-Gin at Agdu deciphered . . . . . . . . | 201 |
| 81. | Sha-Gin's (II) Seal as Lord Gin at Agdu deciphered . . | 201 |
| 82. | Sha-Gin's (II) Seal as Under King-Companion Gan of Great Khamaesh, King Dili the Ruler *Gut*, deciphered . . . | 202 |
| 83. | Bag-Eri's Seal as of the House of Mar, the Lord of the Deep at Uridu Land deciphered . . . . . . . | 202 |
| 84. | Dudu's Seal as Dudu Dan, The Son of Gan-Eri, The Minister of the One Overlord at Agdu Land deciphered . . . | 203 |
| 85. | Dudu's Seal as Dan, The Son of Gan-the-Second of the House of Aha and Ner the Ukus, The Gut, deciphered . . . | 204 |
| 86. | Shudur Kib's Seal as Kibbu-Shuha, Son of the House of Aha at Agdu Land, deciphered . . . . . . . | 205 |
| 87. | Shudur Kib's Seal as Kib the Pharaoh, The Overlord at Agdu Land deciphered . . . . . . . . | 205 |
| 88. | Shudur Kib's Seal 1st line as Kibbu, The devotee of Fire, The *Gut* Kibbu of Šargin the Gut, deciphered (contd. in 89) . | 206 |
| 89. | Shudur Kib's Seal 2nd line continued decipherment as " Son of Dan, Ruler of The Deep Waters at Uriki (or Uri-du) Land " . | 206 |
| 90. | Amulet Seal of Kibbu as Kibbu, Kib, The Gut deciphered . | 207 |
| 91. | Amulet Seal continuation deciphered . . . . . | 207 |
| 92. | Shudur Kib's Seal as Kib, The Pharaoh of The Garden (of Edin) at Agdu Land deciphered . . . . . . | 208 |
| 93. | Shudur Kib's Seal as Kibbu, Lord of The Deep Waters, Son of Aha Men, deciphered . . . . . . . | 208 |
| 94. | Shudur Kib's Seal as Qa, King of Ma-esh-gan (and) Mush(-sir) [Egypt], deciphered . . . . . . . . | 209 |
| 95. | Seal of The *Gut* Shu, The Son of Pharaoh Kib deciphered . | 209 |
| 96. | Uri-Mush's Seal as The One Overlord, The Great Hero, deciphered . . . . . . . . . | 210 |

### MAPS

| | | |
|---|---|---|
| I. | Relation of Koptos and Egypt to Mesopotamia, Asia Minor and India, showing old Trade-Routes . . . . | 4 |
| II. | Relation of Sumerian Indus Valley Colony to Mesopotamia and Egypt . . . . . . . . . . | 36 |

# ABBREVIATIONS

### OF CHIEF REFERENCES

| | |
|---|---|
| AE. | Ancient Egypt. Ed. Sir W. M. Flinders Petrie, London. |
| B. | Origin and Development of Babylonian Writing. G. A. Barton, Leipzig, 1913. |
| BD. | Egyptian Hieroglyphic Dictionary. Sir E. Wallis Budge, 1920. |
| BE. | A History of Egypt. J. H. Breasted, 1925. |
| BHE. | History of the Egyptian People. Sir E. Wallis Budge, 1914. |
| BK. | Book of the Kings of Egypt, I. Sir E. Wallis Budge, 1908. |
| Br. | Classified List of Sumerian Ideographs. R. Brünnow, Leyden, 1889. |
| BSK. | Sea Kings of Crete. J. Baikie, 1920. |
| CAH. | Cambridge Ancient History, I. 2nd Ed., 1924. |
| CIWA. | Cuneiform Inscripts., W. Asia. H. Rawlinson and T. G. Pinches. |
| CT. | Cuneiform Texts in the British Museum. |
| DP. | Délégation en Perse Mémoires. |
| EPM. | The Palace of Minos. Sir A. Evans, 1921. |
| ERE. | Encyclopædia of Religion and Ethics. J. Hastings. |
| FB. | Die Boghaz Koi Text-Umshrift, II, 1. Leipzig, 1922. |
| FD. | Documentes Pre-Sargoniques. A de la Fuye. |
| GH. | Hieroglyphs. F. L. Griffith, 1898. |
| HCC. | Clavis Cuneorum. G. Howardy, Lipsia, 1904 f. |
| HNE. | Ancient History of Near East. H. R. Hall, 1918. |
| HOB. | Old Babylonian Inscriptions. H. V. Hilprecht, 1896. |
| JEA. | Journal of Egyptian Archæology. |
| KC. | Chronology of Early Babylonian Kings. L. W. King, 1907. |
| KHS. | History of Sumer and Akkad. L. W. King, 1916. |
| KTA. | Keilschrift text aus Assur. Inhalts. 1920. |
| LMJ. | Museum Journal. Univ. Pennsylvania, 1920, art. L. Legrain. |
| M. | Seltene Assyrische Ideogramme. B. Meissner, 1910. |
| MBt. | Mahā-Bhārata. |
| MD. | Dictionary of Assyrian Language. W. Muss-Arnolt, Berlin, 1905. |
| MKI. | Vedic Index. Macdonell & Keith, 1912. |
| MDC. | Dawn of Civilization. G. Maspero, 1922. |
| MWD. | Sanskrit-English Dictionary. Monier-Williams, 1899. |
| PB. | Babylonian Tablets, Berens Collect. T. G. Pinches, 1915. |
| PH. | Egyptian Hieroglyphs. Lady H. Petrie, 1927. |
| PHE. | History of Egypt. Sir Flinders Petrie, 1923-1925. |
| PHT. | Historical Texts. Univ. Pennsylvania. A. Poebel, 1914 f. |
| PRT. | Royal Tombs, I and II. Univ. Pennsylvania. A. Poebel, 1901. |
| PSL. | Sumerian Lexicon. J. D. Prince, 1908. |
| RA. | Revue d'Assyriologie. Paris. |
| RB. | Early Babylonian History. H. Radau, New York, 1900. |
| RV. | Rig Veda. |

## xx EGYPTIAN CIVILIZATION OF SUMER ORIGIN

| | |
|---|---|
| SMR. | The Mediterranean Race. G. Sergi, 1901. |
| STE. | Textes élamites-sémitiques. V. Scheil. |
| TDC. | Les Chronologie des Dynasties de Sumer et d'Accad. F. T. Dangin, 1918. |
| UE. | Ur Excavations, I. H. R. Hall and C. L. Woolley, 1927. |
| WAOA. | Aryan Origin of the Alphabet. L. A. Waddell, 1927. |
| WBC. | Weld-Blundell Collection Cuneiform Texts. Oxford, 1923. |
| WBE. | The British Edda. L. A. Waddell, 1930. |
| WISD. | Indo-Sumerian Seals Deciphered. L. A. Waddell, 1925. |
| WMC. | Makers of Civilization in Race and History. L. A. Waddell, 1929. |
| WPOB. | Phœnician Origin of Britons, Scots and Anglo-Saxons. L. A. Waddell, 1924. |
| WS. | The Sumerians. C. L. Woolley, 1928. |
| WSAD. | Sumer-Aryan Dictionary, A-F. L. A. Waddell, 1927. |
| WSC. | Seal Cylinders of W. Asia. W. H. Ward, Washington, 1900. |
| WVP. | Vishnu Purana. Trans. H. H. Wilson; ed. F. Hall, 1864. |

# THE SUMERIAN ORIGIN OF EGYPTIAN CIVILIZATION

I

MENES' HISTORICITY DISCOVERED WITH ANCESTORS AS PREDYNASTIC PHARAOHS

*Disclosing Menes as son of the world-emperor " Sargon-the-Great " of Mesopotamia & his Date, about 2704 B.C.*

> " All that we know of the first of the Pharaohs—Menes—beyond the fact of his existence is practically nil."—MASPERO, *Dawn of Civilization*, 1922, 233.
> " Menes appears to be a ' conflate ' personage of legend."—*Cambridge Anc. Hist.*, 1924. I, 267.

HITHERTO Menes, the traditional founder of the First Dynasty of Egypt, although regularly cited in the native Egyptian king-lists from the old chronology of Sety I downwards to Manetho as the founder of the First Dynasty in Egypt, has been so shadowy and so little known, that notwithstanding the discovery of his " tomb," with contemporary inscriptions, by Sir Flinders Petrie in the royal cemeteries at Abydos in 1900, he is still regarded by the latest historical text-books as " a conflate personage of legend." And beyond the finding of his name in a few contemporary and later inscriptions, and the inference that he possibly arrived in Upper Egypt either from Libya on the west, the Sudan on the south, Arabia on the east or from Elam in Persia on the north-east by way of the Red Sea, and that he is the traditional uniter of Upper and Lower Egypt and founder of Memphis city, nothing whatever is known to Egyptologists of his origin and ancestry, achievements, personality, portrait and race.

The manner in which I was led to discover the truly historical character of Menes, his lost epoch-making history and pre-history, his genealogy continuously back through

## 2 EGYPTIAN CIVILIZATION OF SUMER ORIGIN

seven centuries to the first Sumerian or Aryan king who was the traditional founder of civilization and builder of the first city, his Aryan race, his date, and the fact that he was at one and the same time the Sumerian emperor in Mesopotamia and the first dynastic king or Pharaoh in Egypt as a crown colony of his world-empire, has been broadly indicated in the Preface.

The first clues to these discoveries were gained by my observation that Menes (as he was called by the Greeks) or *Manj* (as he is usually called in his own Egyptian inscriptions)[1] appears in his due chronological position along with his dynasty in the official king-lists of the Early Aryans from the first king onwards, as preserved in the ancient Indian epic chronicles, the Purānas. In the latter he bears the name of *Asa Manja*, or " *Manja* the shooter " in the solar version of these lists, and *Manasyu* or *Manas*-the-Uniter in the lunar version.[2] And the great Indian epic, the Mahā-Bhārata, in supplementing the Purāna chronicle account, describes him as " Manasyu of the line of the Prabhu [*Parāa* or ' Pharaoh '], the royal eye of Gopta [Kopt or Egypt] and of the four ends of the earth."[3] The Indian epic king-lists further record that he was the son and successor of the mighty world-emperor, King Kuni or Sha-Kuni or Sagara, whom I had fully identified with the Mesopotamian world-emperor, whose name is variously spelt Kin, Gin, Gani, Guni, or Shar-Guni, a name which is arbitrarily semitized by Assyriologists into " Sargon," in order to equate it with the Hebrew name " Sargon " of the much later notorious Semitic Assyrian king of that name in the eighth century B.C. who carried the Jews into exile, and from whom they distinguish the former as " Sargon-the-Great."

On comparing these Early Aryan king-lists with those of the Sumerians in Mesopotamia,[4] I observed that the latter documents also recorded in the self-same chronological position the dynasty of King Gin or Guni (" Sargon-the-Great "), bearing substantially the same names and titles as in the Indian lists and in exactly the same order ; and that the names and order from " Sargon's " son Manis onwards were identical with those of Menes' dynasty of Pharaohs on

[1] See later.  [2] See pp. 4 f.  [3] See p. 4 and App. I.  [4] Kish Chronicle.

## MENES AS SON OF SARGON-THE-GREAT 3

their own Egyptian monuments. Menes or Manj in his Egyptian inscriptions usually bears the title of "Manj-the-Warrior," and in the Sumerian king-lists and in his own inscriptions in Mesopotamia, the son and successor of "Sargon-the-Great" is styled "Manis-the-Warrior." And the last king of this dynasty, bearing the same name in both Sumerian and Egyptian inscriptions, has his name significantly written on his own Egyptian inscription by the self-same Sumerian pictographic signs as in the Sumerian king-lists and in his own inscriptions as Sumerian emperor in Mesopotamia.

Further comparison disclosed that Menes' father, "Sargon-the-Great," along with the latter's father and grandfather were identical in names and titles with the three Predynastic Pharaohs who immediately preceded Menes in Egypt; and who have left there their records, seals or sealings in Sumerian script. And these identities are confirmed by their own Sumerian inscriptions in Egypt, and by their official seals in their Indus Valley colony, in which most of them bore also the title of "Pharaoh," and mention Egypt by name as being within their empire.

Let us now examine the detailed proofs for these identities of Menes or Manj and his "predynastic" ancestors in Egypt with those of Manis and his immediate imperial Sumerian ancestors in their contemporary inscriptions in Mesopotamia and the Indus Valley and in the Indian epic records of the Early Aryan kings.

### MENES OR MANIS-TUSU AS MANASYU THE "PHARAOH OF GOPTA" (EGYPT) IN THE INDIAN EPICS

The name of this Aryan king under the form of *Manasyu* is found in the lunar version of the Indo-Aryan King-Lists, and corresponds to the solar form of his name as Asa Manjas or Asa Manja in the solar main-line lists in which he is No. 38 (see Table, p. 151)—the solar lists [1] being the most complete and in undisturbed chronological order. And "Sargon" in this Puru version is called Pra-Vīra or "Foremost hero," in which *Vīra* corresponds to his Sumerian title of *Pir*,[2] V being a very late invented letter.[3]

[1] Lists of the purer Sun-worshippers. [2] WMC. 200. [3] See WAOA. 49 f.

## 4 EGYPTIAN CIVILIZATION OF SUMER ORIGIN

One of the Indian Epic records of this King Manasyu and his ancestry states according to my revised reading : [1]

"PURU had by his wife Paushti three sons PRA-VĪRA, Ishwara and Raudr-āshwa, all of whom were mighty charioteers.[2] Amongst them Pra-Vīra had by his wife ACCHURA Seni a son named MANASYU of the line of the PRABHŪ ['Pharaoh'], the royal eye of GOPTA [Kopt or Egypt] and of the four ends of the earth. Manasyu by Su-Vira's daughter begat three sons Shakta, Samhana and Vagmā, all heroes and mighty charioteer warriors."

Here we have fortunately preserved to us in the Indian epic the concentrated tradition of the Aryan King Manasyu as "Pharaoh of Gopta" or Egypt, all in a nutshell. His genealogy is fully authenticated back to his grandfather Puru II, who is Puru-Gin of the Sumerian Isin lists and his Egyptian and Indus inscriptions, and Uru-ka Gina of his Mesopotamian monuments.

Manasyu's father Pra-Vīra, identified as Sargon, here bears the title of Vīra corresponding to his *Pir* title in the Old Isin Sumerian king-list ; whilst the *Pra*, in series with the longer form Prabhū, now appears to be the equivalent of the Egyptian *Parāa* or "Pharaoh." [3]

His mother's name of *Acchura Seni* also confirms Manasyu's identity with Manis-Tusu. Her Indian name substantially equates, as we shall see, with the Mesopotamian name for Sargon's queen of "Lady *Ash-nar*," also read *Ash-lal;* and *l* and *r* are freely interchangeable and Egyptian has the same letter for both. And we shall find that Sargon in his own Egyptian inscription calls his queen "The Lady *Ash*."

His designation as "of the line of the *Prabhū*" clearly defines him as "of the line of the Pharaohs." *Prabhū*, the Sanskrit word here, means "ruler, master, lord," [4] and it is in series with his prefixed title of *Pra*, obviously derived from the Sumerian *Par, Bar* or *Baru*, "lord" [5]—the form

---

[1] The Sanskrit text of this critical record in the Mahā-Bhārata epic is given in App. I.
[2] Sargon in his war records states that he rode in "a brazen chariot."
[3] See WSAD. 34 and cp. BD. 238—the Egyptian name had its first syllable latterly spelt with the Sumerian house-sign *Bar* or *Par*, so as to mean "The Great House"; and in Sumerian *Bar, Bara*="great house or palace or temple" (WSAD. 29), and Pl. XVIII.
[4] MWD. 684.   [5] WSAD. 34.

MAP I.

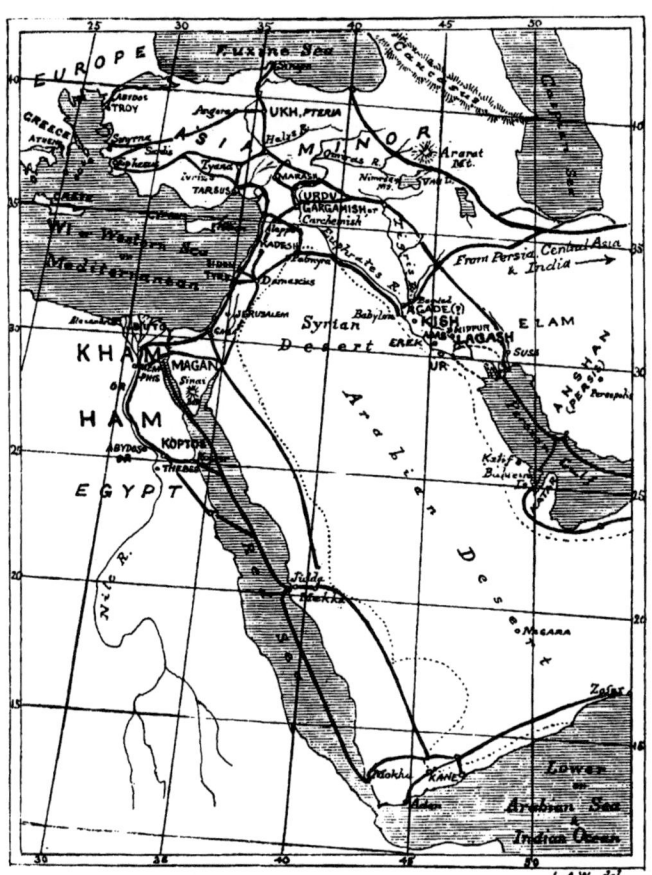

RELATION OF KOPTOS AND EGYPT TO MESOPOTAMIA, ASIA MINOR
AND INDIA, SHOWING OLD TRADE ROUTES.

Prabhū adopted by the Indian scribes was presumably to make this " Pharaoh " title intelligible to Indian readers. And the fact that he is described as " of the line of the Prabhū " is obviously to denote that his father (Sargon) before him was also a *Pra* or *Parāa* or Pharaoh. And we shall find that Sargon in one of his Indus seals calls himself " Pharaoh," and in another (No. 8) " The Son of Egypt (or Khamaesshi) Land," implying his birth in Egypt.[1]

The title " Royal Eye " for Manasyu is a strikingly Egyptian metaphor and in series with the name *Asar* (Greek Osiris) for the traditional deified ancestor of Menes, which name is written in Egyptian and Sumerian by the same pictograph and phonetic value of an Eye over a Throne,[2] another instance of the Sumerian origin of a fundamental Egyptian word with the same meaning, word-form and hieroglyph writing. And Menes, in one of his inscriptions in Egypt, actually uses this Eye-Throne Sumerian hieroglyph for his title, see Fig. 12, p. 58.

The title " Eye of the Four ends of the Earth " for Manasyu is, we shall find, the equivalent of Manis-Tusu's Mesopotamian imperial title and of his son Naram Enzu's title of " King of the Four Quarters of the World." [3]

The place-name *Gopta* [4] is of great historical importance. It equates with the Ancient Egyptian *Gebt* or *Gabt* name for Koptos ; [5] and it survives in the modern " Copt " title for native Egyptians as opposed to immigrant Arabs ; and it is clearly cognate with *Kopt-os* of the Greeks, the name of the oldest immemorial trade-city in Upper Egypt on the Nile, to the east of Abydos (see Map I). It was, presumably, the first capital of Menes in Upper Egypt. This name Gopta or Copt is probably, I suggest, the real source of the name " Egypt," the " Aiguptos " of the Greeks.

In his name " Manasyu," as it occurs in this Indian text, it is significant that the affix *yu* means in Sanskrit " uniter " [6] so the name would thus be " *Manas*-the-Uniter " ; and Menes is designated by Egyptian tradition as " The *Uniter*

---

[1] This is significant *re* his legend of birth on the Nile, see later.
[2] See pl. XVIII, and WSAD. p. 20.    [3] RB. 7, and PHT. iv. 213.
[4] Now recognized as a territorial designation for the first time, it previously having been translated as a mere grammatical expression.
[5] BD. 1044.    [6] MWD. 853.

## 6 EGYPTIAN CIVILIZATION OF SUMER ORIGIN

of the two crowns of Upper and Lower Egypt." Under his other Indian name as *Asa-Manja*, or "*Manja* the Shooter," is described in the Indian Chronicles, his quarrel with, and disinheritance by, his father, Sagara (Sargon), which, we shall find later, appears to relate to his declaration of independence in Egypt during the lifetime of his father in Mesopotamia ; and thus explaining why Sargon's younger son succeeded his father on the Mesopotamian throne and not Manis-Tusu, his eldest son, who only succeeded later.

### IDENTITY OF MENES WITH THE ARYAN EMPEROR MANASYU & MANIS-TUSU, SON OF SARGON, CONFIRMED

It was this startling and revolutionary discovery by me, about a quarter of a century ago, that Menes, the founder of the First Dynasty of Egypt, was clearly identical with the Aryan Emperor Manasyu of Gopta, or Asa-Manja or Asa-Manjas, and with Manis-Tusu, the son of Sargon, disclosed by the Indian Chronicles and King-Lists, that chiefly forced me to take up seriously the gigantic task of mastering the Sumerian language and its linear and cuneiform script, in order to revise the spelling of the names at first hand, after observing the totally different forms of the names which different Assyriologists " restored " from the same Sumerian writing in the same texts. All the more so was I prompted to take up this Egyptian side of the research, as the marvellous civilization of Ancient Egypt had captivated me ever since I had spent some weeks at the Boulaq Museum in Cairo in the eighties, and had acquired even then an amateurish acquaintance with the Egyptian hieroglyphics.

On gaining a working knowledge of all three scripts, Sanskritic, Sumerian with cuneiform, and Egyptian, the detailed examinations and comparisons of the critical names in the several texts with the associated histories of the kings thus made possible, fully confirmed the identities of the latter as now demonstrated in detail.

## The Name "Menes," Manj or Aha-Manj compared with the Sumerian Manis-Tusu & its Indian forms

One of the earliest critically-important historical results of this trilingual comparison of the Sumerian, Indian and Egyptian proper names was that which emerged from my comparison of the names for Menes (as the Greeks called him, and the *Manj* or *Aha-Manj* of his own inscriptions) with its Sumerian and Indian forms. This disclosed identity in all three. And as this trilingual identity is of critical importance not only for the identity of Menes with Manis-Tusu, but also for the rest of Menes' Dynasty as well, it is desirable here to examine it in detail.

## Identity of the name "Menes," Manj or Aha-Manj in Egyptian, Indian & Sumerian

It is necessary to premise in my comparison of the Egyptian language and writing with other cognate Aryan languages and writing—for I have demonstrated that the Ancient Egyptian language is radically Aryan in its roots and writing,[1] although it adopted latterly a Semitic idiom in using these Aryan roots, as the subjects of Menes, like those of Sargon in Mesopotamia were mostly Semitic-speaking people—that Ancient Egyptian writing, like its Aryan cognates Sanskrit, Pali, Hindi, etc., and Phœnician alphabetic writing, does not usually express the short vowel *a* in its writing. The hitherto unknown reason for this, as I have demonstrated in my *Aryan Origin of the Alphabet,* is that the short vowel *a* is inherent as an affix in each consonantal letter.

Thus "Menes," as the Greeks called him, spells his name (as also do later Egyptians) by the "Egyptian" hieroglyphs reading alphabetically M-N and M-N-J. Egyptologists recognized that in order to sound the words written by this consonantal way of spelling, it was necessary to introduce a vowel after each initial and medial consonant. But unaware of the reason for this consonantal spelling with its absence of short vowels, they agreed on the expedient of arbitrarily introducing the vowel *e* after each initial and

[1] WSAD. *passim.*

## 8    EGYPTIAN CIVILIZATION OF SUMER ORIGIN

medial consonantal sign in rendering the words into "Roman" or European alphabetic writing.

But, as I have shown in my *Aryan Origin of the Alphabet*, the unexpressed vowel in Ancient Egyptian was not *e*, but was the *a* inherent in each consonant as in the other Aryan languages which used this consonantal form of writing. Thus the Egyptian name for "Menes," written M-N and M-N-J does not usually read *Men* or *Menj*, as "restored" by Egyptologists, but reads properly *Man* or *Manaj* or *Manj ;* just as in the Indian Sanskrit his name is written M-N-S-Y-U and A-S-M-N-J, which are universally transcribed into Roman characters by all Indianists as *Manasyu* and *Asa-Manja*.

The fuller Egyptian form of Menes' name as *Manj*, strikingly confirms the literal identity of the Egyptian with the Sanskrit *Manja* (or Asa-Manja), the son of the Emperor Sagara, that is Sargon; and it equates also phonetically with the *Manis* name of Sargon's son in Sumerian—the affix *Tusu* meaning, as seen below, "The Warrior." This fuller Egyptian form of Menes' name is usually disguised by many English Egyptologists as *Mena*. But the alphabetic value of the last letter is rightly rendered by the Berlin school as *J*,[1] which is now seen to be its proper value by our trilingual comparison ; and this is confirmed by the pictorial form of this Egyptian hieroglyph which pictures a flowering reed, which I observed was the same sign, form, sound, and meaning as the Sumerian pictograph of the flowering reed word-sign with the phonetic value *Gi*[2]—thus affording another of the many instances I have demonstrated of the derivation of the Egyptian hieroglyphs from the Sumerian pictographs, with the same pictographs, form, phonetic value and meaning.

We thus get the trilingual equation of Menes' name as follows :

| Egyptian. | Sumerian. | Sanskrit. |
|---|---|---|
| *Man* or *Manj*   =   | *Manis* or *Manisi*   =   | *Manasyu* and *Manja*. |

Similarly is it with the title of *Aha* or *Akha* which "Menes" uses sometimes along with his proper personal name of *Manj* or abbreviated into *Man*, and giving him a

[1] GH. xi.      [2] Br. 2385.   This soft *Gi* being parent of *J*.

PLATE II.   SUMERIAN.           EGYPTIAN.

**A, Ā, "Hand."**
Pictures hand & embroidered sleeve.
Br.6542. P.1.            B.293.

= **Ā, "Hand."**
Pict. hand & forearm.
G.12, fig.100. BD.105ᵃ.

**A, Ā, "Ground, foundation, dwelling."**
From Udug's Bowl, BOB.108-9.
Br.10495, 10523. M.79756. B.481.

= **AA, YA, "Island, district, place."**
G.31. fig.50. BD.16ᵃ.

**AG, AKA, "Fire within" (Brazier)**
Pict. brazier in enclosure.
Br.4734-5. M.8218. P.21f. B.195.

= **AKH, "Brazier."**
Pict. brazier & smoke.
G. 42.

**AKH, "Wind-Bird"—Eagle, "strength."**
Pict. winged disc (eagle) & a talon or claw.
B.8124; 8128, 8290.   B.346.

= **ĀKHA** -MIST, "Eagle".
(Mist - ? "passage, way," c.p.
BD. 287ᵃ. designating the Eagle as a "Bird of passage".)
BD. 135ᵇ. Fig. after G. Fig. 1.

**AKHA, EKHA, "War, mighty, kill, fight."**
Pict. arm holding shield with battle-axe inside.
Br. 7269-71 & see Dict.   B.312.

= **AKHA, AHA, "Fight, Fighting."**
Pict. arms holding shield & mace or battle-axe.
G.15. fig.177.

**ALA, ALAL, "All, full, the full collection of wood, bind, hang."**
Br. 5965, 6007. MD.46. B.270
& see Ala in Dict.

= **AU, AUI, (AAL), "All, totality, full."**
Pict. tied bundle of wood.
BD.2, & c.p AAL, UAL. "Bind".
BD1ᵃ,146ᵇ. Fig. from G. Nᵒ 160.

**AN, AS, "Star."**
Br. 418, 432.   B.13.

= **ANKH, "Star."**
BD. 125ᵃ, G.30

**AR, UB, "Shackle—Plough, cause earth to go up (&. ear or plough)."**
Pict. a diagram of a plough.
Br. 5780-84. WPOB.49,345,1   B. 261.

= **AR, HAB, "Plough."**
c.p. BD. 130ᵃ, 441ᵃ and see Dictionary article
AR. "plough to ear."
L.A.W. del.

SUMERIAN ORIGIN OF EGYPTIAN HIEROGLYPHS (A).
(For continuation, see Plates XVIII-XXI.)

form of name with title which is usually spelt by English Egyptologists as *Aha Men* or *Aha Mena;* but which should now be properly spelt *Aha* (or *Akha*) *Manj*, though, as we shall find, Menes himself sometimes spells his name on his Indo-Sumerian seals as *Men*, see Plate V, Nos. 2, 3 and 10.

Here again our trilingual comparison confirms the identity of this title *Aha* or *Akha* in all three languages, Egyptian, Sumerian and Indian, in meaning and generally in word-form. This title *Aha* or *Akha* means in Egyptian " The Warrior," and is derived, as I have shown, from the Sumerian root *Aha* or *Akha* " Fight, strike down," a Sumerian root which runs in the same word-form and meaning throughout the whole family of Aryan language including the English.[1] And the Egyptian hieroglyph for this sign, which is a picture of two arms holding a shield and a battle-mace, is significantly derived as I have shown from the similar Sumerian sign for this pictograph *Aha or Akha*, again showing the derivation of the Egyptian hieroglyphs from the Sumerian with the same pictograph signs, word-form and meaning.[2] Thus it is demonstrated that the Sumerian title of Sargon's son, namely, *Manis-Tusu* or " Manis-the-Warrior," is the equivalent of the Egyptian *Aha-Manj* or *Akha-Manj*, for *Tusu* in Sumerian also means, as I have shown, " War or Fight " and is the Sumerian origin of our English word " Tussle."[3]

So also, the Indian form of Menes' title as *Asa-Manja* means " *Manja*-the-Shooter "—*As* meaning in Sanskrit " Shoot at, cast, throw,"[4] thus showing that the Indian scribes had translated the Sumerian title *Tusu* into Sanskrit to render it intelligible to Indian readers, just as Menes himself had translated it by *Aha* to render it more intelligible to Egyptians to whom *Tusu* was presumably unknown.[5]

We thus find that besides Menes' identity of name in all three languages—Egyptian, Sumerian and Indian—his title also of " Warrior or Fighter " also is identical thus :

| Egyptian. | | Sumerian. | | Indian. |
|---|---|---|---|---|
| *Manj*-the-Warrior | = | *Manis*-the-Warrior | = | *Manja*-the-Shooter. |
| (*Aha-Manj*) | = | (*Manis-Tusu*) | = | (*Asa-Manja*). |

[1] WSAD. 9.    [2] Pl. II.    [3] WSAD. 9-10.
[4] MWD. 117.    [5] Cp. WSAD. 10.

And we shall find that Menes calls himself "the son of Gina or Sha-Gina" in his Indus Valley and Egyptian records, in agreement with the Sumerian king-lists of the official Kish Chronicle *re* Manis. And several of his descendants in the First Egyptian Dynasty likewise claim the same ancestry in their Egyptian inscriptions. Thus no proof of identity could be more complete in regard to "Menes," the founder of the First Dynasty of Egypt, being the son of "Sargon-the-Great" or King Gin, to whom as a predynastic Pharaoh of Egypt we now turn.

## II

### "Sargon-the-Great" & his Father and Grandfather as Predynastic Pharaohs

*Disclosing his Annexation or Reconquest of Egypt, c. 2714 B.C.,*
*His Egyptian Tomb Inscriptions deciphered,*
*His titles " Pharaoh," Kad (" Ka "), Ukus, " Goth " & Aryan Race,*
*His father & grandfather as Predynastic Pharaohs " Ro " & " Khetm,"*
*With their real Dates about 2765 and 2780 B.C. respectively.*

THE father of Menes, now disclosed as the mighty Mesopotamian emperor King Gin, Gani or Guni, the so-called " Sargon-the-Great " of Semitists, repeatedly calls himself in his own records and is called in the later Babylonian Omen literatures : " King of the Four Quarters of the World " ; that is in series with Menes' Indian epic title of " The Royal Eye of Gopta and of the Four Ends of the Earth." That this was no mere idle boast, but was justified to a very considerable extent in fact, is shown in my *Makers of Civilization*, wherein is collated the evidence for the vast extent of his empire, extending from the Indus Valley on the east to the British Isles on the west, and embracing a " world-empire " considerably larger than that of Alexander or the imperial Romans ; and thus entitling him to be styled " world-emperor," as he usually is. And it was through this vastness of their monarchic and colonizing sway that he and his immediate descendants were enabled to diffuse so effectually and rapidly their Sumerian civilization throughout the greater part of the known old world of their time, from about 2725 B.C. onwards.

The records of " Sargon's " conquests of the West and his conquest or reconquest of Egypt are contained in the old official copies of his edicts and chronicles in the archives of the oldest Sun-temple in Mesopotamia at Nippur (see map, p. 4), and repeated in the later Omen-tablets of the Babylonians, which latter give the dates of those conquests with reference to the year of his reign, which is now found to have begun about 2725 B.C.

SARGON'S CONQUESTS IN THE WESTERN OLD WORLD TO THE TIN-MINES (? OF BRITAIN) BEYOND THE WESTERN SEA OR MEDITERRANEAN

In his inscriptions at Nippur temple "Sargon-the-Great" claims that : " Unto King Gin, king of the Land (or Earth), Lord Sakh gave no foe from the Upper Sea [Mediterranean] unto the Lower Sea [Persian Gulf and Indian Ocean], Lord Sakh . . . subjected the lands to him." And the Omen version of his Chronicles states : "King Gin who marched against the Land of the West, and conquered the Land of the West, his hand subdued the Four Quarters of the World." [1]

Further details of his conquests in the West are given in others of his inscriptions, and in his Chronicles in their Babylonian copy and in the Assyrio-Babylonian extracts in the Omen-literature. Thus the Chronicles state the particular year in which he achieved these conquests, in almost literal agreement with the Omen version, and make the complete conquest to have occurred in the eleventh year of his reign, while the Omens place it in his third year. This is supposed to imply that his first expedition was in his third year and the full conquest in his eleventh.

This Chronicle copy reads : [2] "King *Gin*, king of Agudu City, through the Weapon [3] of Lord Sakhar Tar [4] (or ? Lady Ish-Tar) was exalted. And he possessed no foe or rival. His glory over the world he poured out. The Sea in the East [? West] [5] he crossed. And in the eleventh year the Land of the West (or Sunset) in full his hand subdued. He united them under one rule. He set up his images in the West. Their booty he brought over as arranged."

[1] KC. 2, 27.   [2] Text in KC. 2, 3 f.   The reading is as revised by me.
[3] *Bal*, Br. 278-9.
[4] Br. 5081.   On *Sakhar Tar* v. *Ishtar*, see WMC. 220.
[5] The Omen version says "The Sea of the West he crossed." KC. 2, 31.

## SARGON AS PREDYNASTIC PHARAOH IN EGYPT

Some particulars regarding these conquests are given in one of his edicts on the boundaries of his empire.[1] This refers amongst other things to his "conquest of the land of the Muru (Amorites)" and mentions his suzerainty over "*the Tin-land country which lies beyond the Upper Sea* [Mediterranean]." This obviously refers to Sargon's sovereignty over the tin-mines of Cornwall,[2] and I have adduced evidence for the introduction of the Bronze Age into Britain by Amorites before his epoch or about 2800 B.C. And it mentions that "*the produce of the mines* is taken, and the produce of the fields to King Gin has been brought." And Egypt or *Mishir* or *Mizir* is mentioned as being within his frontiers.

### SARGON AS A PREDYNASTIC PHARAOH WITH INSCRIPTIONS & TOMB AT ABYDOS

Although "Sargon" is admitted by a leading Assyriologist to have held Egypt and to have included Egypt within his empire by its name of "Mizir"[3] and by others under its hitherto unidentified Semitic title of "Dilmun,"[4] none of the text-book writers on Babylonian or Egyptian History refer to the subject at all.

But we now find Sargon's own inscription, as the "oldest" of the inscriptions of Predynastic Pharaohs that have been found at the royal tombs at Abydos, and attesting that his own tomb was there along with that of his queen. And it now appears that Sargon, with his vast world-empire, had selected for his mausoleum for himself, his queen and his dynasty that relatively cool semi-temperate part of his realm in Egypt on the Mediterranean, presumably because it was a more natural resting-place for him and his Caucasian race than the torrid sun-baked mud plains of Mesopotamia. And we shall find that both Sargon-the-Great and his son Menes and their dynasty call themselves *Gut* or "Goth" in their Indus Valley seals, as well as *Bar* or *Par* or "Pharaoh."

This discovery of Sargon as a Predynastic Pharaoh was made through the Indian Chronicle account of "Sargon's" son under his title there of *Manasyu*, identifying him with Manis-Tusu and Menes.

[1] Text in KTA. 1920. No. 92.
[2] See WPOB. 413 f.
[3] Sayce in *Ancient Egypt*, 1924, 2-5.
[4] See refs. later.

### THE "PREDYNASTIC" PHARAOHS OF EGYPT

The kings or "Pharaohs" of Egypt before Menes are termed by Egyptologists "Predynastic." This is because the late Egyptian priest Manetho, who compiled in the 3rd century B.C. a list of the Pharaohs for Ptolemy II Philadelphus, for the great library of Alexandria (of which work only fragments are now found in the works of later classic writers), heads his long list of the Pharaohs with Menes, whom he calls the founder of the First Dynasty in Egypt. And similarly Sety I (whose beautiful alabaster sarcophagus is now a chief treasure in the Soane Museum in London), the father of Rameses-the-Great, also begins his list of Egyptian kings with Menes, who was the traditional uniter of the crowns of Upper and Lower Egypt into one kingship and nation.

But Manetho prefixes to Menes a list of ten kings, who it was said reigned before Menes at Thinis near Abydos for a period of 350 years before Menes, and who may be nine pre-Sargonic Sumerian suzerains with Sargon as the tenth. And before these again he prefixes a long list of gods and demigods as kings with fabulous ages, just as did his more or less contemporary Babylonian priest Berosos in his list also compiled for the Seleucid Greek king of Babylon, and somewhat like the Isin priests prefixing fabulous chronology to the historical kings of Mesopotamia. The early list of Egyptian kings, also on the Palermo stele of the Fifth Dynasty, enumerates ten kings before Menes, the names of whom are mostly illegible. But no inscribed remains of any of these ten legendary pre-Menes kings are said to have been found.

The only inscribed objects with personal names recovered at Abydos and other old Egyptian sites which are considered by Egyptologists to be "Predynastic," give the names of eight kings or "pharaohs" who are believed to be Predynastic from the archaic form of the writing and the relatively early-culture form of the objects inscribed, coupled with the absence of their names in the First Dynasty list. And these eight historical "Predynastic" kings have been arranged by Egyptologists in serial order according to their supposed relative archæological ages.[1] But as the last

[1] PHE. 1, 6.

## PREDYNASTIC KING "RO" IS SARGON'S FATHER 15

two are written in a later style and classed as belonging to the period of "Narmer" who is within the First Dynasty, this leaves only six "Predynastic" kings of whom inscribed remains have been found; and three of these are doubtfully Predynastic.

*Now, the very first of these historical Predynastic Pharaohs, and heading the list, proves by our new Sumerian and Indian keys to be none other than the father of Menes, "Sargon" himself!* And the other two who are placed by Egyptologists immediately after him are disclosed to be his father and grandfather, who preceded him as predynastic Pharaohs.

### Sargon's Father & Grandfather as the Predynastic Pharaohs hitherto called "Ro" & "Khetm"

The three earliest of the Predynastic Pharaohs who have left inscriptions are those whose names have hitherto been read *Ka-Ap, Ro* and *Khetm*. They are now disclosed to be respectively in reality Sargon himself with his father and grandfather; but chronologically they are in the reverse order to what they have been placed by Egyptologists on archæological grounds—another instance of the unreliability of archæological dating.

### Inscriptions of King "Ro"

The inscriptions of King "Ro" were found in his great tomb at Abydos, roughly scratched on large votive funereal jars of pottery which were placed alongside large alabaster

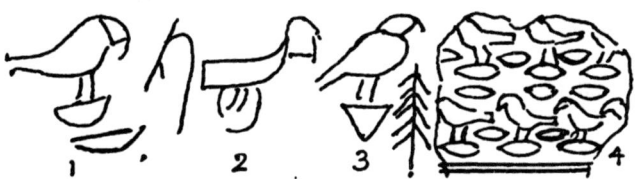

1, 2, 3. On Pottery.    4. On Sealing.
Fig. 1.—King "Ro's" Name from his Tomb at Abydos.

jars,[1] and another was impressed on a clay sealing by a cylinder seal of Mesopotamian style and engraved in finer fashion.[2] They are shown in the above figure.

[1] PRT. I. xliv. 2-9.    [2] PRT. II. xiii. 96, and PHE. I, 5.

# 16 EGYPTIAN CIVILIZATION OF SUMER ORIGIN

### Decipherment of the Real Name of Predynastic Pharaoh "Ro," identifying Him with Sargon's Father

For decipherment, I here place the Egyptian writing of this king's name alongside the standard Sumerian writing of the Sargonic period in Mesopotamia in the conventional style of pictographs used for lithic engraving there.

It is seen that the Egyptian writing is not in the

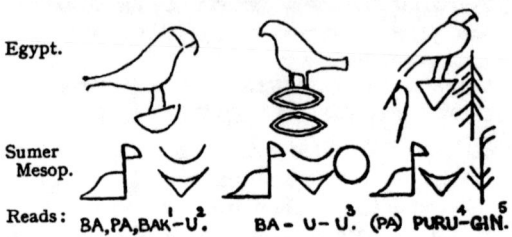

Transl. BAU, BAUU or BAKU or Hawk-king PURU-GIN.

Fig. 2.—Name of Predynastic Pharaoh "Ro," deciphered as BAU, BAUU or BAKU or PURU-GIN.

conventional Egyptian style of hieroglyphs, which was developed after Menes' epoch, but it is essentially in Sumerian linear pictographic script, with the hawk-sign drawn somewhat more naturalistically than in the conventional diagrammatic form generally used in Mesopotamia; and that the signs have their Sumerian phonetic syllabic values and are not alphabetic, which accounts for the name not having been hitherto deciphered or read.[6] For our decipherment the signs are given in the usual direction for reading, namely from left to right, as in Sumerian, English and all Aryan languages.

[1] B. 83; Br. 2047-8.     [2] B. 365; Br. 8645.
[3] The crescent sign is also written as a circle. B. 365.
[4] Br. 8632-4. On *Puru* value cp. Br. 8632, 7501-2, 6971.
[5] B. 92; Br. 2384.
[6] The "Ro" value assigned to it by Egyptologists was obtained from the later Egyptian value of $R$ borne by the oval sign, as representing "a mouth" or "entrance" *Ra* (B.D. 416, G.H. 12). This is obviously derived from S. *Ri, Rin* "a ring, circle, enclosure, periphery, orifice" (Br. 10167 f.), with sign conventionally differentiated from the circle as a square.

## KING "KHETM" IS SARGON'S GRANDFATHER

His name it will be noticed is spelt in Egypt in three different ways, namely as *Ba-u* (or *Bak-u*), *Ba-u-u* and *Puru-Gin*. These forms of his name thus equate with the form of his name as the 36th king on the main-line lists in the Indian Chronicles and in the old Sumerian prefixed lists in the Isin Chronicle and on his Indus Valley seal, as is displayed in the following equations:

| Egypt. | Old Sumerian Lists (Isin [1]). | Indus Valley Seal.[2] | Indian Lists. |
|---|---|---|---|
| Bau or Bauu | = | = Bu or Buz | = Bāhu |
| or Baku | = | = | = Bāhuka |
| or Pau-Gin | = Bara-Gin | = Par-Gin | = Pra-Cin-wat |
| or (Pa) Puru-Gin | = Buru-Gina | = Buru or Puru | = Puru (II) |

It is also seen that whilst the later Indian scribes have preserved substantially the same spelling of the name as in the Egyptian inscriptions they have Sanskritized them slightly in order to extract a meaning from them. Thus they have made *Bauu* or *Baku* into *Bāhu* and *Bāhuka*, both of which latter names mean in Sanskrit "The arm" or "mighty." And *Par-Gin* and *Puru-Gin* they have Sanskritized into *Pra-cin-wat* or "The collector or gatherer," with the tradition that "he conquered the eastern countries to the confines of the rising sun."[3] And in one of his Indus seals he calls himself "Son of Egypt and Magar (Sinai Peninsula)."[4] In his inscriptions in Mesopotamia, where he was a famous builder and law-giver, he calls himself Uru-ka *Gina*.[5]

THE PREDYNASTIC KING "KHETM'S" REAL NAME IN EGYPTIAN & SUMERIAN, IDENTIFYING HIM WITH SARGON'S GRANDFATHER

Similarly, the name of the Predynastic Pharaoh [6] hitherto read "Khetm" or "Khatm" is now disclosed to be written in Sumerian hieroglyph and with the Sumerian phonetic value of that sign. That sign pictures a Sumerian cylinder-seal (*Tukh* or *Dukh*) in its realistic form with its attached loop of string, as contrasted with its diagrammatic form in Mesopotamian Sumerian for rapid writing with straight

[1] WMC. 140.  [2] App. II.  [3] MBt. 1, 95.  [4] App. II.  [5] WMC. 190 f.
[6] It is on a clay sealing. Petrie, *Naqada and Ballas*, lxxx. 1, and PHE. 1, 5. See Fig. 3, over page.

## 18 EGYPTIAN CIVILIZATION OF SUMER ORIGIN

lines, on wet clay-tablets, as seen in the annexed figure, where the Sumerian form of this sign is placed beneath the Egyptian for comparison.

It is thus seen that this predynastic Pharaoh's name, hitherto read "Khetm,"[2] reads in Sumerian *Tukh, Tukhu, Dukh* or *Tekhi,* which equates with the name of the 35th king

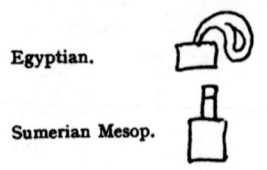

Egyptian.

Sumerian Mesop.

Reads: TUKH, DUKHU or TEKHI.[1]

FIG. 3.—King "Khetm's"[2] Name deciphered as *TUKH, DUKHU* or *TEKHI.*

on the main-line list of the Indian Chronicles, who is made therein the father of the king above-named and the grandfather of Sagara or Sargon, and it also equates with the name for this king in the old Sumerian King-Lists. Thus:

| Egypt. | Old Sumer Lists. | Indian Lists. |
|---|---|---|
| Tukhu or Tekhi | = Tuke[3] = | Vri-*Taka* or Dhri-*Taka.* |

The Indian prefixes *Vri* and *Dhri* were obviously added for descriptive purposes by the early Indian scribes who converted the Sumerian syllabic pictographic writing into the Indian alphabetic writing. For *Vri* in Sanskrit = "to cover, check, conceal," that is the sense of "a seal," which this *Tekhi* literally means in Sumerian. And *Dhri* has the analogous meaning of "keep down, restrain, preserve" (which are also secondary meanings of this Sumerian "seal" word. Indeed *Dri-Tīkr* is a Sanskrit word for "seal"[4] and we shall find that Sanskrit frequently intruded an *r* Cockney-

---

[1] B. 157. Br. 3921, spelt *Di-* (or *Ti*)-*ukh* (or -*ukhu* or -*akh*) giving the form *D(i)ukhu* or *T(i)ukhu* or *T(i)akh* or *Dikh*, cp. Br. 8289-90. On *Tekhi,* Br. 3922.

[2] "Khetm" or "Khatm" is the later Egyptian descriptive title for this seal sign, as "the cut or engraved," and is derived from the Egyptian *Khat* "cut or engrave" (BD. 569); which Egyptian word is seen to be obviously derived from the Sumerian *Khat* "cut" (Br. 5581), which I have shown to be the parent of our English word "Cut," and of its equivalents in the Aryan family of languages, Sanskrit *Chid*, etc.

[3] WMC. 140,587.    [4] Apte's *English-Sanskrit Dict.* 381.

## SARGON'S EGYPTIAN INSCRIPTS. ON HIS TOMB 19

wise into the old Aryan or Sumerian roots. This *Takhi* "seal" word is also obviously the source of the modern Indian *Tika* for the caste mark on the forehead of Hindus.

And incidentally this Sumerian "seal" word, which has also meaning "written tablet," is, as I have shown under its *Dikh*, *Tikh* and *Dukh* values, the parent of our English words "Tick-et, Tok-en, Dock-et, Docu-ment," etc., and the corresponding words of this form and meaning which run throughout the Aryan family of languages [1]—another instance of the Sumerian origin of the Aryan languages.

### "SARGON'S" INSCRIPTIONS AS PREDYNASTIC PHARAOH GIN OR SHA-GIN IN EGYPT

*(the so-called King "Ka-ap")*

That this startling discovery of "Sargon's" inscriptions in Egypt was not made before, is now seen to be owing, partly to the narrow outlook of Egyptologists, with their

FIG. 4.—"Sargon's" Sumerian Inscription as Pharaoh at Abydos. (On a jar, after Sir F. Petrie, PHE. 1, 5.)

FIG. 5.—Sumerian Inscription of "Sargon's" queen, "The Lady ASH," at Abydos. (On a jar, after Sir F. Petrie, PHE. 1, 5.)

theory that Civilization and the Egyptian hieroglyphs originated in the Nile Valley, and partly to the fact that these predynastic inscriptions are written in the Early Sumerian script and language, and not in the later derived conventional form of the Egyptian hieroglyphs with which alone Egyptologists are familiar. As a result these Sargonic inscriptions have hitherto remained undeciphered and unread.

[1] WSAD. 55 f.

## 20 EGYPTIAN CIVILIZATION OF SUMER ORIGIN

These highly critical inscriptions of this king, now disclosed to be the great emperor "Sargon" (see Figs. 4 and 5) as a Predynastic Pharaoh of Egypt, were discovered by Prof. (now Sir) Flinders Petrie in one of the oldest tombs at Abydos in Upper Egypt. In this tomb the queen of this king was buried, and also it seems himself.

In summarizing the discovery and contents of this tomb Prof. Petrie says:[1] "The tomb of this king is a brick-lined pit about twenty feet long and half as wide. It had been entirely plundered anciently; but many cylinder jars of pottery remained in the sand, bearing inscriptions [Fig. 4-5] which gave the name of 'Horus Ka,' with the personal name of 'King Ap.' Besides these there are other similar inscriptions [Fig. 5] of 'Ha, wife of the Horus Ka.' In the same tomb was an impression of a small seal of Ka. From these remains we see that the system of inscribing the royal property, *of sealing on clay with a cylinder seal and the free use of writing*, were already in course of development, leading on to the civilization which followed."

### "Sargon's" Sumerian Inscriptions at Abydos

When I first saw these inscriptions about twenty years ago, in the light of my Indian keys to Menes' Mesopotamian origin and with some acquaintance with Egyptian hieroglyphs and Sumerian writing, I observed that the writing generally resembled the Early Sumerian script and differed considerably from the conventional Egyptian hieroglyphs and contained some signs which were absent in the latter.

On scrutinizing the inscriptions in detail some years later, I found that the writing was radically of the old cursive Sumerian type (such as I later found written regularly on the Indo-Sumerian seals of the Sargonic and later period); and that it was obviously intended to be read with the Sumerian phonetic values of the signs, that is syllabically. Moreover, it was clear that both inscriptions were to be read in the retrograde direction, as the Sun-Hawk sign in both faced to the right, a feature which indicates the direction for reading to the left through the beak or nose of bird or

[1] PHE. I, 4-5.

PLATE III.

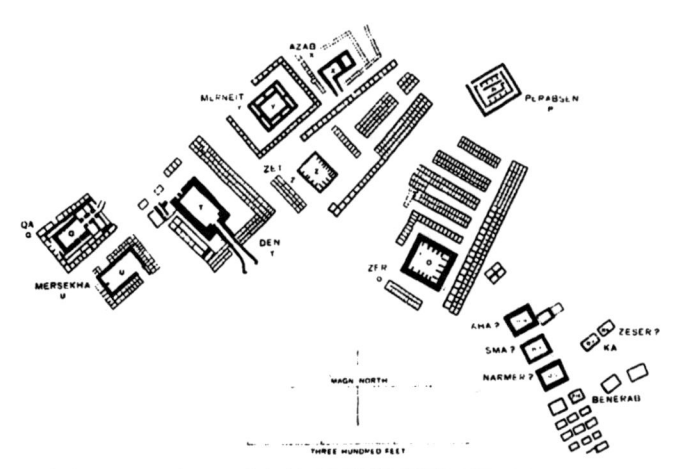

GENERAL PLAN OF TOMBS OF PREDYNASTIC AND FIRST DYNASTY
PHARAOHS AT ABYDOS.

(After Sir F. Petrie, PRT., II, Pl. LVIII.)

Note the tomb of Sargon-the-Great as King "Ka" to the right of that of Menes' (Aha); and the tombs of Menes' descendants on the South and North become more and more extensive and developed. See Pl. XIII for details of Pharaoh Dudu's or "Den's" tomb; and Pl. XVI for details of King Shudur Kib's or Qa's tomb.

# SARGON AS AN UKUSI LINE ARYAN

animal in archaic Hittite and in Egyptian inscriptions, and also as we now find on the Indo-Sumerian sealings.

On reading the signs with their Sumerian syllabic values, I found that the King's personal name read GIN-UKUS, or GIN-UKUSSI[1] (see decipherment table, Fig. 6). This strikingly confirmed his identity with King Gin or "Sargon"; for the usual title of "Sargon" in the Indian Epics is *Kuni* (or *Shakuni*) *Aikshvaka, i.e.* "Kuni descendant of Ikshvāku" —the latter being as we have seen the solar title of the first Aryan king and the equivalent, as we have found, of his Sumerian title in the Kish Chronicle of *Ukusi*. And "Sargon" as Kuni or Shakuni in the Indian Epics is repeatedly called by this proud title of "Descendant of Ikshvāku," and his descendants also bear this title.[2]

## The Shield for the Solar Title of the Pharaohs on "Sargon's" Tomb Inscription at Abydos and its Sumerian Meaning.

At the outset it is noteworthy that the king's *Solar title* is enclosed within a sign consisting of an upright panelled frame with three vertical bars in its top register (compared with two in the queen's inscription) and surmounted by the Sun-Hawk, while his solar title occupies its lower register. The Solar title of Pharaoh is called by Egyptologists "the Horus name" from "Horus" or *Haru*, the title of the Sun and of the Sun-Hawk, which is presumably derived from the Sumerian *Hu* or *Ha* name for the Hawk.[3] And this "Horus" title is given the first place of all the plural titles used by subsequent Pharaohs, each of whom claimed to be "Son of the Sun." It is significant that already Sargon had adopted this heraldic shield-like enclosing device for framing his Solar title; and it was evidently the model copied by the latter Pharaohs for this purpose, with the alteration that the vertical bars were relegated to the lower register, thus giving more prominence to the Solar title. The vertical bars have suggested to some Egyptologists that this design, which they call *serekh*, represented a banner with fringes, because in the later forms the bottom bars

[1] Br. 11184 gives the complement -*si* to the *Kus* value.
[2] See WMC. 196.   [3] Br. 2053.

have sometimes free ends; but their early position as erect bars above is against this view. Much more probable, it seems to me, is the suggestion that the figure represented the hieroglyph of a temple; for this seems confirmed by the fact that the sign resembles the upper portion of the Sumerian pictograph of the temple-sign, which has the value of *Bar* or *Bara*,[1] which designated him as the *Parāa* or "*Pharaoh*" in Egyptian inscriptions of the First Dynasty, as we shall see, and also in the Indus seals. And in its developed forms in the stele of the fourth king of the First Dynasty it is figured realistically as a temple or palace (see Fig. 6, p 23).

This temple or palace sign, or the upper portion of that sign, is placed within the square sign, which in Sumerian has the value of *Rin*, and meaning primarily "Ring," and secondarily "enclosure, dwelling-place"; and it has the Semitic value of *Saru*,[2] which is thus presumably the source of the later Egyptian name *serekh*; I have accordingly translated it as "of the House of the Pharaoh."

### DECIPHERMENT OF SARGON'S INSCRIPTION AT ABYDOS

In the decipherment of this Sumerian inscription of "Sargon," in order to enable the reader to follow it, I have, in the accompanying Decipherment Table in Fig. 6, arranged in the first line the signs in their usual orthographic Sumerian order for reading from left to right; and in the second line are placed for comparison the corresponding forms of these signs in the standard Early Sumerian script of Mesopotamia, in which it will be noticed the signs are given a slightly more cursive and somewhat abbreviated form for rapid writing; in the third line are placed the Sumerian phonetic values of each sign in roman type, each duly attested from the standard Sumerian lexicons; and in the fourth line is the literal translation all duly attested for each word by the references in the preceding line. The language is Sumerian.

Here it is seen that "Sargon" uses, or is given, for his personal name at Abydos in Egypt precisely the same

[1] Br. 6871-2; WSAD. 29.   [2] B. 443; M. 7683.

## SARGON'S EGYPT INSCRIPTIONS DECIPHERED 23

personal name *Gin* which he uses with the variant *Gani* in his inscriptions in Mesopotamia, and which is used for him in most of the Babylonian inscriptions. And his title of " The *Ukus* or *Ukussi*," we have seen designates him as a descendant of the first Sumerian king Ukusi of *Ukhu* (Sun-Hawk City), or the first Aryan king under his solar title of Ikshwāku of the Indian Epics and Vedas, in keeping with the references to him in the Indian Epics as an *Aikshwaka* or " descendant of King Ikshwāku," *i.e.* " Ukusi of Ukhu."

Predynastic.

Mesopot. Sumerian.

Reads :  SHA¹  PA -RIN²-BARA³KAD⁴ GIN⁵ U-⁶KUS⁷

Transl. : The Shepherd of the (Sun-)Hawk, of the House of the Pharaoh. KAD (the lofty) GIN, the Ukus (or Ukussi).

FIG. 6.—Sargon's Tomb Inscription as the Solar KAD, GIN, or SHA-GIN, the UKUSSI at Abydos deciphered.

The *Sha*[8] prefix to his solar title is in series with his name and title spelt *Sha-Gin* in the Old Sumerian King-Lists above noted and in series with his fuller Indian form of name as *Sha-Kuni*. The sign for his solar title " KAD " is the pictogram of an uplifted hand with the fingers erect. In its conventionalized Egyptian hieroglyph form this sign is pictured by two uplifted hands conjoined and is given the phonetic value of *Ka*, whence Egypto-

---

[1] *Sha,* " The shepherd." B. 93 ; Br. 2552 and see note 8.
[2] B. 83 ; Br. 2045, 2047, and see *Bak, Pak,* in WSAD. 25. *Rin* 443. Br. 10167.
[3] B. 301 ; Br. 6872.
[4] B. 311 ; *Kad* or *Shu,* Br. 7063-5.
[5] B. 283 ; Br. 6506.
[6] B. 273 ; Br. 6020.
[7] B. 508 ; Br. 11184, *Kus,* with complement -*si.*
[8] This *Sha* sign means " protect," " protector," also " shepherd," and " shining," Br. 2560, 2572, 2577. It is clearly not the reed sign *Gi*, with the meaning of " king," from which it differs by its curve below.

logists have called the solar title of this king "King *Ka.*" This *Ka* value in Egypt is obviously derived from the Sumerian value of this sign as *Kad* or *Kat*,[1] wherein the final *d*, as is often the case, has dropped out ; and affords another illustration of the derivation of the Egyptian hieroglyphs from the Sumerian in pictographic form and phonetic sound. This title *Kad* is used by Sargon also in his beautiful Bull signet (Pl. IV, No. 1) from the Indus Valley. And *Kad* as we have seen was a not infrequent title used by the Phœnicians, and we have seen that Sargon was an Aryan Phœnician.

The simplicity in the titles of the great world-monarch "Sargon," without any reference to his empire on this funerary votive vase is noteworthy. Possibly his temporal titles were recorded on his main epitaph (as in those of his descendant Pharaohs as we shall see) which has been lost. Here it should be noted that, this inscription was presumably written by his son Menes, who we shall find revolted against his father and was in revolt against him at the time of the latter's death, and thus lost the immediate succession in Mesopotamia. In such circumstances, if Sargon's body were really buried in this tomb, which was the tomb of his queen (the mother of Menes), who obviously died before him, his body must have been embalmed for its transport from Mesopotamia to Abydos to repose beside that of his queen. On the other hand, no embalming or mummification is found in Egypt before the Second Dynasty, nor customary till the Third Dynasty, nor has any been found in Mesopotamia or elsewhere in the civilized old world outside Egypt.

We now turn to the inscription of the Queen of "Sargon" found in the same tomb.

### Sargon's Queen's Tomb Inscription at Abydos Deciphered

The inscription on Sargon's Queen's tomb vase (Fig. 5) is likewise written in the reversed direction or towards the left, and in the Sumerian language. When arranged for

[1] Br. 7063.

# SARGON'S QUEEN'S EGYPT INSCRIPTION 25

decipherment in the usual Sumerian order of reading from left to right it reads as follows:—

Predynastic.

Mesopot. Sumerian.

Reads: PA - RIN- BARA KAD MA-ASH NIN - I

Transl.: (Of) The (Sun-)Hawk House of the Pharaoh KAD, my Lady ASH.

FIG. 7.—Sargon's Queen, the Lady Ash (*Ash-Nini*), Tomb inscription at Abydos deciphered.

The name of Sargon's Queen here as "The Lady *Ash*" is of immense critical importance. In later Babylonian records the name of Sargon's Queen is given as *Ash-nar*(-tum) or *Ash-lal*(-tum)—*tum* meaning "the exalted," and *l* and *r* are freely interchanged dialectically. And in the Indian Epics her name as the mother of Manasyu, *i.e.*, Menes, is given as *Acchura*(-*Seni*) (see p. 4). Thus both Babylonian and Indian substantially agree with the Abydos inscription, and confirm her identity as the Queen of "Sargon" or King Gin.

The third sign, that immediately following the "Horus" *Kad* title, is the ship-sign as the pictograph of a Nile boat, as distinguished from the high-prowed ship-sign in Mesopotamian Sumerian. It has the phonetic value of *ma*, with the literal meaning of "my" or "me," and is, as I have shown, obviously the Sumerian origin of these English words. This gives the reading, "Of the (Sun-)Hawk House of the Pharaoh Kad, my Lady Ash," and shows that Sargon's Queen died within his lifetime and was here buried by him.

KING GIN'S OR "SARGON'S" SEALING AT ABYDOS AND ITS DECIPHERMENT

I find another of King Gin's or "Sargon's" inscriptions amongst the sealings unearthed at the Abydos tombs by

---

[1] As in previous Fig.  [2] B. 137; Br. 3682.
[3] B. 1; Br. 2; WSAD. 19.  [4] B. 532; Br. 11949.  [5] B. 533.

## 26 EGYPTIAN CIVILIZATION OF SUMER ORIGIN

Sir F. Petrie, included by the latter in " Sealings of King Ka and Narmer,"[1] and here reproduced in Fig. 8.

FIG. 8.—Sealing of King GIN or "Sargon" at Abydos.
(Photo after Petrie.)

It will be noticed that this royal sealing (for a jar or other article of the royal property) consists of a tenfold repetition of two alternating signs, namely a circle with matted line interior and a branched twig or reed ; and from exigencies of space for the circles two of the reeds belonging to the lower row of circles are squeezed into the top row of signs. Now, these signs are the well-known Sumerian

Predynastic

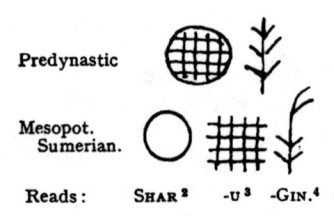

Mesopot.
Sumerian.

Reads: SHAR[2] -U[3] -GIN.[4]

FIG. 9.—King Gin's or "Sargon's" Sealing from Abydos deciphered. Here it is seen that King Gin calls himself *Sharu-Gin*, suggesting that this seal was for use in Mesopotamia.

syllabic signs for *Shar*, *U* and *Gin* as seen in the above decipherment table, which also shows that the sealing reads *in the retrograde direction*, from right to left.

Thus these three inscriptions from the tomb of the Predynastic Pharaoh, Gin, Sha-Gin or Sharu-Gin at Abydos, the tomb of himself and his Queen, with his solar title of *Kad*—and we have seen that "Sargon" was a famous

[1] PRT. II., pl. XII, 95.  [2] B. 353; Br. 8208.
[3] B. 273; Br. 6020.   [4] B. 92, as before.

## SARGON'S RECONQUEST OF EGYPT

Sun-worshipper—now identify him clearly with the mighty world-monarch "Sargon" or King Gin of Mesopotamia, whose empire included Egypt, and with the father of King Manasyu or Asa-Manja " the Prabhu of Gopta " and son of Sha-Kuni and Queen Acchura(-Seni) of the Indian Epics, who was, we have found, identical with Manis-Tusu or " Manis-the-Warrior " of Mesopotamia, and with Manj or Aha-Manj or " Manj - the - Warrior " of the Indian epics, or the Egyptian *Manj* or " Menes."

### SARGON'S ANNEXATION OR RECONQUEST OF EGYPT, & ROUTE & DATE

Some light also is thrown on the date and route of Sargon's annexation of Egypt by the references in his chronicles and in the extracts preserved in the Babylonian and Assyrian Omen-literature, and in his traditional autobiography. While the former gives the specific year of his reign for his first expedition of conquest to the Mediterranean as his third year of reign and his culminating conquest of " all the lands of that Western Sea of the Setting Sun " in his eleventh year, his autobiography says: "To the Western Sea-coast thrice did I advance," and it adds, " *Iatu* (or Itu)-Land-Mouth submitted," wherein the word now read as *Iatu* (or *Itu*) has hitherto been read by its Semitic synonym of " Dilmun."[1] And that Sargon regarded this *Iatu*-Land-Mouth (also defined as Pu-Land,[2] a Semitic title for Lower Egypt,[3] presumably from *Pu*, the old name for the early sacred city of Buto in the Delta [4] and the centre of the aboriginal predynastic Serpent cult) as one of his greatest conquests in the West, seems evidenced by its being given the first place of the only two places, both in the West, actually named as conquered by him in his autobiography.

Now it is significant that the old and usual Egyptian

---

[1] This territorial name has hitherto been conjecturally read *Ni-tuh(-ki)*, with the Semitic synonym Dilmun (Br. 5372). But the standard Sumerian bilingual glossaries give for the first sign the chief value of *I* or *Ia* (Br. 5305; M. 3664-5), and *Iau* is the name of this sign. And the definition of this land name is prefixed by " *Pu*-Land," and it bears the suffix *ka* or " Mouth " (Br. 5372). It thus obviously designated *Iatu* Land as " The Land of the Mouth of the Iatu River or Nile."

[2] Br. 5372; M. 7799.  [3] MD. 789.  [4] BD. 981 a.

hieroglyphic name for the River Nile is *Iatur*,[1] a name also applied to the Land of Egypt.[2]

This "*Iatu* Land-Mouth," therefore, one of the greatest of Sargon's new conquests in the West, made by him in his eleventh year of reign, appears to designate "The Mouth-Land of the Iatur or Nile," that is Lower Egypt. And this identity is confirmed in the next chapter. This conquest (or reconquest, as it now appears from the new evidence), of Egypt by Sargon, *via* the Mediterranean, from the north is also in agreement with Sargon's records, which make his conquests of "The Lands of the Western Sea (or Mediterranean)" begin from the Muru or Amorite Land in Northern Syria. His penetration to Upper Egypt would doubtless follow from his possession of Lower Egypt with his "predynastic" capital there, presumably at Pu or Buto.

### Sargon on the Nile *re* his Birth Legend

Sargon's later Babylonian title of *Ni-lu-ba-ni*, which occurs in the Isin literature of about 2000 B.C., may thus, I think, possibly refer to his having been "born on the *Nile*"—*Nilu* in Assyrian meaning "Flood or high-tide water"[3] and *bani*="beget."[4] So, after all, the legendary story of his being sent adrift in a basket of rushes by his mother on "The River" may thus have occurred on the banks of the Nile, where his father and grandfather before him were the Predynastic Pharaohs.[5] And the Hebrews in borrowing this legend for their Moses, would appear to have helped themselves to the local floating legend of the Aryan Pharaoh Sargon surviving on the Nile. There seems no doubt that this absenteeship of these Mesopotamian emperors in Egypt must have contributed to the usurpation of the Mesopotamian throne by Zaggisi, who dethroned Sargon's father there.

[1] MDC. 6; and see BD. 97 b; and cp. later *Itru*, BD. 99 b.
[2] Lower Egypt was called *Itur*-meh, and Upper Egypt was *Itur*-res, cp. BD. 97 b.
[3] MD. 678.   [4] *Ib.* 173.   [5] Details of Birth-legend, WMC. 205 f.

## SARGON'S INDUS VALLEY SEALS WITH TITLES OF "PHARAOH," &C.

In his Mesopotamian records, King Gin or Gana or "Sargon-the-Great" refers repeatedly to his conquest or reconquest of the Indus Valley as detailed in my *Makers of Civilization*, and those records are shown to be in full agreement with the details of that event preserved in the Indian epic chronicles. It was therefore not surprising to find that no less than six of the great collection of several hundreds of official Sumerian signet-seals, unearthed by Sir John Marshall at the two ancient Sumerian city-ports of the Indus, at Mohenjo Daro and Harappa, were seals of this mighty emperor who held that Indus colony for the greater part of his long reign of fifty-five years.

In one of these seals he bears the title of "Sagara," identical with one of his solar titles in the Indian epics;[1] and in another "Sag" which is obviously a contraction for the same. In three of these his name is spelt "King Gin" (*Shar-um Sharu-Gin*) and in two it is spelt "Gan" or "Gana." In three of them he adds the title of *Gut* (or "Goth"), and in one he calls himself "The Great *Khāti*" (or *Khatti* or "Hitt-ite").

The spelling of the same king's name occasionally by different pictographic signs bearing the same or nearly similar phonetic values in the case of Sargon's and of other Sumerian kings' names is noteworthy. The reason seems to have been to introduce other meanings, heroic or poetic, into the names, analogous to the Chinese practice by poets of spelling emperors' names by hieroglyphs different from those usually employed for spelling the name so as to yield new poetic or complimentary meanings. Thus Sargon's *Gin* name by its sign here has the meaning of "The Ruler," and his title *Sharu* by this sign here written means "The Universal Lord," instead of "King."

As the fully detailed decipherment of these new Indus Valley seals is given in Appendix II with duly attested proofs for the reading of each sign, it is only necessary here to record the literal reading of the inscriptions on these Indus seals of Sargon. Their inscriptions, as usual in all

[1] WISD. 63 f.

## 30 EGYPTIAN CIVILIZATION OF SUMER ORIGIN

these Indo-Sumerian seals, as well as in the similar Early Sumerian seals from Mesopotamia, are graven so as to give the writing in their sealings or seal-impressions in *the reverse or retrograde direction* from left to right. In the following literal translations, the writing is given in the usual Sumerian or Aryan direction for reading from right to left. For convenience of reference I cite these seals in the order in which they are arranged in Plate IV.

His beautiful Bull signet (Plate IV, Nos. 1 and 2, for seal and its impression) admirably portrays as its central figure the sacred Indian Bull, the Brahmin Bull of modern India, adorned with a wreath or garland as in Indo-Aryan festivals at the present day. But this Bull is here used as the pictograph of his title *Gūt*, and the prominence given to it indicates the importance which the king attached to that title. The inscription reads :—

" SAG, The Seer, The lofty *Kad*, the tablet (seal) of the One Lord, The GŪT (Goth)."

This title *Sag* is spelt by the identical sign which Sargon uses on his seal previously deciphered by me,[1] in which its fuller form of *Sagara* is given, that is in literal agreement with his solar title as preserved in the Indian chronicles, as we have seen. His title of " Seer " or " Diviner " is in keeping with the Babylonian records of his initiation into the priesthood as a priest-king. *Kad* is a Phœnician title which we shall see is used repeatedly by members of his dynasty; and the prominence given to his *Gut* title here is noteworthy, and in No. 6 he calls himself Khāti or " Hittite."

Of his other seals, No. 5 inscription reads :—

" SHARU-GIN of *Uri* (or *Akkadu*) Land."

No. 6 reads :—" SHAR-GIN, The Great *Khāti* of . . . Land."

No. 7. reads :—" SHAR-UM-GIN, The *Gūt* (or Goth) of *Agdu* Land."

Here the Sumerian form with the syllable *um* (or " overlord ") is significant as it is in agreement with that in his early Mesopotamian tablets.

Seals Nos. 8 and 9 also appear to be " Sargon's " by his

[1] *Ib.* 69 f.

PLATE IV.

INDUS VALLEY SEALS OF SARGON AND HIS FATHER AS "PHARAOHS,"
c. 2760-2720 B.C.

(Photographs after Sir J. Marshall.) For decipherments and translations, see pp. 29 f.,
179 f.

name Gan or Gana; though there is a doubt as to whether they may not be those of his great-grandson and namesake Shar-Gani-Eri, who also spells his name occasionally Gan and Gana, and who we shall find is the so-called King "Kenkenis" or "Khent" of Egyptologists, and the son of Narmar, son of Menes.

No. 8 reads :—" GANA, The Son of *Khamaesshi* (Land) at Agdu (Agade)."

On the great historical significance of the name of this land as a name for Egypt, see next chapter.

No. 9 reads :—" GANA, The Son, The ' Pharaoh,' The Gut of Agdu (or Abudu) Land."

### Summary of Discoveries regarding Sargon as Predynastic Pharaoh of Egypt

Thus we find through the keys supplied by the Indian King-Lists and Chronicles, that the "earliest known" of the Predynastic kings of Egypt of whom any contemporary inscriptional evidence has been found, the so-called "King Ka," is the great Sumerian or Aryan emperor King Gin of Agudu, the so-called "Sargon"; that his father and grandfather there before him were the so-called Predynastic Kings "Ro" and "Khetm"; that his son, the emperor Manis-Tusu or "Manis-the-Warrior" of Mesopotamia is identical with Asa-Manja or "Manja-the-Shooter" and Manasyu "the Prabhu of Gopta," son of the world-emperor Kuni or Sha-Kuni of the Indian Epics and Chronicles, and identical with the Pharaoh Manj or Aha-Manj or "Manj-the-Warrior" or "Menes" the founder of the First Dynasty in Egypt; that Sargon's Queen, the Lady Ash, and probably himself were buried at Abydos as attested by his three tomb inscriptions there; that by these discoveries is found the first synchronism between Egypt and Mesopotamia by which is now fixed with comparative certainty the date of Menes, hitherto the most disputed of all fundamental dates in Ancient History, at a no earlier period than about 2704 B.C.; and that the Civilization of Egypt was of Sumerian or Aryan Origin.

The further identity of Sargon's son Manis-Tusu with "Menes," the founder of the First Dynasty of Egypt, now requires a special chapter.

# III

## Menes' Lost History & Achievements in Egypt Recovered

*Disclosing his identity with King Manis of Mesopotamia,*
*His Sumerian Governorship of Elam & Indus Valley,*
*His Seizure of Egypt from his Father-emperor,*
*His Establishment of First Egyptian Dynasty, c. 2704 B.C.,*
*With a fully-fledged Sumerian Civilization,*
*His Sea- & World-Empire, Sun-worship & Aryan Race.*

MENES or Manj or "Manj-the-Warrior," although the traditional founder of the First Dynasty in Egypt with his tomb and contemporary inscriptions at Abydos in Upper Egypt, has hitherto been so shadowy a personage that, as we have seen, Egyptologists confess that "all we know of the first of the Pharaohs, Menes, beyond the fact of his existence is practically nil"; and the very latest text-book on Ancient History says: "Menes appears to be a conflate personage of legend."

Now, however, we recover Menes as a truly historical personage through our new keys, with his lost history and portrait and the leading details of his epoch-making achievements, his blood-relationship to the predynastic Pharaohs, his manner of establishing the First Dynasty in Egypt, with its civilization and hieroglyphs derived from the Sumerian, and his real date at about 2704 B.C.

### Menes identical with Manis of Mesopotamia

In the previous chapters we have found that Menes or Manj-the-Warrior was identical with the famous Mesopotamian world-emperor Manis-the-Warrior, the eldest son and successor of the Sumerian world-emperor King Gin or Guni, the "Sargon-the-Great" of Semitists; and identical with Manasyu or "Manas-the-Uniter," the Prabhu (or

# MENES' HISTORY & PREHISTORY RECOVERED 33

Pharaoh) of Gopta (Kopt or Egypt) of the Indian epic chronicles of the Early Aryan kings, also called in the solar version of those chronicles "Manja-the-Shooter" (Asa Manja), the son of the world-emperor Kuni or Sha-Kuni ("Sargon"), which chronicles are in full agreement with the Sumerian and Egyptian records regarding him and his dynasty and their achievements.

His Egyptian inscriptions like those of his father are written in Sumerian script and language and not in the later conventionalized hieroglyphs, and hence have hitherto remained unread. They are now deciphered, and found to be in agreement with his Mesopotamian and Elam records and his official seals from the Indus Valley colony, where he was Sumerian governor before he revolted against his father and annexed Egypt ; and they are in general agreement with the Indian chronicles.

### CULTURE OF MENES IDENTICAL WITH THAT OF MANIS

The fully-fledged culture which Menes and his father and predynastic forefathers introduced into Egypt and which formed the basis and fabric of Egyptian civilization is identical with the Sumerian civilization of the period of Manis-the-Warrior and his dynasty in Mesopotamia. This agreement in the Egyptian and Sumerian culture of that period comprises amongst many other things similarity in agriculture with plough and hoe and irrigation works, brick buildings with recessed walls, metallurgy and copper chisels, etc., cylinder-seals, stone-mace-heads, polished stone-vases, carved slate-palettes, potter's-wheel pottery, painted pottery, incised pottery decoration, animal and bird-form vases, clay-figurines, lapis lazuli beads and inlayings, style of jewellery, use of cosmetics, weaving of linen, chambered tomb-burials with votive offerings of food, dress and tomb-furniture, stone sculptures and statues, Sumerian hieroglyph writing, radical words in Sumerian language, Sun-worship and symbolism, mythology, etc. The identity even extends into the inhuman revolting practice of immolating in royal burials attendants and slaves, as disclosed in the tombs at Ur by Mr Woolley about two centuries earlier, and similarly found at Abydos in Egypt in First Dynasty tombs.

### MENES' SUN-WORSHIP

The Sun-worship of Manis in Mesopotamia is significant with reference to Menes' adoption of the Sun-Hawk in Egypt as his royal line emblem, following in this respect his father and grandfather as predynastic Pharaohs there, and followed by the descendants in his dynasty, and by the subsequent three Egyptian dynasties until the Fifth Dynasty, when the Sun-Hawk was replaced by the Sun-Goose. Some details of his Sun-worship are given below.

### HIS ARYAN RACE

His Aryan race is fully established by the complete agreement of his genealogy in the Sumerian Kish Chronicle with that of the Early Aryan kings in the Indian king-lists and chronicles, and by his and his father's and descendants' use of the patronymic Ukus or Ukush after the title of the first Sumerian king Ukusi of Ukhu city, that is the first king Iksh-Vaku of the Early Aryans, and use of the title of "Goth." Blue eyes are also inlaid in several statuettes and figurines of this period and are painted in frescoes; and the contemporary statue of Manis (Plate I and Fig. 10) is believed to have had the eyes inlaid with lapis lazuli stone.

The racial type of the early dynastic ruling race with broad foreheads is seen in the sculptured portraits of Menes and his son Narmar or Naram and found also to some extent in the skeletal remains. It is distinguished by Sir Flinders Petrie from the aborigines of Egypt (Mediterranean and other) as being "marked by a face wholly different from all the other types. The forehead and nose are in almost a straight line, the head massive, the ear large and flat, the nose straight with rounded tip and slight slope beneath, the jaw long and square."[1] And the sculptures and skeletal remains show that the race was tall.

The head-form, which is the best criterion of racial type, is in the Aryan *broad-browed* and long-headed. This broad-browed feature distinguishes the Aryans, along with the

[1] "Migrations," *Jour. Anthrop. Inst.*, xxxiv, 1906 [12].

ancient Greeks, Amorites, Phœnicians, Hamites, Indo-Aryans, Nordics and other branches of the Aryan race from the Iberian or "Mediterannean" Race properly so-called, the head-form of which is *narrow*-browed and long-headed with dark complexion. Colour is of less importance than head-form. Although the Aryan complexion is naturally white, slight darkening to brunette may result from prolonged residence for generations in southern climates, even without much admixture with darker blood. The ancient Greeks, who were of this Aryan and non-Mediterranean race, have their heroes and heroines described by their classic writers as tall, golden-haired, and blue or grey or "glaucous" eyed.

## Genealogy of Menes & his Descendants

The genealogy of Menes or Manis and his descendants back to Manis' great-grandfather in the Sumerian king-lists is found to be in strict agreement with his genealogy in the official king-lists of the Early Aryan kings in the Indian epics.[1] Here I tabulate for convenience of reference his genealogy as Manis-Tusu in Mesopotamia, according to the Babylonian record in the Kish Chronicle, and we shall see in next chapter that the descendants of Manis-Tusu are identical with those of Menes in the First Dynasty of Egypt.

King Kin (*Sharru*-Kin or "Sargon"),
r. 55 yrs. in Agadu.

| Manis-Tiśśu,[2] | Uri-Mush, |
| eldest son, r. 15 yrs. in Kish after brother Uri-Mush. | younger son, r. 15 (9?)[3] in Kish before k. Manis-Tiśśu. |

Narâm Lord Enzu ("Narâm Sin")
son, r. 56 yrs. in Agadu.

Shar-Gani-Eri,
son, r. 24(?) yrs. in Agadu.
[Anarchy].
(For continuation of
Dynasty, see p. 77).

---
[1] See table, p. 151, and for further details WMC. 140 f.
[2] This is the dialectic variant spelling of this king's name by the Babylonian scribe of the Kish Chronicle about 2200 B.C., but it is spelt Manis-Tusu in his own inscriptions.
[3] Fifteen years is given in Legrain's fragment, *loc. cit.*, No. 1, 7; and nine years in WBC. 444.

### MENES' OR MANIS-TUSU'S REVOLT AGAINST HIS FATHER "SARGON" re HIS SEIZURE OF EGYPT

It will be noticed that although Manis-Tusu (spelt phonetically in the Kish Chronicle "Manis-Tis's'u,") was the eldest son of King Kīn or "Sargon," he did not immediately succeed his father on the Mesopotamian throne; but the succession passed to his younger brother Mush or Uru-Mush, who reigned as emperor of Mesopotamia for 15 (or 9?) years, and claimed in his inscriptions to be King of the Upper Sea (Mediterranean) and of the Lower Sea (Persian Gulf and Indian Ocean) "[1] just as his father Sargon did, though that claim could be only partial as regards the Mediterranean. And Manis-Tusu did not gain the Mesopotamian throne until his brother's death in "a palace revolution," the real character of which is disclosed by the Indus seals as his dethronement by his brother Menes.

Of his brother Uru-Mush's rule in the Indus Valley colony of the Lower Sea, I have discovered evidence in one of his official seals in the second batch of seals unearthed there. This proves that he, like his father Sargon and his grandfather, held the rich Indus Colony as an appanage of the Sumerian empire. In this seal he calls himself "The One Lord," that is emperor. This seal (see Plate XV, No. 8) inscription I read as follows as detailed in Appendix V:—

Reads : *Umun-ash lu-gal-uru uri-mush.*
Translation : The One Lord, The great hero, Uri-Mush.

The reason for Manis-Tusu's non-succession in Mesopotamia immediately on the death of his father Sargon, and not until the death of his younger brother Mush, we now find in the Indian Chronicle record regarding him. This, which is cited in detail below, states that he was disinherited by his father, owing to his having revolted against him. And this revolt now appears to have been his seizure of Egypt from his father, and his declaration of independence there as "Menes" or Manas-yu, King of Upper and Lower Egypt.

The Indian account of the revolt of the young prince Menes or Manis-Tusu against his father "Sargon" is thus

[1] PHT. 4, 200 f.

MAP II.

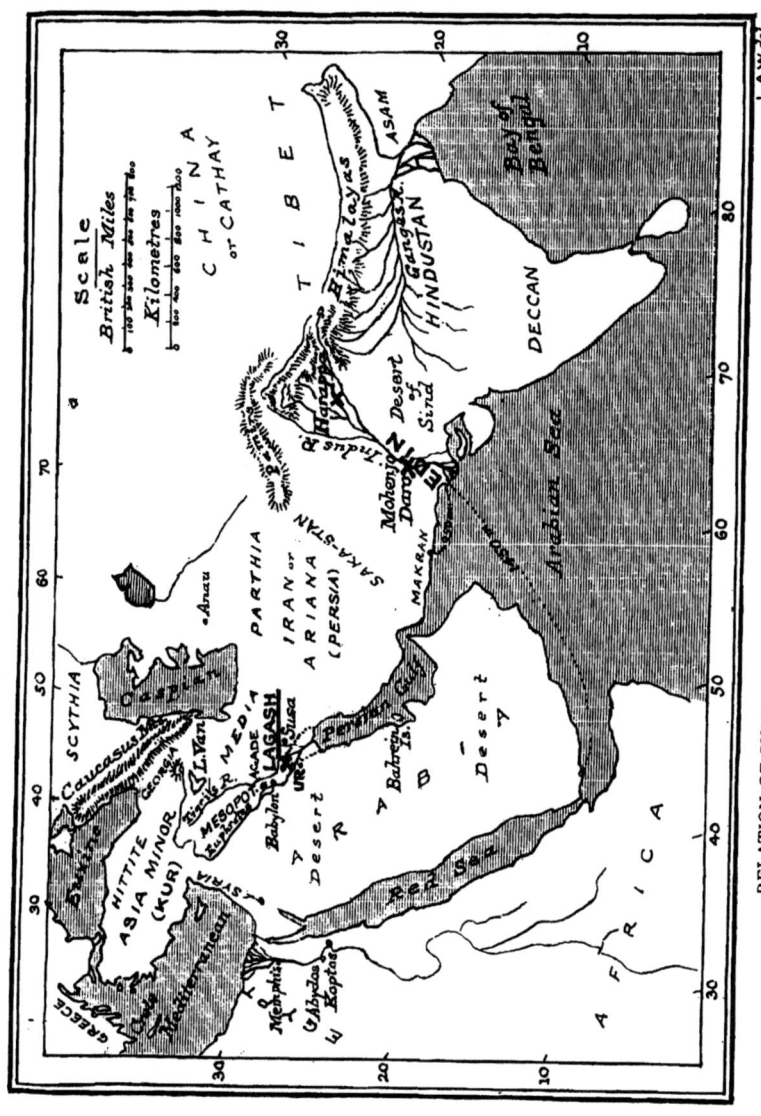

RELATION OF SUMERIAN INDUS COLONY TO MESOPOTAMIA AND EGYPT.

## MENES' SEIZURE OF EGYPT FROM HIS FATHER 37

related in the solar version of the Indian Epic Chronicles, under his title of Asa-Manja, the eldest son of the world-monarch Sagara (*i.e.* as we have seen, " Sargon "). This record is in the somewhat expanded sacerdotal form it has been given by the later Brahman priests ; it states [1] :—

" Asa-Manja—son of Sagara by his queen Keshinī [2]— the prince through whom the dynasty continued, was from his boyhood of very wayward [3] conduct. His father hoped that as he grew up to manhood he would reform ; but finding that he continued addicted to the same habit Sagara abandoned him. The sixty thousand fed troops (?) [4] of Sagara followed the example of their ' brother ' Asa-Manja. The path of virtue and piety was obscured in the world by the 'sons' of Sagara." [Here the narrative goes on to relate in diffuse Brahmanist fashion, that King Sagara, in order to remedy this disaster, commenced preparations for the horse-sacrifice [5] for a world-monarch's conquests, presumably in anticipation of his recovery of the lost provinces. But this sacrifice did not materialize until his grandson's day. It was obstructed by " the world-monarch's " horse—a late Brahmanist sacrifice—being stolen. And for its recovery other loyal " sons " of Sagara had to dig a chasm in the earth, where the " sons dug downwards each for a league," and were thereafter killed. The world-monarch's horse was eventually recovered only by Sargon's grandson, in the person of *Ansu*-mat (*i.e.* Narām *Enzu*) the son of Manis-Tusu (or Menes) whom his grandfather Sagara adopted. And the chasm which Sagara's " sons " had dug was called " The Ocean " (Sagara), a false Brahmanist etymology of Sagara's name.]

This is obviously a somewhat allegorical tradition of the successful revolt by prince Manis-Tusu (Manis-the-Warrior or Menes), against his father, and his retention of Egypt against the expeditions sent by his father ; so that the complete "world-monarchship," including Egypt, was not

[1] WVP. 3, 298 f.
[2] Here Menes' mother, who in the lunar version is called Acchura Seni, is descriptively styled " The Fine Haired " (Keshinī), and is called " a daughter of King Vidarbha."
[3] *Apavritta* = " gone out of the way, deport, turn away." MWD. 52.
[4] *Sagaraiva padhvasta.*
[5] Horse-sacrifice was also performed by victorious Greek heroes.

recovered until the accession of Sargon's grandson Narām Euzu, the son of Manis-Tusu, who we shall find succeeded his father, Menes, as second king of the First Dynasty in Egypt as "Narmar," and combined with it the imperial throne of Mesopotamia.

The digging operations referred to were, I venture to suggest, a memory of canals connected with the Mediterranean dug by Sargon's expeditionary force in the Suez Canal region in their attack on Menes' position in Upper Egypt, as the Sumerians were great experts in digging canals. And we have seen that Sargon, in his record of his attack on King Zaggisi, speaks of his canals for military purposes.[1] At that early period the Gulf of Suez, arm of the Red Sea, probably extended up to the Bitter Lakes, and Lake Timsah to the site of the modern Ismailia, that is only about six miles from the Bala Lake, which is continuous with Lake Menzaleh, an old arm of the Mediterranean and presumably then the open sea of the Mediterranean, as geologists find that the Red Sea extended to the Mediterranean in this line in former times. Thus the cutting of a relatively short canal might have connected it with the Mediterranean sufficiently for the passage of the galleys of those days. For Lower Egypt was presumably not originally under Menes; but had to be conquered by him later on, and probably continued to be held by Sargon's governors for a time.

What seems to be historical confirmation of Manis-Tusu's quarrel with his father, Sargon, is found in a record which states Manis-Tusu, King of Anshan (*i.e.* Persia), was deported as an enemy by King "Shar-Gani- (?) Sharri"[2]—for Shar-Gani or Sargon is often confounded with his great-grandson of the former name. And Sargon's son, Manis-Tusu, we shall find was King of Anshan as well as governor of the Indus Valley to its east in the reign of his father, Sargon, as attested by his own seals recently unearthed in the latter region, and now deciphered; and numerous contemporary statues of him have been unearthed in Elam in S.W. Persia of which he was for a time governor and latterly emperor.

[1] WMC. 213. [2] Cp. KHS. 244.

## PORTRAIT OF MENES, MINOS OR MANIS

### Menes' Portrait as Manis-Tusu or "Manis-the-Warrior"

Amongst the many particulars now recovered of Menes and his personality, through his identification with Manis-Tusu, are his portraits as found on several of his statues that have been unearthed in Mesopotamia and Elam, from which latter province is the one shown in Pl. I and Fig. 10. From the inscription engraved upon it, it was

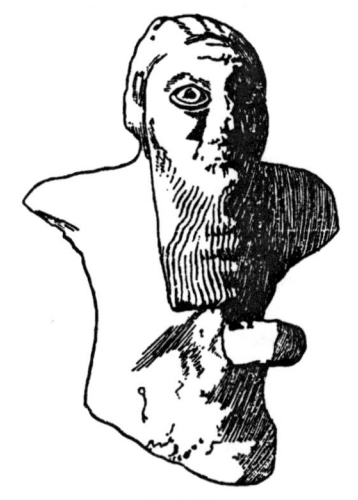

Fig. 10.—Statue of King Manis-Tusu (or Menes) in alabaster from Susa in Elam and now in the Louvre. (After DP. x. pl. I, 1907, 398.) See Frontispiece for photograph.

erected by an official in the service of King Manis-Tusu during the latter's suzerainty over Elam.

This fine artistic statue in alabaster is sculptured in the round, and shows the king bearded and like his Sumerian Aryan ancestor King Madgal, founder of the Indus colony, who was also governor and latterly King of Elam, which was a colony of the Sumerian Empire along with the Indus Valley Colony, in his day—the shaven face was obviously adopted for sacerdotal purposes under the *ex-officio* priest-kingship. And it is noticeable that his upper lip is shaven, a Sumerian and Ancient Hittite custom which distinguishes those from the Semites who wore a moustache as well as beard.

The staring effect of the eyes is owing to the eyeballs having been made of white limestone inset into the eye-sockets of the alabaster image, and to the inlaid iris and pupil being lost. The iris was inlaid it is believed with lapis lazuli stone, as is found in other similarly inlaid eyes, to represent the blue eyes of the early Aryan race.

## MENES AS MANIS-TUSU IN MESOPOTAMIA, ELAM, PERSIA & INDUS VALLEY

The reign of Menes in Mesopotamia as well as in Egypt is implied by the record in the Indian Epics that Manasyu was " the royal Eye of Gopta *and of the four ends of the Earth*," as already cited; though in none of his Mesopotamian inscriptions yet found does he call himself like his father and like his son a " world-monarch."

The existing contemporary records of Manis-Tusu in Mesopotamia, Elam, and Persia seem to date only from the period in which he gained the Emperorship as " King of Kish " there, in succession to his younger brother Mūsh or Uri-Mūsh. And Manis-Tusu, as " King of Kish," was amongst the earliest recovered names of a king bearing that imperial Mesopotamian title, and as a Sun-worshipper. But in the Indus Valley I have discovered his seals there as crown prince governor of that colony before his attainment of kingship as detailed below, and see Plates IV and V.

Most of his original inscriptions in Mesopotamia are characteristically carved on the extremely hard mineral called diorite, a stone not found in Mesopotamia and brought there by sea, as we shall find, from the north of the Red Sea *via* the Arabian Sea and Persian Gulf. Others are inscribed on votive vases and on a stone-mace-head, on a cruciform monument, and on the famous Black Obelisk, while others are certified copies in the old Sun-temple at Nippur.

The most historically important of these inscriptions is that of which many multiple copies, more or less fragmentary, exist in which he records as " King of Kish " his vast cam-

## MENES AS PHARAOH IN INDUS VALLEY 41

paign of reconquests of revolted colonies to the east of Mesopotamia, in Persia, the Indus Valley and across the Indian Ocean or Arabian Sea, through the Red Sea to the Sinai Peninsula on the borders of Egypt, as now definitely established for the first time in these pages. This campaign occurred after he became King of Kish, that is after his gaining the imperial throne of Mesopotamia on the death of his younger brother ; and we shall find that it was a reconquest of revolted colonies of his father's, Sargon's, empire. Before examining this record of his vast reconquests with the important geographical information they contain of the extent of his empire, it is necessary here to refer to my discovery of his official seals in the Indus Valley.

### OFFICIAL SEALS OF MENES OR MANIS-TUSU DISCOVERED IN THE INDUS VALLEY DISCLOSING HIM AS CROWN PRINCE GOVERNOR THERE, AS SON OF " SARGON " WITH TITLE OF " PHARAOH "

Startling concrete confirmation of all the foregoing identifications of Menes, Egyptian, Babylonian, and Indian, now emerges, fortunately for History, in my *discovery of no less than nine official seals of Menes in the Indus Colony in the second batch of seals unearthed there, and in several of these he already bears the title of* " *Bara* " *or* " *Pharaoh* " *and* " *Aha Men.*"

In my pioneer decipherment of the first batch of the Indus Valley seals, I supplied for the first time the key to the signs of these seals in that linear variety of Sumerian writing hitherto undeciphered. With those keys to the script, I experienced little difficulty in deciphering the freshly-found seals.

The previous Indus Valley seals disclosed that it was a custom of the Mesopotamian emperors to send the crown prince for a time as governor of that rich and favourite crown colony on the Indus.[1] The new seals, which included others of Sargon and other Mesopotamian emperors, show that Sargon also followed this practice.

[1] WISD. 35 f., 55 f.

## The Title of "Under-King Companion" or Viceroy in the Indus Colony Seals

Striking confirmation of my observation, in my *Indo-Sumerian Seals Deciphered*, that it was the custom for the Sumerian emperors of Mesopotamia to send their eldest son as Viceroy to the Indus Colony of Edin is now found in the second batch of seals unearthed there, and now deciphered for the first time.

Whilst the names on many of these fresh seals are those of the crown princes of Mesopotamia of Sargon's dynasty who latterly became emperors, the title which these bear in many of their seals is not "king" or "emperor," but "Under-King Companion," in the form of *Shag-man, Shab-man,* or *Sha-man.*

The first element in this title, namely, *Shag, Shab* or *Sha,* is very interesting. Its pictograph (see initial sign in Plate V, Nos. 1, 3 and 7) represents and means "Heart"; and its secondary meaning is "interior, midst, within," and also "below, lower, under"; [1] and it is, in the latter sense, the usual sign employed to designate the Persian Gulf and Indian Ocean as "The Lower Sea." Hence the meaning of the full title might be "King-Companion of the Persian Gulf and Indian Ocean." The second syllable *Man* literally means "Two, Second, or Companion," and also "King"; [2] and it is significant that it is formed by two short straight strokes like those in the first batch of Indus seals which I deciphered, and not written by its usual crescent form as in ordinary Mesopotamian writing. This title of *Shag-man* thus means literally "The Under-King Companion," and so is the equivalent of our modern "Viceroy."

Most of the crown princes of Sargon's or Menes' dynasty in their Indus seals carry this title on some of their seals, thus indicating those seals as belonging to the period of their governorship or viceroyship of the Edin colony. Whilst others of their seals bear the title of "Lord Companion," in which the sign for this "Lord" has the sense of "Emperor," and thus implies a more advanced rank, presumably corresponding to "Co-Regent." And others of their seals in

[1] Br. 7988 f.  [2] Br. 9952 f.

INDUS VALLEY SEALS OF PHARAOH MENES AND HIS SON NARMAR
OR NARAM.

(Photographs after Sir J. Marshall.) For decipherments and
translations, see pp. 41 f., 184 f.

## MENES' SEALS IN INDUS VALLEY DECIPHERED

which they are called "The One Lord," belong to their period of emperorship.

### MENES' INDUS VALLEY SEALS DECIPHERED

The nine seals of Menes or Manis thus discovered in the Indus Valley are figured in Plate IV, No. 10, and Plate V, Nos. 1-8.

In these new Indus seals here deciphered, Menes or Manis calls himself by his names and titles variously spelt as *Men, Ash-Mānshu, Aha* or *Akha* and *Aha-* (or *Akha-*) *Men*. And while styling himself *Bara* or "Pharaoh" and son of *Shar-Gin* or *Sara-Gin* (*i.e.* "Sargon"), he also significantly spells the latter name as *Shagāni* or *Shakunu*, thus using substantially the dialectic form of the Indian epics *Shakuni*, a form which is also used in Menes' ebony label at Abydos as we shall see. *Aha* we have seen has in the Sumerian the meaning of "Warrior," just as *Tussu* has, and thus confirms the identification of Menes or Aha Men with Manis Tussu of Mesopotamia. And his title of *Gut* or "Goth," like that of his father Sargon, in his Indus seals is noteworthy.

These Indus seals of Manis, Menes or Aha Men, the detailed decipherment of which is given in Appendix III, are here enumerated in the order in which they are figured in Plates IV and V, for convenience of reference.

PLATE IV, No. 10 SEAL (and App. III, Fig. 59)

Reads : *Umun-man a-ha mar sha-ga-ni bara gu-edin-ash.*

Transl. : Overlord Companion AHA, the son of SHAGANI, The Pharaoh at Edin Land.

PLATE V, No. 1 SEAL (and App. III, Fig. 60)

Reads : *Shag-man ma-anshu bara gu-edin* (or *ag-du*)-*ash.*

Transl. : Under-King Companion MĀNSHU, The Pharaoh at Edin (or Agdu) Land.

No. 2 SEAL (and App. III, Fig. 61)

Reads : *Umun-man a-ha-men . . . gu- . . .*

Transl. : Overlord Companion AHA-MEN . . . at . . .

No. 3 SEAL (and App. III, Fig. 62)
Reads : *Shag-man a-ha-(?)men gut gu-ag-du-ash.*
Transl. : Under-King Companion AHA-(?) MEN, The *Gut* (or " Goth ") at Agdu Land.

No. 4 SEAL (and App. III, Fig. 63)
Reads : *Umun-ash a-ha mar gut gin gu-ag-du-ash.*
Transl. : The One Lord AHA, son of the *Gut* GIN, at Agdu Land.

No. 5 SEAL (and App. III, Fig. 64)
Reads: *Umun-man a-ha-(?)man mar(?)azu (ma)-esh-tar Gin.*
Transl. : Lord Companion AHA-(?)MAN, son of the Priest-Seer Esh-tar GIN. (On "Seer" table cp. p. 227).

No. 6 SEAL (and App. III, Fig. 65)
Reads : *A-ha sig uku mush.*
Transl. : AHA, The Overthrower of King MUSH.

No. 7 (and App. III, Fig. 66)
Reads : *Shag-man Aha ma-(es)-gan-mush.*
Transl. : Under-King-Companion AHA of Mā-(es)gan and Mush (-sir) [Egypt].

No. 8 (and App. III, Fig. 67)
Reads : *A-ha men-a gu uri-du* (or *ki-*) *-ash.*
Transl. : AHA MENA at URIKI Land.

The place-name on the smaller seals does not always clearly differentiate the name Edin from the very similar pictograph of Agdu, or " Agadu " (or Agade).

EVIDENCE OF INDUS SEALS ON IDENTITY OF MENES & MANIS-TUSU & HIS GOVERNORSHIP OF INDUS COLONY

This critically important historical series of official Indus seals of Manis-Tusu, the son of Sargon-the-Great, whilst disclosing his hitherto unknown governorship of the Indus Colony of his father's vast empire, as crown prince, and also as emperor and with the title of Pharaoh in his own seals, confirms absolutely his identity with Pharaoh Men, or Aha Men, the first king and founder of the First Dynasty of

Egypt. These seals also confirm his identity with the Aryan world-emperor Manasyu or Asa-Manja, the son of the world-emperor Shakuni of the Indian Lists; and disclose original Sumerian variants in the spelling of "Sargon's" name in series with the phonetic forms of spelling current in the Indian Lists and in Egypt. And the repeated use of the title *Bara, Para* or "Pharaoh" on these seals evidences the free intercommunication of the Indus Valley with Egypt in his reign.

MENES' OR MANIS-TUSU'S CONQUESTS IN PERSIA, INDUS VALLEY, ARABIAN SEA-LANDS & *via* RED SEA TO SINAI PENINSULA

From the vast extent of his victorious conquests, as recorded in his own records, we can now see how Manis-Tusu or Menes earned his title of "Menes-the-Warrior."

There are several instances of Manis-Tusu having crossed the Persian Gulf or Indian Ocean to the Arabian coast with a victorious army;[1] but his greatest expedition there was his reconquest of the lost provinces stretching along the Arabian coast and Red Sea to Sinai.

The fullest text of this inscription is preserved in a series of certified copies set up in the old Sun-temple at Nippur, which are found to be in literal agreement with the texts of his campaign records on his original monuments, as far as the existing fragments of the latter go. One of his original diorite inscribed monuments with the critical paragraph about his defeat of the thirty-two kings actually exists. The fullest text reads as follows [2]:—

"Manish Tusu, King of Kish City, when Anshan [Persia] and Shu-Edin-hum ["The Garden of Edin, the Fruitful" =Indus Valley] he had smitten, the Lower Sea [Persian Gulf and Arabian Sea] in ships he (crossed). Thirty-two kings of cities on the other side of the sea had rallied to battle and he defeated them, and their cities he smote, (and) their lords he cast down, and the whole country . . . as far as the Silver Mines he destroyed. The mountains beyond the sea, their (diorite) stones he broke and his statue

[1] PHT. iv. 238.
[2] Text and translation in PHT. iv. 205 f. His transliteration of *Shiri-hum*, I have already proved in WMC. x, reads *Shu-Edin-hum*, or "Garden of Edin, the Fruitful."

## 46  EGYPTIAN CIVILIZATION OF SUMER ORIGIN

he fashioned, and to Lord Sakh he dedicated it. The Sungod and Zagaga. . . . Who shall destroy this inscription, may Lord Sakh and the Sun-god tear out his foundations and destroy his seed."

This critical record by Manis-Tusu of his crossing the Arabian Sea in ships with his great armies after his reconquest of the Indus Valley and his conquest on the Arabian side of thirty-two confederate kings, and his advance to a country of Silver Mines, the name of which is lost, and to "the mountain *beyond the sea*" of the diorite rocks, which we shall find is Magan, in the Sinai Peninsula at the head of the Red Sea, which was afterwards regularly reached by ship from Mesopotamia, is all of immense historical importance with reference to the Red Sea route by which Menes reached Upper Egypt with his metal-armed warriors and Sumerian civilization.

We observe that this expedition took place after Manis-Tusu, who repeatedly calls himself in other inscriptions "The Smiter of Elam," had conquered (or reconquered) Anshan (that is as admitted by the best authorities, Persis, the old central province of Persia) immediately to the east of Elam, and after he had conquered (or reconquered) The Garden of Edin Sumerian colony in the Indus Valley. See Map II.

This great conquest of the thirty-two confederate kings on the Arabian coast-land was esteemed by Manis-Tusu so important an achievement that he records it in identical words in the monuments he set up in the chief cities and temples all over Mesopotamia. The expedition, we are informed on his Cruciform Monument—symbolic of the Sun-Cross of which he was a worshipper—took place "when all the lands . . . revolted against me." It was thus a *reconquest* of the lands within his father's former empire.

For the Arabian and Red Sea portion of the campaign, he probably marched his victorious army, after recovering the Indus Valley colony, westwards from the Indus Valley along the coast of Baluchistan and Mekran to the narrow Straits of Oman or Ormuz, just as Alexander-the-Great, over two millenniums later, in returning from his inglorious adventure in India from the Indus to Persepolis, marched his troops along the shore with his fleet under Nearchus

## MENES' CONQUESTS IN RED SEA & SINAI 47

in the offing, past the Straits of Oman to Persis or Anshan, or Persepolis with its beautiful palaces which he destroyed.

His point of crossing the Lower or Arabian Sea was probably effected at the Straits of Oman, where on the peninsula the first pitched battle with the confederate kings was likely to be fought, and with his fleet he could attack them in the rear, in a battle which, judging from the great number of kings engaged, must have been one of the greatest in the old world.

The number of the hostile confederate kings and their cities which he " smote," thirty-two, implies the conquest of a vast stretch of the Arabian coast, which is so sparsely peopled and the towns are almost entirely located on the coast and at great distances apart. The statement that he reached the diorite mountains " beyond the sea," *i.e.* beyond the Red Sea arm of the Lower Sea or Arabian Sea, absolutely identifies the limit reached by his expedition with Magan which we shall find was at the base of the Sinai Peninsula in the neighbourhood of Suez. It is thus indicated that he voyaged from the Indus Valley and Persia through the Arabian Sea and the Red Sea to Sinai on the borders of Lower Egypt to the east of Suez.

### MAGAN, THE LAND RECONQUERED BY MANIS-TUSU, A NAME FOR THE SINAI PENINSULA

Magan,[1] the famous sea-port of the mountainous country whence the Sumerians obtained by sea their diorite blocks for statues, is located by Assyriologists in the Sinai Peninsula at the head of the Red Sea.[2] And we shall find by the inscription of Pharaoh Narmar, now deciphered for the first time in next chapter, that it was on the borders of Lower Egypt. It was so very distant from Mesopotamia by sea that King Gudia, about four centuries after Manis-Tusu, records that the voyage took *a whole year* to and from Magan to bring back diorite blocks and precious woods and stones to the sea-port of Lagash in Mesopotamia, by way of the Persian Gulf.[3] And we shall find that it is repeatedly referred

[1] The name by its Sumerian signs means " Receptacle of Ships," implying that its chief town or city had a harbour.
[2] MD. 538.
[3] On products of Magan, copper, etc., Br. 3692 f. ; and MD. 886, 537 f.

to along with Egypt in the Indus seals of the descendants of Manis or Menes, cited below.

## Manis-Tusu & Egypt in Mesopotamian Literature re " Khamasi " Land & " Kham " or " Ham "

In none of the existing inscriptions of Manis-Tusu in Mesopotamia, nor in those of his dynasty, nor in those of the later Sumerian king Gudia, is there any reference to Egypt by its usual Babylonian name of *Misri* or *Musri*,[1] the equivalent of its modern Egyptian and Arabic name of *Misr*. Nor does it appear to be mentioned by them as *Pu*, nor does Manis-Tusu mention *Iatu* (" Dilmun ") Land in his existing inscriptions in Babylonia. It is possible that his omission to mention Egypt by name, if it be not the missing name in all the copies of his victory inscriptions, may have been owing to his having for so long held the Land of the Nile outside of, and independently of, the Mesopotamian empire as his personal possession, that he wished his favourite land to continue so ; or that it probably remained faithful to him when all the other lands revolted. But we have seen that Sargon in one of his Indus seals (No. 8) called himself " The Son of *Khamaesshi* Land, which we shall find was a title of Egypt, and several of his descendants in their Indus seals mention Egypt as their land, as seen below.

What now seems to be a Babylonian reference to Manis-Tusu in Egypt we find in the Old Sumerian King-List wrongly prefixed by the Isin priests to the Kish Chronicle, in which we have an old version of Sargon's Dynasty as Kings of Kish (see WMC. Table facing p. 140 and App. III). In this the succession is recorded as here shown on the left, and on the right are placed their usual titles for identification :—

    1. Ganni-*Pur* (or *Pir*), the horizon-quartering = King *Ganni, Kin*, or " Sargon."
    2. Mu, in whose r. Kish was smitten by weapons = *Mush* or *Uru-Mush*, s. of 1.
    3. Ha-(?)Manish or " *Danish* " of *Khama-si* Land = *Aha Manj* or *Manis-Tusu*, s. of 1.
    4. Nerra-*En* or Enugge    = *Narām Enzu*, s. of 3.

---

[1] Its name as *Misri* and *Misir* occurs in the Amarna Letters of about 1400 B.C.

## EGYPT AS KHAM, HAM, KHAMASI, &c. 49

In this Old Sumerian King-List, the Isin scribe writes the name of this third king (that is the King of *Khama-si* Land who succeeded Sargon's son Mu whose reign was ended by " Kish was smitten by weapons " just as we know that Sargon's son Mush's reign ended by his being killed at Kish in a revolution, and his overthrow is disclosed by the Indus seal to have been by his brother Menes Aha) as " Ha-Da-ni-ish." But this second sign *Da* very closely resembles the ship-sign *Ma ;* and as this king in question occupies the identical position of Manis-Tusu or Manish-Tusu in all the other lists of the same dynasty, it is certain that he was Manish-Tusu, and that the Isin scribe mistook *Ma* for *Da ;* and that the real name on the Old Sumerian List which he copied was *Manish*. The corruption of this entry is also presumed by the prefixed title written *Ha* by the scribe, instead of *Aha*, which we have seen is the synonym of Tusu or " Warrior," and the prefixed *Aha* title used by Menes in both his Egyptian and Indus inscriptions. And we have seen that this scribe wrote King *Mu* for " King *Mush*," presumably through carelessness.

This Old Sumerian List records that after " Kish was smitten by weapons," at the end of the reign of King Mu(sh), " the kingship passed to *Khama-si* or *Hama-si* City-Land," where King Ha-Danish, properly *Aha-Manish*, reigned.

This Land [1] of *Khama-si* or *Hama-si* is clearly not the *Khmazi* City-Land of Udu's Bowl, which I have shown was an ancient title of Carchemish or Kar-Khamish or " Fort-Khamish," and which never was a capital of the Sumerian or Babylonian kings of Mesopotamia.

On the other hand, it appears to be the Land of *Kham* or *Ham*, the oldest traditional name for Egypt, and a usual name for that land and its people in the Hebrew Old Testament, where the Phœnicians are called " Sons of Ham " ; and Sargon and his son Menes we have seen were direct descendants of the First Phœnician Dynasty of Aryans. The Greeks called Egypt sometimes *Khemia* or *Khīmia*.[2]

Now this *Khama-si* Land is obviously the *Khama-esshi* Land, of which Sargon claims to be " The Ruler " in the

---

[1] *Ki*=" Land." Br. 9636.
[2] Plutarch, *De Iside et Osiride*, 33.

## 50 EGYPTIAN CIVILIZATION OF SUMER ORIGIN

aforesaid Indus seal; and we shall find that the latter land is repeatedly mentioned in the Indus seals of the later members of Sargon's dynasty, and is several times used alternately with Egypt or *Mush-sir* and *Pu* (or Buto).

In the name *Khama-si*, the affix *si* is defined in the bilingual glossaries as (*a*) dialectic for *shar*, great, luxuriant, fat [1]—suggestive of "the flesh-pots of Egypt," and also (*b*) as "bile," perhaps in series with the later traditional Egyptian explanation of the old name of Egypt as *Kami*(-*t*) or *Kam* [2] meaning "dark-coloured or black" in allusion to the darkish colour of its soil, and it is spelt with the Crocodile hieroglyph *Kam*.[3]

Moreover, the country to the west of Mesopotamia across the Arabian desert, *i.e.* in the direction of Egypt, is called by the later Sumerians and Babylonians *Kimash*, a land from which couriers came overland with merchandise, including sesame oil, to the capital of Dungi at Lagash, and from the mountains of which Gudea obtained copper. It seems to be a later phonetic spelling of this name for Egypt. The country of Kimash is placed by Assyriologists "to the west of Babylonia,"[4] and there is no inhabited country west of Babylonia until Sinai and Egypt are reached.

Altogether the identity of *Khamasi* and *Khamaesshi* and *Kimash* Land with Egypt seems now clear.

### MENES *re* MANIS-TUSU AS SUN-WORSHIPPER

Menes was essentially a Sun-worshipper, as evidenced by his inscriptions in Egypt. Manis-Tusu likewise was significantly an ardent Sun-worshipper, like his father Sargon, who we have seen regularly invoked the Sun-god, and called himself in his Egyptian inscription an "Ukussi" or descendant of Ukusi of the city of the Sun-Hawk, the first Sumerian king.

One of Manis-Tusu's best-known monuments is his massive Cruciform Monument dedicated to the Sun-god at the Sun-temple of Sippar, and its form symbolizes the Sun-Cross.

[1] Br. 4198.  [2] BD. 1044-5. Also spelt *Qam*, 770-1.
[3] BD. 787 b. It is also significant that the Crocodile is called in Egyptian *Khams* or *Khems*, BD. 485 b.
[4] PB. 11. There it is stated S.W., but Prof. Pinches informs me "it should be in all probability west."

## MENES AS MANIS-TUSU SUN-WORSHIPPER 51

Its twelve sides are inscribed with long texts recording his conquest of Anshan (Persia), "when all the lands . . . . revolted against me," and in which his gifts to the Sun-god and his temple are detailed, including choice Date fruits— a simple fruit-offering which recalls that of his famous ancestor "Cain," the son of King Ukusi or "Adam,"[1] who incurred the wrath of the Semitic god for not offering the sanguinary Chaldean sacrifices, as did his "brother" Abel. In his inscriptions also in the Sun-temple at Nippur Manis invokes the Sun-god along with King Sakh, Zagg or Zagaga, who we have seen was his deified ancestor Ukusi of the city of the Sun-Hawk. And on the back of the great ebony label in Menes' tomb is painted with red pigment a Sun-Cross like a pedestalled Red Cross of St George.

As an Aryan Sun-worshipper, Menes or Manis appears to be the king called in the Indian Vedic psalms *Manasa* or *Mayin* (*i.e.* Menes or Men) who invoked the Sun and the Sun-Hawk, and significantly for "boons abiding in the Sea." He is associated with *Yayati* and *Evāvada*, apparently his descendants, who may represent *Ata* or *Zetata* and *Ousaphaidos*, the third to fifth kings of the First Dynasty of Egypt in Manetho's list (see p. 78). And it is noteworthy that Manasa bears the title of *Khattiyo*, that is, as we have seen, a title for "ruler," and which as *Kat* or *Kad* is borne by Sargon and the 1st Dynasty Pharaohs in their tomb inscriptions (see later). This Vedic hymn, which was evidently composed in the fierce heat of a torrid clime, such as Egypt is in the hot season, from its appeal for a "heat-sheltered house," joyously says [2]:—

> "O Sun! sage One, free as the unwedded hero, in love of battle moving o'er the foes. . . .
> Self-excellent, grant us a sheltering home, a house that wards off fierce heat!
> Thy Name sung forth by bards soars up to Thee, the loftiest One, with this swift-moving (Fire-offering's) flight.
> One (by thy Name) wins the boon his heart is set on :
> He who bestirs himself (by thy Name) shall bring the thing to pass.

[1] WBE. 17 f.   [2] RV. 5, 44, 7-10. Translation based upon Griffith's.

> The chief best (boon) abideth in the Sea, nor does (thy) long libation ever fail (to win it).
> The heart of him who praiseth (Thee) trembles not in fear, when his hymn is sung by the pure (in heart).
> This (singer) is he with thoughts of the *Khattiyo* [1] MANASA, of YAYATI and *Sadhri* and EVAVADA :
> This priest Avatsāra's sweet songs strive to win for us the mightiest strength known.
> The (Sun-) Hawk, girth-stretching, is the full source of (the prayed-for boons) as by the libations of the all-bestowing MAYIN and YAYATI.
> Sadā-Prina the holy, Tarya, Sruta-vit and Bahu-Vrikta joined with you have slain their foes."

This agreement in his Sun-worship, Egyptian, Mesopotamian, and Indo-Aryan, forges, therefore, another link in the chain of the personal identity of Menes with the Sumerian or Aryan emperor Manis-the-Warrior of Mesopotamia.

### MANIS-TUSU OR MENES AS A FREE CONSTITUTIONAL RULER & LAW-GIVER

One of the most interesting and important of the monuments left by King Manis-Tusu is his famous " Black Obelisk," so-called from its black diorite stone. It was discovered by M. de Morgan in 1897 in the French excavations at Susa, the capital of the Elam province of the Sumerians in south-west Persia, where it had been carried off as booty, presumably from Kish, in a raid by a revolted king of Elam of later date, who has endorsed it accordingly and it is now treasured in the Louvre Museum.

Its record [2] is a striking illustration of the very advanced free constitutional government which King Manis-Tusu administered ; and discloses him as a most enlightened ruler and respecter of the free institutions and rights of private citizens, and quite on a par with our most " modern " times, although about forty-six centuries ago. The text occupies sixty-nine closely-written columns, and records the purchase of several large estates in the neighbourhood of

---
[1] This old Indian Pali name here, is Sanskritized as usual in the modern Vedic MSS. into *Kshatra*.
[2] STE. 1, 1 f. ; and for Summary, KHS. 206 f.

Kish City, his capital, which he required for his official buildings and settlements for his officials and for the estate of his son, wherein, instead of confiscating the necessary land and buildings already occupied, he purchased it legally at its full market-value, by shekels of money, with in addition lavish gifts and payments for the goodwill of the tradesmen and others who were dispossessed, *just as if he were a mere private citizen himself*. The precise area of each estate, as accurately measured, with their defined boundaries, is given, and its value then reckoned in standard measures of grain and afterwards converted into its equivalent in silver: one *bur* of land being reckoned as worth sixty *gur* measures of grain, and one *mana* of silver.[1] An addition of one-tenth the purchase price was paid to the owner or joint-owners of each estate, who also received from the king presents of cattle, garments, vessels, etc., varying in value according to the rank of each recipient and his share in the property. And all the names of the sellers, with their addresses, as well as their receipts with the names and addresses of the witnesses, are all duly recorded. And the names and duties are detailed of the forty-nine government overseers entrusted with the administration and cultivation of the lands thus purchased by King Manis-Tusu or Menes.

### ROUTE OF MANIS-TUSU, ASA MANJA OR MENES IN HIS SEIZURE OF UPPER EGYPT, c. 2704 B.C.

We have seen from the Indian Chronicles that King Manis-Tusu as the crown-prince Asa-Manja revolted from his father Sargon, in his early manhood; and this tradition, along with the historical evidence we have gained regarding him, appears to provide material for reconstructing the outline of the lost chapter on his mode of seizing Upper Egypt and the route by which he effected it.

As crown prince of the Sumerian empire, Manis, as we have found, was governor of the Indus Valley colony of that empire.[2] As such, he would have control of the local Sumerian army of occupation in the Indus Valley and of

---

[1] *Mana* in Sanskrit in Vedas is " golden," MKI. 2, 128.
[2] WISD. 35 f., 55 f.

the great merchant-fleet plying between there and the port of Lagash (for the type of ship in this, Menes' period, see illustrations on the ebony labels from Menes' tomb (Fig. 13, p. 62)). This fleet [1] also presumably voyaged to Magan and Egypt *via* the Arabian coast-ports and the Red Sea, as is implied not only in his father Sargon's title of " King of all the Lands of the Lower Sea," but also by Manis-Tusu's own record that the thirty-two kings of this coast-land up to Magan or Sinai had " revolted," thus implying that they had been under the suzerainty of the Sumerian empire ; and Menes, as well as his father, use the title " Pharaoh " on their Indus seals.

The Indian Chronicles record that 60,000 of " the fed sons " of the emperor Sagara (Sargon) followed the crown-prince in his revolt, which is evidently a memory of the great number of Sargon's military and naval forces which flocked to the standard of their young master, Menes, in his great adventure in a more temperate and attractive clime. With such resources, it would be comparatively easy for Manis or Menes, proceeding *via* the Red Sea, to carve out and hold a kingdom in Upper Egypt, and ultimately overpower the local governors of Sargon in Lower Egypt, which was so very remote by the land route from Mesopotamia, while Sargon was deprived of his Lower Sea fleet. For it was clearly by the Red Sea route that Manis-the-Warrior, the Aryan King Manasyu, with his metal-using warriors, arrived in Egypt to become " The *Prabhu* (or Pharaoh), the Royal Eye of Gopta," as Menes, the founder of the First Dynasty in Egypt.

Egyptologists are mostly agreed that Menes must have entered Upper Egypt by the Red Sea, somewhere to the east of Koptos and Abydos, at which latter place is his ' tomb " with his inscriptions. And at Koptos exist the oldest known statues of a god in Egypt, indicating the Red Sea route of their erectors. " The oldest statues of gods (in Egypt) are three gigantic limestone figures of Min at

---

[1] There is no record of the number of ships or size of ships used by Menes. The form of the ships is seen in the hieroglyphs of his ebony-label tomb inscription. In the Third Dynasty King Snefru sent a fleet of forty ships to a Syrian port for cedar wood, and the length of one of these was no less than 170 feet. Baikie, p. 146.

## MENES ESTABLISHES ARYAN CIVILIZATION 55

Koptos; these bear designs of Red Sea shells and swordfish. . . . His worship continued down to the Roman period."[1] This god "Min" would now appear to be either the deified Menes himself or more probably *Min* or *Man*, the twin Sun-gods of the Sumerians, Aryans and Phœnicians.[2]

Koptos was an ancient trade-mart town of immemorial antiquity, to which converged the old caravan routes from the Red Sea, Sudan and Lower Egypt. And its Red Sea seaport was Kosseir (see map), which thus seems to have been the probable port of debarkation of Menes and his Sumerian invading army.

The "Predynastic" kings of Egypt, prior to Menes, are said by Egyptologists to have been all confined to Lower Egypt;[3] though we have found that Sargon's father, as well as himself and his grandfather, as predynastic kings had their tombs at Abydos in Upper Egypt—a more fitting and congenial resting-place for Aryans than the Delta. Thus Menes would probably meet with comparatively little resistance in establishing himself at Koptos, whence he proceeded to annex the more populous and richer Delta, *i.e.* Lower Egypt; and it is as "The uniter of the two crowns of Upper and Lower Egypt" that he comes down to us in Egyptian history. And his name *Manasyu* in the Indian records means "Manas-the-uniter."

### MENES' ESTABLISHMENT OF SUMERIAN OR ARYAN CIVILIZATION IN EGYPT

Menes, the first independent king of United Egypt, is the traditional introducer and establisher of civilization in Ancient Egypt; though we have seen that his father, Sargon, and his grandfather and great-grandfather were also predynastic Pharaohs, and thus possessed the same civilization. What Menes appears to have done was to vastly increase the elements of sporadic Sumerian civilization introduced by his father and other predynastic kings, and to have established it firmly for the first time.

Significantly, the civilization that he brought with him

[1] PHE. 1, 3.
[2] WPOB. 242 f.; and WISD. 51, 89. *Manu* in Indian legend was son of the Sun-god.      [3] PHE. 1, 4.

## 56 EGYPTIAN CIVILIZATION OF SUMER ORIGIN

and established in Egypt is now seen to be of the same general kind as the Sumerian of the Sargonic period in Mesopotamia and in the Indus Valley. His culture, with its metal industries, irrigation by canals for agriculture, pottery [1] and art, alabaster bowls, cylinder seals for sealing on clay, votive ceremonial stone mace-heads, form of tombs, Sun-worship and writing in Sumerian script and in the Sumerian language soon becoming modified by the introduction of aboriginal Semitic idioms and by a local neo-archaism in forming the Sumerian pictographs resulting in the standard stereotyped " Egyptian " hieroglyphs, yet retaining the same phonetic sounds and meanings—all betrays unequivocally its Sumerian or Aryan origin.

The Aryan race also of Menes and his dynasty and dynastic ruling people is evidenced by their physical type on their monuments and in their skeletons unearthed from their tombs. This reveals them to be of the Aryan type, tall, long-headed, with relatively broad brows and large brains, straight bridge to the nose and of a very vigorous type of face, as already noted.

### DATE OF MENES' INVASION OF EGYPT, ABOUT 2704 B.C.

The approximate date for Menes' invasion of Egypt, as evidenced by the newly-found synchronism with the Sargonic epoch in Mesopotamia, and detailed in the Chapter on Chronology, is about 2704 B.C. This indicates from the chronology of Sargon's dynasty preserved in the Kish Chronicle that Manis' or Menes' occupation of the throne in Upper Egypt took place about the twentieth year of the reign of Sargon, when Prince Manis was about twenty-one years of age ; and that he continued to hold Egypt as an independent king, outside the Mesopotamian empire, during the remaining thirty-five years of his father Sargon's reign in Mesopotamia, and continued to do so during the fifteen years of the reign of his younger brother Mush in Mesopotamia, whereafter he himself gained the imperial crown of the latter on the death of his younger brother, the emperor Mush, in a " revolution," which is now seen to have been the result of Manis-Tusu's seizure of the Mesopotamian crown.

[1] Pottery of a " Syrian " type is found in the First Dynasty.

# MENES' EGYPTIAN INSCRIPTIONS DECIPHERED

### MENES' INSCRIPTIONS IN EGYPT IN SUMERIAN LANGUAGE & IN SUMERIAN WRITING

Further striking evidence of the identity of Menes with the Sumerian emperor Manis-the-Warrior of Mesopotamia emerged in the facts, that, as now disclosed, the inscriptions of Menes at Abydos are in Sumerian writing of the Sargonic period and in the Sumerian language ; and similarly so are the inscriptions of the rest of his First Egyptian Dynasty, all of which have hitherto remained undeciphered except for the royal names, most of which also have not been correctly read.

In Egypt several inscriptions of Menes have been found by Sir F. Petrie at Menes' "tomb" at Abydos, engraved on ebony and ivory labels, stone vases, on a gold bar from his treasury, and on clay sealings (reading towards the right), which latter

FIG. 11.—Menes' Title of *Aha* (or *Akha*) in Egypt.
(After Sir F. Petrie.)

were also found along with an ivory label at Nagada.[1] Most of these inscriptions are merely his solar or " Horus " name of *Aha* (or *Akha*), which is pictured by a pair of hands holding respectively a shield and stone-mace, as seen in Fig. 11. And I have shown that this *Aha* hieroglyph with its phonetic value and meaning of Warrior are derived from the Sumerian.[2] Significantly cup-mark inscriptions are also found therein (Pl. VI, *e-f*), as in Ancient Britain and Troy.

The largest and longest inscriptions of Menes in Egypt are engraved on the ebony and ivory labels found at Abydos, of which three of the smaller are shown in Plate VI, and the largest in Plate VII (in duplicate). All of these, with the exception of the smaller ivory label deciphered below, are funereal and now prove to relate to the circumstances of his tragic death as we shall see later on. This small ivory label is of critical historical importance, as in it he uses his title of *Tusu* in Egypt, instead of the usual *Aha*.

[1] PHE. 1, 13.   [2] WSAD. Pl. I. 9 f.

## 58 EGYPTIAN CIVILIZATION OF SUMER ORIGIN

### MENES OR AHA MEN CALLED TUSU MENNA IN ONE OF HIS ABYDOS INSCRIPTIONS

This ivory label of Aha Mena (No. 1, Plate VI) was obtained from the tomb supposed to be that of Narmer[1] (who, we shall find, was Narām, the son of Manis Tusu) the adjoining tomb next but one to that of Aha, which latter had been early rifled and its inscribed objects strewn around near the old surface level, whilst others of Menes' inscribed objects were found in the adjoining tombs of his family.

This small label measuring 2¼ inches in length, and like the other labels pierced by a hole towards its top right

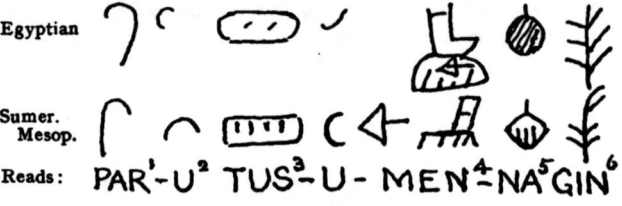

Egyptian

Sumer.
Mesop.

Reads: PAR$^1$-U$^2$ TUS$^3$-U - MEN$^4$-NA$^5$GIN$^6$

Transl. The Pharaoh TUSU-MENNA, The Ruler.

FIG. 12.—Menes' Title of TUSU-MENNA in Egypt Deciphered.

[1] B. 77; Br. 1722.  [2] B. 365, as before.
[3] Tus or Tush. B. 481; Br. 10515="Battle" M. 7999.
[4] Br. 10355; PSL. 237. The high seat of Egyptian throne compared with the low in the diagram in Mesop. Sumerian is noteworthy.
[5] B. 71; Br. 1581.  [6] Gin=ruler, Br. 2400.

border, proves to be of unique historical importance, as it preserves in Egypt this king's title of *Tusu*, and substitutes it for *Aha* (or *Akha*), thus *demonstrating the equivalency of "Aha" and "Tusu."* Like all the other First Dynasty inscriptions it is written in the Sumerian script and language. It reads in the retrograde direction, but in the annexed decipherment table I have arranged its signs for convenience from left to right.

Here it is significant that Menes uses in spelling his *Men* name that compound Sumerian sign of an Eye and Throne, which is now disclosed as the obvious Sumero-Egyptian

[1] PRT. II, 20 f.

PLATE VI.

LESSER LABELS FROM MENES' TOMB IN EGYPT.

In ebony and ivory (from photographs by Sir F. Petrie, PRI. II, Pls. III and IIIA). For decipherments and translations of *a*, see pp. 69 f.; of *b* and *c*, pp. 69 f. and Pl. VIII, facing p. 70. Note in *d* the Revolving Sun Spiral and "Cup-markings," as in prehistoric tomb monuments and "whorls" in Troy and Ancient Britain (see WPOB. 237 f.).

## MENES' MESOPOTAMIAN EMPIRE

source of his title as Manasyu, in the Indian epics as "The Royal Eye of Gopta (Egypt)."

The other larger inscriptions of Menes in Egypt refer to his tragic death as seen later on and in these he is repeatedly called " the son of the Great Pharaoh Gani (or Sha- Gani)."

### HIS MESOPOTAMIAN EMPERORSHIP AT KISH

On becoming emperor at Kish, in addition to his kingship in Egypt, Manis reigned at Kish for fifteen years, according to the Kish Chronicle, when he was succeeded there by his son Narām Enzu. This would give him a total reign in Egypt of thirty-five years independently, and thereafter conjointly with Mesopotamia of fifteen years, or in all fifty years. But the Egyptian traditional chronology of Manetho, which we shall find is proved by the Kish Chronicle to be grossly exaggerated for the successors in Menes' Dynasty, gives him a reign in Egypt of sixty-two years as seen in the chapter on Chronology. Such a long reign seems only possible on the assumption that he abdicated in Mesopotamia and retired to Egypt to reign for twelve more years there, whilst his son Narām Enzu was reigning contemporarily in Mesopotamia, which seems improbable.

## IV

### MENES' TRAGIC DEATH ON SEA-EXPLORATION IN ATLANTIC ISLAND, c. 2641 B.C.

*With Decipherment of the Sumerian Inscriptions on the Ebony Labels in his Tomb in Egypt*

ON succeeding eventually to the imperial throne of his father " Sargon " at Kish city in Mesopotamia on the death of his younger brother, to whom his father had given the succession on disinheriting him for his revolt, Manis (or Menes or Manj) reigned for fifteen years as world-emperor, according to the Kish Chronicle, and he was then succeeded by his son Narām Enzu, the Narmar of the Egyptian monuments, whose hitherto unknown history is described in Chapter VIII. The Indian epic accounts describe him, as Asa Manja, as meeting a violent death; and this is in agreement with the Egyptian tradition, which is now fully confirmed by the actual contemporary inscriptions unearthed from his tomb in Egypt.

### MENES' OR MANIS' DEATH

The Egyptian tradition of Menes' death is that he met with a tragic end. It relates that after reigning for long as an ideal sovereign, architect, warrior, sailor, statesman, promulgator of written laws, and regulator of the worship of the gods, he was killed by a " hippopotamus "[1]—a word *Kheb*, which also significantly, in the light of our decipherment of his tomb inscriptions, means " a wasp."[2]

It has been suggested that Menes was probably identical with a certain king or " Lord " of Magan, called " Mannu-Dannu " or " Mannu-the-mighty," who was " cast down " by the emperor Narām Enzu.[3] And this conjecture of identity has been rejected merely on the assumption that

[1] MDC. 235.   [2] Cp. BD. 539 a.   [3] JEA. 1920, 89, 295; 1921, 80.

## MENES' TRAGIC DEATH IN WESTERN OCEAN

Menes' date was much earlier than that of Narām Enzu; though now it is seen to be also wholly untenable even when, as we have now found, these two emperors Menes and Narām Enzu were contemporary. For apart from Narām being the son of Menes, we find from Narmar's (i.e. Narām's) own Egyptian record in his Slate Palette victory [1] tablet, that Mannu-Dannu was an aboriginal, uncivilized chief of Magan and not of Egypt. Moreover, the contemporary ebony labels on Menes' "tomb" at Abydos tell us the real story of the circumstances of Menes' death elsewhere.

### Tragic Death of Menes disclosed in Inscription on Ebony Labels at his "Tomb" at Abydos

The Ebony Labels found at the "tomb" of Menes at Abydos, which have not previously been deciphered are, I find, written in transitional Sumero-Egyptian hieroglyphs; and contain an account of Menes' tragic death by an accident during a voyage of exploration by sea in the far West. And it is stated that that "tomb" was only the place of "the bored tablet of hanging wood dedicated." It was thus merely a cenotaph.

### The Great Ebony Labels from Menes' Tomb at Abydos

The largest ebony label (see Plate VII), which was found in duplicate by Sir F. Petrie in 1901 at the empty tomb of King Mena or Menes at Abydos,[2] is said to show "the earliest known use of hieroglyphs for continuous writing in Egypt."[3] But it has hitherto remained undeciphered and untranslated because its writing, with the exception of a few characters, is not in the stereotyped form of Egyptian hieroglyphs with which Egyptologists are familiar, and which came into use after the period of Menes. And no Assyriologist has hitherto perceived the very transparent resemblance to, and identity with, the Sumerian hieroglyphs in its writing. For convenience of reference I give here my careful transcript of the inscription from the photograph

---

[1] WMC. 311 f.  [2] PRT. II., pl. III A.
[3] PHE. I, 14. But we have seen that his father Sargon's tomb inscriptions are earlier.

## 62 EGYPTIAN CIVILIZATION OF SUMER ORIGIN

in Plate VII, where some of the signs require the assistance of a lens to make out their full details.

In view of my discovery that Menes or Aha Manj or "*Manj*-the-Warrior" was identical with the Mesopotamian emperor "*Manis*-the-Warrior" (Manis-Tusu), the son of Sargon, and thus an Aryan Sumerian who ordinarily wrote in Sumerian characters and language; and that the conventional

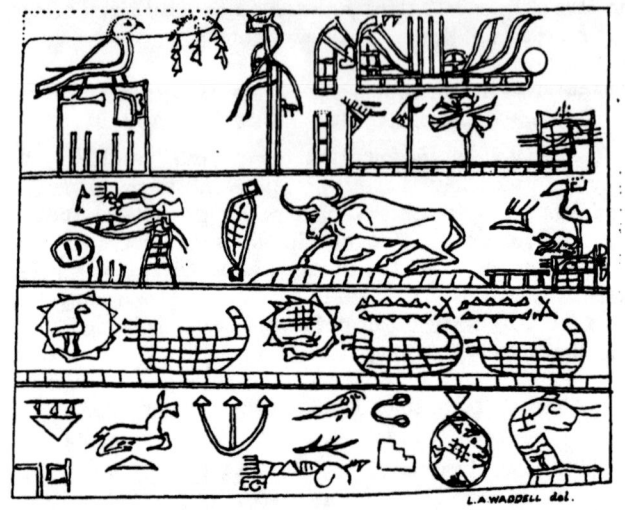

FIG. 13.—Great Ebony Label Inscription from Menes' "Tomb" at Abydos (Drawn from Photograph in Plate VII.)

Egyptian hieroglyphs, with their radical language, were derived from the Sumerian, I several years ago proceeded to re-examine this important sealed label inscription for its decipherment by our new keys.

### DECIPHERMENT OF MENES' GREAT EBONY LABEL INSCRIPTION

I then observed that the writing was in Early Sumerian pictographic writing of the same type substantially as in Sargon's inscription at Abydos and in the Early Sumerian and Indo-Sumerian seals, with some of its pictographic signs written more realistically than in the Mesopotamian dia-

PLATE VII

GREAT EBONY LABEL FROM MENES' TOMB AT ABYDOS.

In duplicate (from photographs by Sir F. Petrie, PRE, II, 7l, IIIA). For decipherment and translation, see pp. 62 f. and 188 f.

## MENES' TRAGIC DEATH IN THE FAR WEST

grammatic style, as for example, in the pictographs for " Fly " and " Ship " and " Ox," see Fig. 13, lines 1 to 3.

On deciphering the signs through their Sumerian values, I found that the record contained a detailed contemporary and official account of Menes' death and its tragic circumstances. It described him as " King Manash or Manshu, the Pharaoh of Egypt, the Land of the Two Crowns," and " the son of The Great Sha-Gana, the Pharaoh," and stated that on his voyage of inspection by ships from Egypt to " The Peak of the Far Western Land," he met his death through the sting of a Wasp or Hornet ; and that this label was merely " The hanging Wood (Label) " of his cenotaph in Egypt.

The full details of my decipherment and literal translation of this extremely important historical inscription are given, sign by sign, and line by line in Appendix IV, with each of the signs deciphered through the Sumerian, along with their phonetic values and literal meanings ; and each and all duly attested from the standard Sumerian lexicons, as in the case of all my previous decipherments.

### The Record on the Large Ebony Labels in Menes' " Tomb," narrating the Tragic Death of Menes in an Exploration in the Far West

Thus the full record on the Ebony Label in Menes' " Tomb " at Abydos records in the Sumerian writing and language literally as follows :—

" *The King Manash (or Minash), The Pharaoh of Mushsir (Egypt), the Land of the Two Crowns, the perished dead one in the West, of the (Sun-) Hawk race, Aha Manash (or Minash) of the Lower (or Sunrise or Eastern) and of the Sunset (or Upper or Western) Waters and of their Lands and Oceans, The Ruler, The King of Mushrim (the two Egypts) Lands, son of the Great Sha-Gana (or Sha-Gunu) of the (Sun-) Hawk race, The Pharaoh, the deceased, the Commander-in-Chief of Ships. The Commander-in-Chief of Ships (Minash) made the complete course to the End of the Sunset Land, going in ships. He completed the inspection of the Western Lands. He built (there) a holding (or possession) in Urani Land. At the Lake of the Peak, Fate pierced (him) by a Hornet (or Wasp),*

## 64 EGYPTIAN CIVILIZATION OF SUMER ORIGIN

*The King of the Two Crowns, Mānshu. This bored tablet set up of hanging wood is dedicated (to his memory)."*

The pathetic simplicity and dignity of this contemporary record of the tragic ending of the life of this great " world emperor " and early Aryan admiral, whilst on a voyage of exploration and discovery to the furthest west islands in the Atlantic, at the ripe old age of about eighty years, and over four and a half thousand years ago, strikingly reflects the businesslike directness, conciseness, precision, restraint and historical and scientific habits of this adventurous enterprising Early Aryan ruling and seafaring race. Indeed, their record is *so thoroughly modern* that it might well have been composed and written at the present day.

### THE FATAL HORNET WHICH SLEW KING MENES

This contemporary historical account of the death of King Menes by the sting of a Hornet or Wasp is significantly confirmed all unsuspectedly by the Egyptian tradition of his death.

In Egyptian tradition or legend, Menes is said, after a glorious reign of sixty to sixty-two years in establishing and developing civilization in Egypt, to have been killed by a *Kheb* beast which came forth from the waters of the Nile.[1]

*a* in Label B.    *b* in Label A.    *c* Sumer pictograph.

FIG. 14.—The Fatal Fly on Menes' Label as a Wasp or Hornet.

This *Kheb* animal in question has hitherto been translated "Hippopotamus." But it does not appear to have been remarked before, in this regard, that *Kheb* in Egyptian also means a "Wasp" (or Hornet),[2] which thus shows that the Egyptian legend actually preserved the true traditional name of the animal which caused Menes' death, though latterly misinterpreted. It is also noteworthy that the beast, according to the Egyptian tradition, came out of the waters of "The Great River" (*Iaur-au*), latterly known as the Nile;

[1] Manetho cited by MDC. 235.    [2] BD. 539a.

and the label records that the death-dealing insect was " at the Lake of the Peak " in Urani Land.

The identity of the " piercing Fly," which ended the life of the illustrious " world-monarch " King Menes in the Far West, is well preserved in its pictograph on the duplicate label, Plate VII B, when examined under a lens. This clearly portrays it to be a winged insect of the Wasp or Hornet kind ; and it has the same general form in the somewhat abraded label (see Plate VII A). These two pictographs are shown in the accompanying Figure (No. 14), alongside of the diagrammatic form of this sign in the old Sumerian writing ; and in the Sumerian glossaries this pictograph is defined as " a voracious or wolfish insect of the field." [1]

### The Word for " Fate " is a Swallow

The word for Fate on this label is pictured by a Swallow which has the ideographic meaning in Sumerian of " swift " and " Fate " as well as a " Swallow." In Babylonian tradition the swallow was also a bird of Fate or augury. In the Chaldean version of the Deluge, the Chaldean Noah says :—

" I caused to go forth a swallow, the destiny bird . . .
The swallow went and turned about,
A resting-place it did not settle upon and it returned." [2]

### " Urani " Land where Menes met his Tragic Death as " Erin " (Ireland)

The later Egyptians in ignorance of the real circumstances and locality of the death of Menes, and interpreting the traditional name of the beast that killed him as an " hippopotamus," naturally placed the scene of his death on the Nile, as that quadruped was and is common in the Nile, and was restricted to Africa in historic times. The later Greek myth-mongering bards on the other hand, who were unaware of the identity of King Minos of Crete with Pharaoh Menes or Minash of Egypt and Mesopotamia, yet aware that he met a tragic end whilst on a sea-voyage to the West, made King Minos to be treacherously and miserably murdered in

---
[1] See footnote to decipherment in App. IV.
[2] W. Houghton, *Natural History of Ancients*, 221.

## 66 EGYPTIAN CIVILIZATION OF SUMER ORIGIN

a hot-bath in Sicily whilst he was there in pursuit of his fugitive architect, Daedalus. This legend was presumably invented in order to account for the Minoa colony of Egyptians in Sicily, with architecture of the traditional Minos or Menes' type—this Sicilian Minoa, like the other ports of that name in the Mediterranean having been doubtless a port of call established by Minos or Menes.

Now, however, this official authentic and contemporary historical record on the ebony labels in his " tomb " at Abydos, definitely places the locality of Menes' death at " the End of the Land of Sunset," that is to say in the furthest western land in the Atlantic known to the adventurous Egyptian mariners of Menes' day. We have already seen that Sargon, the father of Menes and the predynastic Pharaoh who immediately preceded him in Egypt, records that the Tin Land, which lay *beyond* the Upper or Western Sea or Mediterranean, and thus in the Atlantic beyond the Pillars of Hercules, was tributary to him and sent him the products of its mines.[1] And I have shown that the " cup-mark " gravings on the prehistoric monoliths in the neighbourhood of the Tin and other prehistoric mine-workings in the British Isles are in the ancient Sumerian sacred funereal script of the Sargon period, and we shall find them repeated in the tomb inscriptions of some of the members of Menes' Dynasty in the following chapters. Moreover, I have adduced evidence showing that the Tin Land referred to by Sargon was in Cornwall, which was thus already a recognized part of Sargon's empire before the accession of Menes to that empire. And from its uplands the still further western land of Erin is sometimes visible.

But Menes, the greatest admiral of the Old World, who, as we have seen, had repeatedly made with his fleet the long deep-sea voyage of about three thousand miles from the Persian Gulf and Indus Valley to Egypt by the Arabian and Red Seas, and who, as King Minos was the most famous sea-king in Greek tradition, expressly embarked on his last great voyage of exploration, as we are officially told in this

---

[1] There were relatively poor ancient tin-workings in South-western Spain to the west of Gades outside the Strait of Gibraltar, but it is doubtful if they were worked in the Sargonic period.

## SITE OF MENES' DEATH IN ERIN 67

label, in order " to inspect the End of the Sunset Land," in the Far West " going in ships."

This Land of " The End of the Sunset " must have especially attracted a scientific sea-explorer like Menes, who, we are told, " made its complete course," and all the more so, as he was, as we have seen, an ardent Sun-worshipper. For it was the accepted theory of his day, and a theory which continued down through the ages till the comparatively modern time of Copernicus in the fifteenth century A.D., that the Sun moved round the earth ; and that after Sunset in the furtherest western land in the ocean it travelled back to its point of " rising " in the Far East by an underground passage, as the " Night or Resurrecting Sun," as opposed to the " Day or Flying Sun," or " Sun-Hawk." This dual character of the Sun in " going " and " returning " is freely pictured as I have shown in the sacred seals of the Sumerians and Hittites with its respective westing and easting represented by alternating spirals, which as demonstrated in a former work is obviously the unknown source of the decorative "spiral ornament" in the Aegean and elsewhere.[1] And significantly the pictograph for this " End of the Sunset Land " on this Menes label is the Sumerian word-sign for it, representing the Sun entering this supposed dark underground passage, pictured by two curved or wavy lines with the Sun inside (see Fig. 39 in App. IV). And it was presumably to discover this supposed turning-point of the Sun that Menes made his final great adventure.

This " End of the Sunset Land," which was thus reached by ships, lay clearly beyond the Tin land of Cornwall, which was already a colony of the empire and well known. And the furthest land to the west of the latter is the land of Erin—for at this period the Sumero-Phœnicians had evidently not yet reached the Azores or America, which latter now appears to be " The lost Atlantis " of a later age of Aryan-Phœnician explorers.

The name *Urani*, for this furthest west land reached by Menes or Manj or Mena, thus appears to me to be the original form of the old name " Erin " for Ireland ; and we have seen that the vowels freely interchange in Sumerian and

[1] WPOB. 248 f., 285 f., 308 f.

## 68 EGYPTIAN CIVILIZATION OF SUMER ORIGIN

Early Aryan, and that ancient place-names are surprisingly persistent down to modern times. Moreover, I have demonstrated elsewhere that representations of this " End of the Sunset Land" occur in Ireland, engraved on prehistoric cup-marked stones at New Grange on the Boyne River, near Drogheda, which are essentially replicas of the same pictograms as in the Early Sumerian and Hittite sacred seals.[1]

Remarkable confirmation of the identity of this Urani Land with Erin I found about three years ago in the inscriptions engraved on the boulder stones of the prehistoric rude stone grave at Knock-Many or "The Hill of *Many*," near Clogher on the southern border of County Tyrone. This prehistoric grave tumulus practically crowns the central watershed between the Lough Erne arm of Donegal or Galway Bay of the Atlantic or western side of Erin and Lough Neagh of the River Bann on the North-east, which latter lake was penetrated by Norse galleys within historic times. The inscriptions on the two chief standing boulder stones at Knock-Many, as seen in the remarkably fine large photographs taken by Mr R. Welch in 1896, contain, I observed, inscriptions in Sumerian linear writing which, though largely weathered, were mostly decipherable, and were practically identical in their writing and contents with those of the ebony label from the empty tomb of Mena or Manj or Menes at Abydos. In particular the photograph of *one of the stones*[2] *contains the same monogram of the name "Urani," and is written by the same signs as on the ebony label, but on a larger scale ; and the realistic pictograph of the animal which caused the death of Menes in Urani represented it as a Hornet.*

Most unfortunately, however, those venerable engraved stones of this immensely important monument of hoary antiquity were two years ago cleared from their dense incrustation of lichens of thirty years' growth, by coating them with caustic chemicals for some days followed by vigorous scrubbing with brushes and water. Since then, the subsequent photographs now show little or no trace of the majority of the finer inscriptions, and in the larger stone especially a great many defacing additional initials carved

[1] WPOB. 249 f. 287, 308 f.
[2] Stone D. in drawing by G. Coffey, *New Grange*, 104.

DEATH CONFIRMED BY LESSER LABELS 69

by trippers in the interval. The stone of these boulders is composed of millstone grit, a friable rock consisting of grit concreted with natural cement ; and the action of caustic soda and lime tends to dissolve the cement and set free the grit which with the hard scrubbing tends to remove part of the surface of the stone, and with it the loss of the finer lines of the inscriptions.

But Mr Welch's earlier photographs, which are of great technical excellence, are indisputable facts in themselves. And they preserve many vestiges of the old Sumerian and other inscriptions, the decipherment of which I hope to publish later on.

It thus appears that the Land of Urani in " The Land of the End of the Sunset " in the Far West, to which Menes penetrated in ships and where he met his tragic death through the sting of a Wasp or Hornet was Erin, the furthest West land of Europe (excluding Iceland or Ultima Thule, then doubtless unknown) ; and that his tomb survives on the top of Knock-Many or " The Hill of Many " in County Tyrone, in which the name *Many* seems to preserve the name of that great Aryan " world-emperor " and famous admiral Mena or *Manj* down to the present day. And the so-called " tomb " of Menes at Abydos is disclosed to be not his tomb, but his cenotaph.

CONFIRMATION OF MENES' DEATH IN WEST BY LESSER EBONY LABELS, AND RECORDING HIS NAME AS MANI TUSSI AND SON OF SARGON

The three lesser ebony labels from Menes' " Tomb " figured in Plate VI. p. 58, *a*, 2 and 4, fully confirm the larger labels. *Two record that he has " gone in The West," one records that he is " dead," two record that he is " the son of Pharaoh Gani (Sargon)," and one records him under both titles of* MAN and MANI-TUSSI and TISHU.

The detailed decipherments are given in Plate VI.
The record of label B reads literally :—

" The whole (Earth) Protector (or Leader), The (Sun-) Hawk House, AHA, The Water-Lord, reported perished in The West, The son of Pharaoh GANI (or GUNI)."

## 70 EGYPTIAN CIVILIZATION OF SUMER ORIGIN

The record of label C reads literally :—

"The dead (king) MAN, The (Sun-) Hawk Pharaoh in The West, MANI TUSSI, TISHU, the Pharaoh MAN of the (Sun-)Hawk-race House AHA."

*This gives us again absolute contemporary documentary proof from Egypt itself of the identity of Menes or Aha Men with Manis Tussi, as well as his sonship to Sargon-the-Great.*

Significantly also the small labels D–F from Menes' tomb in that plate give us the " cup-mark " script and the reversed solar Spiral, such as are common on the prehistoric funerary monuments in Ancient Britain.[1]

[1] WPOB. 237 f., 249 f., 287 f. And compare with King Dudu's tomb label, Pl. XIV.

PLATE VIII.

## DECIPHERMENT OF MENES' TOMB LESSER LABELS & CUP-MARKS.
(See photographs in Pl. XII, facing p. 280, and Label A decipherment, p. 280.)

*B. l. 1.*
Egyptian
Sumer Mesop.
Reads  ŚAR-KUR AHA E² BURU KUD GU⁸ DU-DU⁵
Transl.: The whole (Earth) Protector, The Hawk-house AHA, The Water-Lord, reported perished

*b. l. 2.*
Egyptian
S. Mesop.
Reads  WI⁶- ES⁷ BUR⁸ BARU PA-RU⁹ GA¹⁰- NI¹¹
Transl.: in The West, The Son of Pharaoh of the Hawk line, GANI.

*C. l. 1.*
Egyptian
S. Mesop.
Reads  MIM¹² MAN¹³ PA-BAR¹⁴ WI MA-NI¹⁵-TUS-SI¹⁶
Transl.: the dead (king) MAN, The Hawk Pharaoh, in the West. MANI-TUSSI,

*C. l. 2.*
Egyptian
S. Mesop.
Reads  TI¹⁷ - SHU¹⁸ BARA MAN PA - RIN  AHA
Transl.: TISHU, The Pharaoh MAN of the Hawk race, AHA.

*D. F.*
Egyptian
S. Mesop
Reads  RA, DAG, ZAL¹⁹ ASH or IMKIN)²⁰   USSA²¹
Transl.: Revolving Sun (RA). Heaven. The bright Field of Tas (Tasia).

1. B. 59, Br. 1146. The unmarked phonetic values have been given in previous tables. 2. B. 263. 3. B. 12. 4. B. 15, Br. 540, pictures face with protruded tongue = "speak, report." 5. B. 207. 6. B. 380. 7. B. 432. 9. B. 1. 10. B. 275. 11. B. 228. 12. B. 116, M. 1923. 13. B. 431. 14. B. 77. 15. B. 532, Br. 11947. 16. B. 175. 17. B. 76. 18. B. 490. 19. B. 337, M. 5741 f. 20. B. 534, Br. 12196-8, 8371. Also value *Mer, Muru*, "Wind or Storm (god)." 21. Br. 11053, 12214, cp. 7527 and WPOB. 243.

## V

### MENES OR MIN AS KING MINOS OF CRETE & REAL DATE OF MINOAN CIVILIZATION

*Disclosing his Son the Bull-Man (Mino-Taur) as Menes' son Narmar or Narām " The Wild Bull Lord "*

IT also now transpires that the famous legendary hero of Greek myth, King Minos of Crete, is all unsuspectedly the great Sumerian or Aryan emperor Menes or Manis-the-Warrior of Egypt and sea-emperor of the Mediterranean, whose achievements in establishing civilization in Crete and the Aegean were afterwards embroidered with romantic fable by the Greek myth-mongering poets.

It is significant that Sir A. Evans, the brilliant explorer of Cretan antiquities, equates the beginning of his Early Minoan Period I, when Cretan civilization suddenly begins at the end of the New Stone Age, with the beginning of the First Dynasty Period in Egypt; yet no one ever appears to have suggested that Minos and Menes themselves might be personally related or identical. On the contrary, the rich harvest of art treasures unearthed at Crete by Sir A. Evans since 1900 onwards of " Aegean " type with Greek affinities has led him to believe that Cretan or " Minoan " civilization was of independent indigenous origin within Crete itself; and was a chief source of Grecian and European civilization; and that Minos and his civilized Cretans were of the same race as the Late Stone Age aborigines of Crete, amongst whom Minos suddenly appears with his Copper or Bronze Age civilization.

The identity of Minos with Menes now becomes apparent, not only from the identity in their personal tradition, and the equation in their names, but also in the essentials of their culture and civilization; and the Sumerian sign for

## 72 EGYPTIAN CIVILIZATION OF SUMER ORIGIN

the *Man* element in Menes' name in the Egyptian and Indus inscriptions reads also dialectically *Min*.

In legend, Minos was a son of Zeus, just as Menes or Manis-the-Warrior, like his father Sargon, was a descendant of the human original of Zeus, namely King Zagg, Sakh or Sax. He was like Menes or Manis a votary and priest of Zeus or Zagg. He was a sea-emperor of the Mediterranean and laid Greece, including Athens, under tribute, just as Menes or

FIG. 15.—Narmar or Narām or "The Strong Wild Bull," son of Menes or Manis, as Minos' son, "Mino-Taur." (From Slate "Palette" of King Narmar, after Quibell, and compare Plate XII.)

Note his cognomen of Wild Bull's head in upper register duplicated for symmetry, and at bottom the king personified as Wild Bull destroying citadel of his enemy, the king of Magan. For detailed decipherment see next chapter. Note giraffes' necks forming pigment well.

Manis was sea-emperor of the Mediterranean and its lands; and a seal of the son of Manis has been found in Cyprus; and the "Minoa" place-names in the Mediterranean from Sicily to the Syrian coast evidently attest former trading stations of the Minoans. Minos was a great sailor, an admiral and builder of ships, just as Manis was. He promulgated wise laws, which he received from Zeus, just as the Sumerians ascribed their laws to King Zagg or Sax, and Manis himself was a famous establisher and observer of constitutional law. His "Labyrinth," the intricate building which he erected and in which his son dwelt, was probably an exaggerated memory of his great palace in Crete, in which his son doubtless dwelt in his voyages of inspection in the Mediterranean; and it is significant that Menes also is credited with the erection of a " Labyrinth " in Egypt.[1] His son was a Wild Bull-Man, so-called " Mino-Taur," just as the son of Menes or Manis was called " The Strong Wild Bull," *Nar-am*—in which *Nar* means in both Sumerian and Egyptian " Strong or Mighty," [2] and *am* or " Wild Bull " is invariably the sign by which Nar-am wrote his name, *and significantly as we shall see he as "Nar-mar" of Egypt represents himself pictorially on his victory Palette as a Wild Bull*.(Fig. 15). Minos' death also was tragic in a sea-voyage in the West, just as Menes' was.

The culture, art and civilization of Minos and his period was generally similar to that of Menes or Manis. Both kings were of the Bronze Age. Both used finely wrought stone bowls in diorite or other hard mineral. Both had black hand-burnished ceramic ware and decorated and painted pottery of the same forms. Both used writing on clay tablets with a style, and the Minoan script resembles many of the signs in the linear script of Sargon and Menes and his dynastic successors in Egypt (my decipherments of the relatively few inscriptions found in Crete I hope to publish in a later work). The button-seals of Crete resemble those found in the Sumerian colony of the Indus Valley in the Sargonic period,[3] and also in Mesopotamia, and cylinder seals [4] and clay sealings were used by both. The jointed terra-cotta drain-pipes in Minoan Crete are similar to the Sumerian found at Ur and in the Indus Valley. And the differences which latterly developed in the mannerisms and local style of Cretan artists are no greater than those which latterly arose in Egypt and other colonies of the Sumerians under local inspiration. Funeral rites and cults of Minoan Crete were similar to Egyptians of Delta.

The Double-Axe sign for the god Zeus in Crete also occurs

---

[1] MDC. 235.
[2] On *Nar*," strong, mighty," see Br. 7263 f.; MD. 720; and in Egyptian, BD. 378 b, which is another instance of the identity of words in sound and meaning in Sumerian and Egyptian.
[3] WISD. 64 f., 68 f.   [4] EPM. 197.

as a sign for the god *Zag* in Sumerian. It is found in the inscription of Manis-Tusu's grandfather;[1] and it is obviously a fuller form of the diagrammatic axe-sign in Sumerian, which has the phonetic value of *Zag* or *Sag*, and is defined as " axe, sceptre, *two-edged* sword."[2] And significantly this axe-sign is a title in Sumerian of " The Great Lord" (Nar-gal),[3] a martial reflex of the Father-god Zagg, Sakh or Sax, *i.e.* Zeus, who became latterly the " God of War " in Babylonia; and Manis' father Sargon worshipped the weapon of God Zagg as we have seen.

*Identity of Minos of Crete with Menes or Manis-the-Warrior*

| Minos of Crete. | Menes or Manis. |
|---|---|
| 1. Son of god Zeus. | Son or descendant of Zagg or Sax (Zeus). |
| 2. Votary and priest of Zeus. | Votary of god Zagg and ex officio high-priest. |
| 3. Of Bronze Age, replacing Neolithic. | Of Bronze Age, replacing Neolithic. |
| 4. Sea-emperor of Mediterranean. | Sea-emperor of Mediterranean. |
| 5. Sailor and builder of fleets. | Sailor with fleets of ships. |
| 6. Introducer of Civilization. | Introducer of Civilization. |
| 7. Law-giver direct from Zeus. | Law-establisher with code credited to Zagg. |
| 8. Built a Labyrinth. | Built a Labyrinth. |
| 9. His son was a Bull-man (Mino-Taur). | His son was named " The Strong Wild Bull " (*Nar-ăm*), and bore title "Men-Narmar" and *Nerāma*. |
| 10. Writing on clay tablets in linear script generally resembling Sumerian and linear Egyptian. | Writing on clay tablets in linear and cuneiform Sumerian script. |
| 11. Used seal-impressions on clay for sealing. | Used seals for clay sealing. |
| 12. Culture and Art generally of Sumerian or Aryan type. | Culture and Art of Sumerian or Aryan type. |
| 13. Funeral rites similar to Egyptian delta. | Funeral rites of delta similar to Cretan. |
| 14. Double-Axe emblem of Zeus. | Double-Axe sign for Zag in Sumerian and Manis' father worshipped the weapon of god Zagg. |
| 15. Physical type of Minoans is Aryan. | Physical type is Aryan. |
| 16. Death tragic on sea-voyage in West. | Death of Menes tragic on sea-voyage in West. |

[1] Cp. B. pl. 160, No. (?) 160.
[2] Br. 5573 f.; M. 3925.
[3] M. 10751. Ner-gal from his fatal smiting still later became the God of the Underworld.

## INTRODUCES ARYAN CIVILIZATION TO CRETE 75

The physical type of the Minoans in Crete as seen in the beautiful " Cup-bearer " fresco shows " The profile of the face is pure and almost classic Greek, the physiognomy has certainly no Semitic cast ; "[1] and similarly so the ivory carved figures and heads and clay sealings from Knossus are of fine Aryan type ;[2] and the Dorians were early located in Crete.

These identities of the legendary King Minos of Crete with the historical King Menes of Egypt or King Manis-the-Warrior, the Sumerian or Aryan sea-emperor of the Mediterranean, are displayed in the preceding table.

### DATE OF MINOAN CIVILIZATION ABOUT 2700 B.C.

We thus obtain a mass of cumulative evidence for the identity of the legendary King Minos of Crete with the historical King Menes of Egypt and the Sumerian or Aryan King Manis, the sea-emperor of the Mediterranean. We also gain for the first time a relatively fixed initial historical date for King Minos of Crete at about 2700 B.C., and thus recover a more solid foundation for the chronological scheme of classification of the strata in Minoan or Cretan civilization, and for the truer appreciation of its racial authorship and affinities.

---

Altogether, our new evidence identifies Menes, the founder of the First Dynasty of Egypt with King Manis-the-Warrior, the Sumerian emperor of Mesopotamia and son of the world-monarch Sargon, with the Aryan King Manasyu, " The royal Eye of Gopta and of the Four Quarters of the World," and with King Minos of Crete, and discovers the hitherto wholly unknown origin of Menes or Minos, his antecedents, ancestry, race and his tragic death on a sea-voyage in the West ; and fixes with relative certainty for the first time his actual date.

As the successors of Menes in his First Dynasty of Egypt are now discovered to be identical with the successors of Manis-the-Warrior in Mesopotamia and in agreement with the Aryan kings in the Indian Lists, this discovery requires a separate chapter.

[1] *Monthly Review*, 1900.   [2] EPM. 8, and see pl. opp. p. 145. BSK.

## VI

### MENES' FIRST DYNASTY OF EGYPT IDENTICAL WITH MANIS-TUSU'S DYNASTY IN MESOPOTAMIA & IN INDIAN LISTS FROM NARMAR ONWARDS

WE now discover that Menes' Dynasty or The First Dynasty of Egypt is identical in names and chronological order of succession with the dynasty of the Sumerian emperor Manis or Manis-Tusu in Mesopotamia and also with that of the Aryan emperor Manasyu or Asa-Manja in the Indian Lists. These identities thus while confirming the personal identities above demonstrated of King Gin or "Sargon" and his Aryan ancestry and descendants, at the same time establish absolutely the Sumerian or Aryan Origin of Egyptian Civilization.

These identities moreover disclose that Egypt was held as a colony of the Mesopotamian empire from the epoch of Sargon onwards to at least the end of his dynasty; with the exception of the reign of Menes or Manis himself, in which it was held independently of Mesopotamia as a separate kingdom by Manis or Aha Men personally. Indeed, the Indian King-Lists and Chronicles make it clear that his younger brother Mush did not reign there, as they omit his name altogether from the main-line Aryan kings, and obviously considered him to be a usurper.

### MENES' OR MANIS-TUSU'S DYNASTY FROM MESOPOTAMIAN LISTS & MONUMENTS, & IN THE INDIAN-KING-LISTS

The genealogical table of Menes or Manis-Tusu from the Kish Chronicle on p. 77, shows that Manis-Tusu's son and successor in Mesopotamia was Narām, Lord Enzu, the so-called " Narām Sin " of Assyriologists, and that he was the grandson of King Kīn or " Sargon " of Agadu. And the

## MANIS-TUSU'S DYNASTY IN BABYLONIA

Kish Chronicle goes on to detail the official list of eight kings from Manis to the end of his, or his father's dynasty, including four temporary kings who reigned in all for only three years during a period of revolt or anarchy on the demise of Narām's successor.

### MANIS-TUSU'S DYNASTY IN BABYLONIAN & INDIAN LISTS COMPARED

In the annexed Table is displayed the agreement between the official Babylonian Lists (Kish and Isin Chronicles) and the official Indian Lists respectively in regard to the dynasty of Manis-Tusu in Mesopotamia and that of the Aryan emperor Manasyu or Asa-Manja. In column 2 are added the forms of the names of those kings as actually found in their own contemporary monuments in Mesopotamia, which is also confirmed by their names in their Indus seals in Plates XI, etc.

*Manis-Tusu's Dynasty in Babylonian and Indian Lists*

| Babylonian. | | Indian Lists. | | |
|---|---|---|---|---|
| Kish Chronicle. | Inscriptions. | Puru. | Solar and Lunar. | No. |
| (Kīn or Sharru-Kīn). r. 55 yrs. Mūsh (Uru-), s. of 37. r. 9 yrs. | (Gani or Gin, Shar-Gani). Mush (Uru-). | Pra-Vīra or Puru II. — | Kuni, Sha-Kuni or Sagara. — | 37. |
| Manis-Tīsshu, s. of 37. r. 15 yrs. | Manis-Tusu (or -Tis's'u). | Manasyu, s. of 37. | Asa-Manja, s. of 37. | 38. |
| Narām-Enzu or Narām-Ba, s. of 38. r. 56 yrs. | Narām-Enzu or Narām-Ba. | Vātā-Yudha, Abha-Yada, or Vāggmin, s. of 38. | Karam-B'a, Ansu-mat or Anjana, s. of 38. | 39. |
| Gani-Eri, Shar-Guni-Eri. r. 24 yrs. | Gani-Eri, Shar-Guni-Eri. | — | Kunti-jit, Rtu-jit or Khat-wanga, s. of 39. | 40. |
| [Anarchy with 4 kings in 3 yrs. of whom 1st was (?) Igigi]. | — | — | [Variation in succession] Bhagī-ratha, s. of 40. | |
| Dudu. r. 21 yrs. | Dudu. | Dhundu, s. of 39 and Bahu-bida. | or Soma or Deva-kshatra. | 41. |
| Shudur-Kib, son of Dudu. r. 15 yrs. [End of Dynasty]. | Shudur-Kib. | Subāhu, s. of 41. | Suhotra II, Shruta or Deva-Kshattra, s. of 41 [Break of Dynasty]. | 42. |

## 78 EGYPTIAN CIVILIZATION OF SUMER ORIGIN

It will be observed that the Indian lists agree with the Babylonian absolutely in chronological order of succession, and substantially in the form of the names, the variations in the latter being merely in phonetic spelling and in the use of one or more titles instead of the personal name. And we thus obtain additional evidence of the identity of the Sumerian and Aryan history.

### Egyptian King-Lists of Menes' First Dynasty compared with Mesopotamian King-Lists of Manis-Tusu's Dynasty & the Indian Versions

In starting to compare the Egyptian King-Lists of Menes' First Dynasty with the Mesopotamian and Indian lists we are met at the outset by the striking fact that there is practically no agreement amongst Egyptologists nor in the traditional Egyptian King-Lists themselves in regard to the names of the kings of the First Dynasty of Egypt.

### Wide Discrepancies amongst Egyptologists & Traditional Egyptian King-Lists in the Names of the Kings of the First Dynasty

Not only are the readings or restorations of the names of the kings of the First Dynasty by the leading Egyptologists more or less totally different, but these again, excepting the name of Menes himself, are totally different from the traditional names of those kings preserved in the lists of Manetho of the third century B.C. and Sety I of the nineteenth dynasty and others (see cols. 1-5 of the following Table).

This wide difference in the readings or restorations of the names in this dynasty by Egyptologists was obviously owing, I observed, to the names being written in the kings' own inscriptions, not in the later stereotyped Egyptian hieroglyphs, but in the parent Sumerian linear pictographic writing and in the Sumerian language with syllabic values for each sign ; and to the fact that Egyptologists treating the signs as Egyptian hieroglyphs read them mostly with alphabetic value, *i.e.* using only the initial letter of the each syllabic sign, and where the latter differed markedly from the later Egyptian hieroglyph, different Egyptologists

## First Egyptian Dynasty of Menes compared with Manis-Tusu's & Manasyu's in Babylonian & Indian

| | Egyptian Monuments. | | | |
|---|---|---|---|---|
| | Waddell (in Sumerian). | Petrie. | Budge. | Mane |
| 1 | MAN, MANJ, AHA-MANJ, MANASH, MINASH, MANSHU, MANI-TUSSI, TUSU-MENA or AHA-MENA, s. of Puru-GANI. | Nor-mer, MEN. | ĀHA. | MĒNĒS. |
| 2. | NARMAR, NAR-AMA or Abatu. | Aha. | NĀRMER. | Athōthis |
| 3. | GUNI, GIN-ERI or Shar-GANI- (or -GUNI) DILI-PA-RIT. | Zer-Ta. | KHENT. | KENKEN |
| 4. | BAG-GID or BAG-GID-GI-RU. | Zet-Ata. | Tcha. | Uenephē |
| 5. | DUDU, DUNU, SHU-DUDU, DANA, or BUSAHAP, s. of Gina Sag. | DEN-Setui. | TEN, Semti. | USAPHA |
| 6. | BI-DI, Lord MAR. | Azab-Merpaba. | Ātab. | Miebidc |
| 7. | SHESHIMMASH, PA or KHAT. | Semerkhet-shemshu. | Hu(?). | Sememj |
| 8. | SHUDUR-KIB, KIBBU, KIBI, QIBI, KIA, QA, or XUDARUR, s. of Gana-Sag. | Qa-Sen. | Qa or Sen. (QEBHU(?)). | Bičnek |

[End of Menes' First Dynasty of Egypt.]

| Egyptian Lists. | | Indian Lists. | |
|---|---|---|---|
| Manetho. | Sety I, &c. | Solar. | Lunar. |
| Mênês. | Mena, Manj. | Asa-MANJA, s. of Kuni or Sakuni. | MANASYU, s. of Pra-Vīra. |
| Athōthis. | Teta. | ANJANA, ANSU-mat, s. of Asa-Manja. | KARAM - B'A, Abhayada or Vātā-yudha, s. of Manasyu. |
| Kenkenês. | Attā. | KUNTĪ-jit, Ritu-jit, or Dili-pa, s. of Anjana. | [Break in Dynasty]. |
| Uenephês. | Ata. | BHAGĪ-ratha, g.s. of Ansu-mat. | — |
| Usaphaidos. | Hesepti. | DEVANA - kshatra, or Arishta - nemi, s. of Kunti-jit. | DHUNDU, SUDYUMNA, s. of Abha - yada ((?) Madhu). |
| Miebidos. | Mer-ba-p. | -- | Bahu-Bida, s. of Dhundu. |
| Semempsês. | Sem-en-ptah(?). | -- | SAMPĀTI, s. of Bahubida, or SOMA (or Aham-yati). |
| Bičnekhês. | Kebh. | SHRUTA, SUHOTRA (III). | (?) Puru-hotra. |
| | | | [Break in Dynasty.] |

|  | Babylonian. | | |
|---|---|---|---|
| Lunar. | Lists: K.=Kish, I.=Isin. | | Monuments. |
| MANASYU, s. of Pra-Vīra. | MANIS-TISSHU (K.), HA (?)MA-NIS (I.),s.of Śar-Gani. | | MANIS-TUSU or Manish-Tussu. |
| KARAM - B'A, Abha-yada or Vătā-yudha, s. of Manasyu. | NARĀM-BA or -ENZU (K.) NERRA, ENUGGE-ANNA (I.), s. of Manis-Tisshu. | | NARĀM-BA or -ENZU. |
| [Break in Dynasty]. | Shar-GANI (or GUNI)-Eri (K.), s. of Narām Enzu. | | Shar-GANI (or -GUNI)-Eri. |
| — | (Anarchy with IGIGI or Nigigi Imi Nanum Iama). | | — |
| DHUNDU, SUDYUMNA, s. of Abha - yada ((?) Madhu). | DUDU (K.) or DUNDU(N). | | DUDU or DUNDU(N) |
| Bahu-Bida, s. of Dhundu. | — | | — |
| SAMPĀTI, s. of Bahu-bida, or SOMA (or Aham-yati). | — | | — |
| (?) Puru-hotra. | SHUDUR-KIB (K.), s. of Dudu. | | SHUDUR-KIB. |
|  | [End of Manis-Tusu's Dynasty in Mesopotamia.] | | |

# FIRST EGYPTIAN DYNASTY OF MENES COMPARED WITH MANIS-TUSU'S & MANASYU'S IN BABYLONIAN & INDIAN

| Waddell (in Sumerian). | Egyptian Monuments. | | | Egyptian Lists. | | Indian Lists. | | Babylonian. |
|---|---|---|---|---|---|---|---|---|
| | Petrie. | Budge. | Maspero. | Sety I, &c. | Solar. | Lunar. | Lists: K.=Kish, I.=Isin. | Monuments. |
| MANI, MANJ, AHA-MAN; MANASH, MINASH, MANSHU, MAN-TUSSI, TUSU-MENA or AHA-MENA, s. of Puru-GANI. | Nar-mer, Mer | Ana | Menes. | Mena, Maj; | Asa-MANJA, s. of Kusi or Sakuni. | MANASYU, s. of Pra-Vira. | Lists: MANIS-TISSHU (K.), HA (?)NA-NIS (I.), s. of Sag-Gani Tussu. | MANIS-TUSU or Manish-Tussu. |
| 2. NARMAR, NAR-AHA or Abatu | Aha. | Nineme | Atoibis | Teta. | ANJANA, ANSUmat, s. of Asa-Manja. | KARAM-PA, Abba-yuta, s. of Vidi-yutha, s. of Manasyu. | | NARAM-BA or -ENZU. |
| 3. GUNI, GIN-ERI or Shar-GANI for -GUNI DILI-PA-RIT | Zer-Ta. | Kenert. | Kenkenes | Atti. | KUNTI-jit, Ritu-jit, or Dalipa, s. of Anjana. | [Break in Dynasty.] | Shar-GANI (or GUNI)-Eri NERRA_ENUGGE_ANNA (K.), s. of Manis-Tissu. | NARAM-BA or -ENZU Shar-GANI (or -GUNI)-Eri. |
| 4. BAG-GID or BAG-GID-GI-RU. | Zet-Ata. | Tcha. | Uenephes. | Ata. | BHAGI-ratha, s. of Amsu-mat. | — | (Anarchy with IGIGI or Nigigi Nanum Iami.) | |
| 5. DUDU, DUNU, SHU-DUDU, DANA, or BUSAHAN, s. of Gina Sag | Der-Setui. | Ter. Semti. | Usaphatdos. | Hesepti. | DEVANA - leshatra, Arishta - aeni, Kasti-jit. | DHUNDU, SUDYUMNA, s. of Abha - yuta (?) Madhu) | DUDU (K.) or DUNDUN). | DUDU or DUNDUN). |
| 6. BI-DI, Lord MAR. | Azab-Merpaba | Atab. | Miebidos. | Mer-be-p. | — | Babu-Bidu, s. of Dhundu. | — | — |
| 7. SHESHIMMASH, PA or KHAT. | Semerkhet-merenkis... | Hu(?). | Semempsis. | Sem-en-puah(?). | — | SAMPATI, s. of Bahu-bidu, (or SOMA (or Ahan-yat). | — | — |
| 8. SHUDUR-KIB, KIBSU, KIBI, QIBI, KIA, QA. or XUDARUR, s. of Gana Sag. | Qa-Sen. | Qa or Sen. (Qanesui(?)). | Bisneehia. | Keuu. | SHRUTA, SUHOTRA (II). | (?) Puru-vorsa. | SHUDUR-KIB (K.), s. of SHUDUR-KIB. Dada. | SHUDUR-KIB. |
| [End of Menes; First Dynasty of Egypt.] | | | | | [Break in Dynasty.] | | [End of Manis-Tusu's Dynasty in Mesopotamia.] | |

# MENES' DYNASTY IN MESOPOTAMIAN & INDIAN

selected arbitrarily the phonetic value of one or other hieroglyph which somewhat resembled it.

Again, as regards the traditional Egyptian list of names of the kings, of Manetho, etc., the almost complete want of equation between these and the monument names was clearly owing, I observed, to the lists having largely used *titles* for the kings instead of their personal names, and thus being in series with the Indian lists which as often as not used different titles, regnal, religious and other, in place of the proper personal names.

### REVISION OF THE READINGS OF THE NAMES OF THE KINGS OF THE FIRST EGYPTIAN DYNASTY ON THEIR OWN CONTEMPORARY MONUMENTS

On realizing the causes of these serious differences in the existing king-lists of the First Egyptian Dynasty, it thus became necessary, before comparison with the Babylonian and Indian lists was possible, that I should revise the readings of the names of each king in their contemporary inscriptions by my Sumerian and Indian keys. The results of these revised readings are given in the first column of the annexed Comparative Table.

### MENES' FIRST EGYPTIAN DYNASTY COMPARED WITH MANIS' OR MANIS-TUSU'S DYNASTY IN THE BABYLONIAN AND INDIAN LISTS

In the annexed Table are compared Menes' First Egyptian Dynasty of eight kings according to the traditional lists of Manetho and others, with Manis-Tusu's Dynasty in the Babylonian Lists and Manasyu or Asa-Manja's Aryan line in the Indian lists. In column 1 are given the names of the kings on their own Egyptian monuments as revised by me, the detailed proofs for which readings are given in my revised readings and translations of the Egyptian inscriptions of these kings. In columns 2 and 3 are given the names as read respectively by the leading Egyptologists, Sir F. Petrie [1] and Sir W. Budge.[2] In columns 4 and 5 are the traditional forms of the names and titles from the lists of Manetho, Sety I and others. And in columns 6 and 7

[1] PHE. 7.   [2] BHE. 251.

80 EGYPTIAN CIVILIZATION OF SUMER ORIGIN

are the forms in the Babylonian king-lists (Kish and Isin Chronicles) and on the contemporary monuments of King Manis-Tusu's (or Sargon's) Dynasty in Mesopotamia.

### RESULTS OF COMPARISON OF FIRST EGYPTIAN DYNASTY KINGS WITH BABYLONIAN & INDIAN LISTS

From this Table is seen the substantial agreement in the names of the kings of Menes' Dynasty on their Egyptian monuments with those of Manis-Tusu's Dynasty on their Mesopotamian monuments and in the Babylonian and Indian lists. The chronological order of the kings also is essentially identical. It is absolutely identical in all three lists—Egyptian, Babylonian and Indian, as far as and inclusive of the third king, *Shar-Guni* or *Gin-Eri*, the *Kenkenes* of Manetho and *Khent* of Egyptologists and *Kunti-jit* of the Indian lists ; and the last king who ended Menes' Dynasty is the same in all three lists : *Kebh* of Egyptian, *Shudur-Kib* of the Babylonian and *Suhotra* of the Indian, who is identical with the king *Shudur Kib* who ended Manis-Tusu's Dynasty in Mesopotamia ; and *Shudur Kib* of his Indus seals.

Of the other kings of Manetho's list and the monuments, Nos. 4 to 7, the 5th, namely *Dudu*, bears the same name in all three lists, Egyptian, Indian (where the name is nasalized) and in the Babylonian. In the latter he immediately precedes the last king of the dynasty. The reason for the extra kings in the Egyptian lists is disclosed to be evidently the anarchy in Mesopotamia which followed on the death of the third king, Gani-sharri, as detailed in the Babylonian Chronicles. In the period following this anarchy the Egyptian lists give two kings (Nos. 6 and 7) who were not kings of Mesopotamia, implying either that they were tributary to the emperor Dudu or held Egypt independently of him, until it was recovered by his successor, the last emperor of Manis-Tusu's Dynasty, namely *Kebh* of the Egyptian and Shudur-*Kib* of the Babylonian. Significantly, certain versions of the Indian lists, which latter exhibit considerable variations in the succession of this period, give between them the names of those two Egyptian kings who are absent in the Babylonian lists.

## MENES' DYNASTY IN BABYLONIAN & INDIAN

The wide differences also in the traditional Egyptian lists of Manetho and others from the names as found on the monuments, are now seen to be owing to these Egyptian lists having largely used *titles* instead of the personal names of the kings. Thus the second king of the dynasty, now disclosed as Narmar of the Egyptian monuments or the emperor Narām of Mesopotamia, is styled in the Egyptian lists *Athōthis* or *Teta* (see cols. 4 and 5 of Table). This is now seen obviously to represent Narām's Mesopotamian title of "*Ati*-enshak,"[1] and corresponding to his Indian title of *Vātā-yūdha* and *Abha-yada*. Similarly the third king, whose name in his monuments reads Guni-Sag and "Khent," the Kunti-jit of the Indian and Kenkenēs of Manetho is called *Atta* in the other Egyptian lists. This seems to represent his *Rtu* and *Khat* titles in the Indian lists, the latter word *Khat* becoming in Sumerian dialect *Hat* and *At* through dropping of the initial letters,[2] as is also seen on the Ancient Briton coins of the Catti.[3] And similarly with others, though some of Manetho's other differences may be errors of later scribes.

Another and extremely important historical result emerging from our Comparative Table is the conclusive evidence afforded that *the total years' reign for the First Dynasty of Egypt given by Manetho is very greatly exaggerated;* and yet Manetho's chronology is implicitly accepted by Egyptologists. Our identification of Menes with Manis-Tusu enables us to recover the actual length of the reign of this dynasty through the Mesopotamian chronicles. Manetho makes Menes' Dynasty reign for 253 years; but the Babylonian chronicles agree in giving the reign of Manis-Tusu's Dynasty in Mesopotamia from and including Manis himself down to the end of the reign of the last King Shudur-Kib as only 134 years. And we find in the Chapter on Chronology that although Manetho gives Menes a reign in Egypt of 62 years, the utmost that can be allowed for his reign in Egypt prior to his accession in Mesopotamia is 35 years, making, with his 15 years in Mesopotamia, a total of 50 years in all in Egypt. This would give the total reign of Menes and his dynasty in Egypt, including his previous

[1] Cp. PHT. 4, 132.    [2] WAOA. 33.    [3] WMC. 8.

## 82 EGYPTIAN CIVILIZATION OF SUMER ORIGIN

35 years' rule there as 169 years instead of the 253 of Manetho. That is to say that Manetho has evidently exaggerated the reign of the First Dynasty by 84 years, or one-third more than its approximately actual years. And as it seems probable that most of Manetho's other dynastic reigns are equally exaggerated in length and as many of his dynasties are now admitted to have been contemporary and overlapping, it should not be impossible to adjust the chronologies of Egyptian dynasties to the newly-found date for Menes of about 2704 B.C.

### Records of Individual Kings of Menes' Dynasty confirm Identities with Manis-Tusu's Dynasty

The records of the individual kings also of Menes' Dynasty in Egypt fully confirm the identities of the kings with those of Manis-Tusu's Dynasty. Menes himself we have already identified with Manis or Manis-Tusu, so we now take up the other kings of his dynasty, commencing with the second king of that dynasty, Narmar.

## VII

2ND KING OF 1ST DYNASTY, NARMAR, IDENTICAL WITH NARAM, 2ND KING OF MANIS' DYNASTY IN MESOPOTAMIA, c. 2640 B.C., & WITH INDO-ARYAN KING-LISTS & INDUS VALLEY SEALS

*Disclosing the equivalency of " Narmar " and " Naram." His Sonship to Menes. His pre-history and achievements. His Sumerian Inscriptions in Egypt & Indus Valley deciphered for first time & his title " Goth."*

THE identity in the names and in the same successive order of the kings or Pharaohs of Menes' or Manj's First Dynasty in Egypt with those of Manis' imperial dynasty in Mesopotamia has been established in the previous chapter. In now taking up the identities of each of Menes' successors in detail in Egypt and Mesopotamia, we begin with the second king of Menes' dynasty, Narmar. The new evidence includes the decipherment for the first time of his Sumerian inscriptions in Egypt, and of his official seals from the Indus Valley colony of the Sumerian empire, of which colony he was as crown-prince the governor under his father Menes before his own accession to the imperial throne as world-emperor. For the new evidence shows the blood-relationship of all the Pharaohs of the First Dynasty which hitherto was wholly unknown; and Narmar in both Egyptian and Sumerian inscriptions is recorded to be Manj's or Manis' son. In Mesopotamia his name is usually spelt Naram or " The Wild Bull Lord," though in his seals it is sometimes spelt " Ner-Mar " and " Mar-Nar." The meaning of his name as " Wild Bull Lord," coupled with his cruel character in war, accounts for the Greek legends of his destructive ferocity as the notorious Mino-Taur, son of King Minos of Crete.

## 84 EGYPTIAN CIVILIZATION OF SUMER ORIGIN

NARMAR, SECOND KING OF MENES' EGYPTIAN DYNASTY
IDENTICAL WITH NARĀM ENZU OR NARĀM BA (" NARAM
SIN ") OF MESOPOTAMIA

King Narmar of Egypt is now definitely placed by our
new evidence as the second king of the First Dynasty, and
as the successor of Menes, of whom we have found him to
be the son. He was rightly placed as the second king by
Budge; whilst others have conjecturally made him the
first king and identical with Menes, or have made him a
predynastic king, because they could not find his name in
the lists of Manetho and the others which called him only
by his titles and not by his personal name (see foregoing
Table).

He is found by the comparative king-lists and genealogies,
Sumerian and Indian, to be identical with the Mesopotamian
emperor Narām Enzu or Narām-Ba (" Narām Sin ") the
son of the emperor Manis-Tusu and grandson of " Sargon-
the-Great." This identity is now fully confirmed and
established by Narmar's own inscriptions in Egypt, not only
in his name but also in his records regarding his paternity
and Mesopotamian empire and by his portraits resembling
those of Narām Enzu in Mesopotamia (see Plates IX and X).

NARMAR'S NAME & EGYPTIAN EMBLEMS OF " THE WILD
BULL " & " FISH-MONSTER " re NARĀM ENZU'S MESOPO-
TAMIAN TITLES OF " WILD BULL " & " FISH-MONSTER "
(" CUTTLE-FISH ")

In Egypt King Narmar usually writes his name by the
two hieroglyph signs of *Nar* and *Mar*, which have the same
pictographic forms, phonetic values and meanings as the
corresponding signs in Sumerian, another illustration of the
Sumerian origin of Egyptian hieroglyphs. But he also
spells his name in Egypt as *Nar-ama*, as we shall find,
which is identical with the usual spelling of his name in
Mesopotamia as *Narām* or *Narāma ;* and in his Indian seals.

In Egyptian, the initial *Nār* syllable of his name is written
by the pictograph or hieroglyph of a monster fish supposed
to be a cuttle-fish ;[1] and the second syllable *Mar* is written

[1] BD. 347 a.

NARAM-ENZU'S (MINOTAUR'S) STELE OF VICTORY.
c. 2600 B.C.

Found at Susa, whither it had been carried from Mesopotamia as a raid-trophy, and now in the Louvre (DP. I, Pl. X). The king is represented of heroic size, with horned hat, climbing with his warriors a high mountain rising to the stars and storming a hill fort. His helmet is adorned with horns of a bull (his homonym). He carries a club or battle-axe and a bow and arrow, and with one arrow he has shot an enemy and tramples on a fallen foe, whilst others plead for mercy. His followers bear standards and weapons. Compare with Narmar's palette of Victory, Pl. XII, p. 92, with its Bull emblems.

## NARMAR'S NAME IN EGYPT & MESOPOTAMIA 85

by the pictograph of a drill or borer,[1] the latter being, as I have shown, derived from the Sumerian *Mar* sign for a drill;[2] and similarly we shall find that the first sign also is of Sumerian origin.

This monster fish or "cuttle-fish" sign has in Egyptian generally the same pictograph form as in Sumerian, with tentacles projecting from its mouth (see Fig. 16 and the top of Figs. 15 and 17). This fish-sign in Sumerian has the

FIG. 16.—Naram's Name in Egypt as "Narmar" (after Petrie).

FIG. 17.—Sealing of Narmar (after Petrie).

usual value of *Pish* or "Fish,"[3] and is defined as "mighty fish" and as a title of the Babylonian god of war or death named *Ner* or *Nar*,[4] presuming that the sign also had this value *Ner* or *Nar* in Sumerian. It has also the Sumerian value of *Kar*,[5] which obviously explains the Indian variant of this king's name as *Karam*-B'a instead of *Narām*-Ba, by the Indian scribes selecting the former value *Kar* instead of *Nar*, which latter was its value in Egypt.

The second element in his Mesopotamian name of *Narām* or *Narāma*, namely, *Am* or *Ama*, which also occurs in his

[1] GH. 49.  [2] WSAD. *Mar*, Pl. IV.  [3] WSAD. 80.
[4] MD. 553 and B. 303. Significantly in Egyptian *Nark* is also a god of death, BD. 343.
[5] Br. 6927.

inscription in Egypt, designates him as "The Wild Bull,"[1] which has also the synonym of "strong lord" or "warrior,"[2] and was a common title of the Father-god and of heroic kings in Sumerian, Babylonian and Indian as well as Egyptian literature; and the Bull was a source of the colossal man-headed Bull-gods of Babylonia. That King Narām actually used this "Wild Bull" element of his name realistically is evidenced by his figuring the Wild Bull on the top of both sides of his Egyptian victory Palette as Narmar (see Plate XII and Figs. 15 and 17), and significantly in the lowermost compartment on the reverse of his Palette *he pictures himself as a Wild Bull* destroying his foes and their citadel. The Bull is also figured beside him on his great stone mace-head. And this title of his, as Wild Bull, we have seen was obviously the source of his being called by the Greek myth-mongering bards "Mino-Taur," or the Bull-man, in his Cretan legend, as the son of King Minos of Crete, who, we have seen, was Menes of Egypt.

The reason why King Narām of Mesopotamia changed his name in Egypt to *Nar-mar*, now apparently transpires in the fact that there is no *Am* or *Ama* word in Egyptian meaning "Bull" or "Wild Bull" or "strong lord." Whereas in Egyptian, *Mar* means "hero,"[3] and it is pictured by the hieroglyph sign of a drill, that is the same sign which in Sumerian with the value *Mar* has the meaning of "pierce, throw down, destroy,"[4] in the same sense as the Wild Bull metaphor.

We thus find that the evidence of King Narmar's name and his own victory Palette in Egypt conclusively confirms his identity with the Mesopotamian emperor Narām or Narāma, who was the son of Manis or Manis-Tusu, who was, as we have found, Menes the founder of the First Egyptian Dynasty.

The Semitic title of "Sin" arbitrarily applied by all modern Assyriologists to King Narām, instead of his Sumerian title of *Enzu* or *Ba* in his own Mesopotamian inscriptions is merely an unjustified attempt, as we have seen, to claim

---

[1] See WSAD. 12 for its occurrence in the leading Aryan languages, including English. Also B. 183; Br. 4545.
[2] Br. 4543-4.  [3] BD. 314 a.  [4] Br. 5818-9.

PLATE X.

NARAM-ENZU OR PHAROAH NARMAR.

Contemporary portrait on basalt bas-relief, c. 2600 B.C., found near Diarbekr, in Kurdistan, and now in Imperial Ottoman Museum, Constantinople. *Compare with Narmar's portrait on his Egyptian Slate-Palette, Pl. XII, p. 92.* It records his victories, including Magan, which he ascribes to God Induru or Ia (Jah). He carries a club in right hand and a whip in left and wears bracelets, and a tall Phrygian hat, as in his Egyptian portrait, see p. 91 and Pl. XII. His upper lip is unshaved, presumably as he was campaigning in Kurdistan, and his nose is of non-Semitic type.

# NARMAR'S NAME IN MESOPOTAMIA & EGYPT

him with his father and grandfather Sargon as Semites in order to suit their erroneous theory. But that theory is conclusively disproved by the documents of these Sargonic kings themselves and by the cumulative evidence of the Sumerian and Indian genealogies and records, including the fact that they were Sun-worshippers, a wholly non-Semitic cult. And this false Semitic attribution of Sargon's great Aryan Dynasty has formed one of the chief obstructions to the discovery of the truth in regard to the origin and affinities of the Sumerians and Aryans and the origin of the World's Civilization.

## Narām's Inscriptions in Mesopotamia

In Mesopotamia many inscriptions of King Narām have been unearthed on votive vases, plaques, his famous stele of victory statues, seals and stamped bricks, etc.,[1] and in old certified copies of his inscriptions at the Sun-temple of Nippur.

In these inscriptions he claims the title of "King of the Four Quarters of the World," and refers to his booty from "the Land of Magan" and elsewhere. In one of these inscriptions preserved in a copy in the Nippur temple describing his conquests,[2] in which the names of the countries and kings are mostly missing, he ascribes his conquests, like Sargon, to Lord Sakh, and in his curse against those who would destroy his inscription he invokes besides Sagaga, Lord Sakh and the Sun-god, also Lady Inanna, the wife of Sakh, of whom he styles himself "the servant or (?) descendant," also the great god Nar (or Ner) and even the Semitic Moon-god and several others, showing that he had an enlarged pantheon, or that he included as cursers the local tribal gods of the would-be destroyers.

## Narām's Conquests in the West, including Magan, Syria & Asia Minor

His conquest of Magan or the Sinai Peninsula, and his defeat of its king Mannu-dannu (supposed to have been possibly Menes of Egypt) have been detailed in the previous chapter.

In the Hittite cuneiform version of his conquests found

[1] TDI. 236 f.  [2] PHT. iv. 210 f.

## 88 EGYPTIAN CIVILIZATION OF SUMER ORIGIN

at the old Hittite capital at Boghaz Koi in Cappadocia in script of about 1400 B.C. or earlier,[1] and which is fragmentary, we find amongst the list of vanquished kings and countries extending from the West Land, and Asia Minor of the Hittites and Syria to Persia, a king of the West Land named *Mana-ila*, who may possibly be identical with this Mannu-dannu. The fragment records:[2] "And I (Narām Enzu) at that time against all the enemy lands made war. Mana-ila king of the Western Land,[3] Bunana-ila, king of Pāgki, Lapana-ila, king of Ulliui, ... innipa-ila king of ..., Pāmba king of the Khatti ("Hittite") Land, Khutuni king of Kaniesh, Nur ... [Dagan king of Burushkhanda], Akwāru-wash king of the Ammuri (Amorites), Tīshenki king of Parashi (Persia) ... Madakina king of Armani, Iskibbu king of the Cedar Mountains (Amanus), Teshshi..., Urlarāg, king of Larāg, Urbānda king of Nīgki, Ilshunna-īl king of Dur city, Tisbinki king of Kūrshaura. Altogether 17 kings who formed an alliance I overthrew them. I entrusted the troops to a *Khar-i* (*Har-i* or *Uru-i*)." And the second fragment records the tribute received in talents of silver and copper and in lapis-lazuli precious stone which was brought to Agadu.

### NARAM OR NARMER'S SEALS IN INDUS VALLEY

Amongst the second batch of seals unearthed from the old Indus Valley colonial capital at Edin, I found the following five seals figured in Plates V and XI, which presumably belong to Naram, see especially No. 3. The detailed decipherment is given in Apps. III and V. Here the literal translation of their inscriptions is given. It is seen that in these seals the name is spelt variously *Nera* and *Marru* and *Mar-Nera*, and also *Ner-Amma*.

### 1ST SEAL (PLATE V, 9 and App. V, Fig. 76).

" Of the Lower (Eastern) Land, the Gut (Goth or "Warrior") NERA, The Gut at Agdu Land."

[1] FB. 2-3.
[2] This translation is based on Sayce's in AE. 1923, 99, with revision of names from texts.
[3] *Gu-shu-a* in which *Gu*=land (M. 2027), *shu*=Setting of Sun, B. 490.

PLATE XI.

INDUS VALLEY SEALS OF FIRST DYNASTY PHARAOHS FROM
NARMAR TO SHUDUR-KIB OR QA, c. 2640-2535 B.C.

Including Gan-Eri (Khent), Bagiru (Bhagiratha) and Dudu or Dan. (Photographs after Sir J. Marshall.) For decipherments and translations, see pp. 88 f., 102 f., 107 f., 109 f., 196 f.

NARMAR'S INDUS SEALS DECIPHERED 89

*Nera* is evidently coined so as to give the meaning of Lord of the Deep Waters (*Ner*), the *Nārāyana* of the Sanskrit.

2ND SEAL (PLATE V, 10–11 and App. V, Fig. 75).
THE ELEPHANT SEAL.

This seal with the Elephant as its chief device reads :—
" Under-King Companion MAR-NERA, The Gut AMMA."

Here significantly the Elephant, which is called in Sumerian *Amsi* or " Horned (Toothed) Wild Bull," is clearly introduced for the Bull element in Naram's name. The Elephant is called sometimes in the east " The Great Ox," and our modern name for it is derived from the Greek *Elephas* through the Semitic *aleph* " an ox." This *Nar-amma* name for him is repeated on seal, Fig. 91.

3RD SEAL (PLATE XI, 1 and App. V, Fig. 77).

" Under-King Companion MARRU, The Lord, Son of the Gut, the *Ara*, The Lord of the Deep Waters GIN (" Sargon ").

It is noteworthy that Naram is called by Nabonidus and late Babylonians " the son " of Sargon.

4TH SEAL (PLATE XI, 2). " Under-King Companion, The heavenly Pharaoh NERA, the Lord at Agdu (or Edin).

5TH SEAL (NOS. 3–4, PLATE XI), THE TIGER SEAL. " Under-King Companion MARRU, the Lord Gut of Tiger Land." This seal as seen in App. V apparently belongs to Nar-Mar.

NARAM AS " THE DEMON-KING " NĀRMARA OF THE INDIAN VEDAS

In view of such wholesale intestine wars waged by Narām—for several of these kings were of kindred Sumerian or Aryan stock, such as the Hittites—it seems to me practically certain that he is the King Nārmara referred to in the Indian Vedic Psalms as a " demon " king, who harassed the loyal and orthodox Aryans and was destroyed in consequence by Indra. This Vedic hymn sings :—

" Thou Indra, who broughtest Nārmara with all his wealth of Ūrjayantī to slay him, so that the demons might be destroyed." [1]

[1] RV. 2, 13, 8.

Here his identity with King Narām or Narmar of Egypt seems to be clearly proved by the name of his chief fort called *Ūrjayantī* or " Ūr-the-Victorious." For *Uri* is the Sumerian, that is Aryan name for the Semitic *Akkad* or *Akkadu*,[1] which Assyriologists suppose to be the Semitic name of Agade, the Mesopotamian capital of Narām-Enzu ; and we shall see that Narmar in his Egyptian Palette calls himself " king of Uri." And Narām, much more than any other king of his Sargonic dynasty, adopted Semitic idioms into his Mesopotamian inscriptions, and as evidence of his reactionary backsliding we have seen that he had adopted the Semitic Moon-god, the human sacrifices to whom are being revealed by the excavations at Ur.

His inveterately destructive character with the abuse of his royalty is pictured by himself as Narmar in his great Palette and stone mace-head, in which he is gloating over his slain and beheaded victims. And his atrocious destructiveness was his leading trait, as we have seen in his Cretan legend as the ravaging Mino-Taur, son of King Minos (or Menes) of Crete.

### Narām's Inscriptions as "Narmar" in Egypt

The chief monuments of Narmar in Egypt are his famous great sculptured slate Palette of Victory (Plate XII and Figs. 15 and 18) and his magnificently carved great stone mace-head, both from Hierakonopolis, and his name on an ebony tablet, several vases and clay sealings by a cylinder-seal, found in his " tomb " at Abydos. But apart from the few short pictographic inscriptions or labels on his great Palette, now read for the first time, and his name-marks, there appear to be no other inscriptions of him yet found in Egypt ; whereas his successors in the dynasty have left several more or less longish inscriptions.

### Narmar's Palette Inscriptions celebrate his Victory over the King of Magan & confirm his identity with Narām of Mesopotamia

His magnificent victory slate Palette,[2] which is practically his only Egyptian monument containing inscriptions besides

---
[1] Br. 7:04-5.
[2] Discovered by Mr J. E. Quibell at Hierakonpolis or "Hawk City " in 1898; and generally described by Sir F. Petrie in Hierakonpolis, 1900-10.

# NARMAR'S EGYPT INSCRIPTIONS DECIPHERED 91

his mere name, is disclosed by its written labels, now deciphered for the first time, to celebrate his victory over the King of Magan, and thus strikingly confirms his identity with the Sumerian emperor Narām of Mesopotamia, who repeatedly boasts of his conquest of Magan in his imperial inscriptions in Mesopotamia.

This monument is shaped in the form of the indigenous Egyptian palette of the two-knobbed-head type, with a well or saucer in its centre for grinding cosmetic pigments (here malachite), the use of which for toilet purposes was common

FIG. 18.—Narmar's Slate Palette, Reverse.

in prehistoric Egypt and Mesopotamia, as it still is in the Orient at the present day. The rest of the surface of the Palette on both sides is finely and artistically carved with figures, scenes and a few hieroglyphs.

Its front or face (see Plate XII, A) is arranged as in Sumerian composite drawings into compartments separated by horizontal lines. In the first compartment, below the duplicated man-faced Bull emblem of Narmar with his name in a cartouche between the Bull-heads is pictured the king wearing the crown of Lower Egypt in procession. The procession is coming from a fort or building bearing the Sumerian pictograph of *Uru*, meaning "Guard," [1] and

[1] B. 290, pl. 183; M. 4587.

## 92 EGYPTIAN CIVILIZATION OF SUMER ORIGIN

presumably it is his famous fort, which is called in the Indian Vedas " Ūrjayantī, the fort of Nārmara." [1] This procession was supposed by Sir F. Petrie to be " formed by the four chiefs of nomes (or provinces) bearing the standards, the high priest Thet, the king Nar-mer [with hieroglyphs of his name in front of him] and the 'king's servant' behind them. They seem to have come from a building named *deb*. In front of the procession lie the bodies of enemies bound and decapitated. The heads, placed between the legs, are all bearded," [2] and above them is a hieroglyph description. Below these are two mythological camel-leopard-like animals, with their necks enclosing the pigment basin. And below is the Bull, symbolizing Narām breaking down a fort, scattering the bricks and trampling upon a fleeing foe. The picture inside the fort is supposed to be the hieroglyph for the name of the town.[3]

The reverse (see Plate XII, B) with the same Bull emblems and name above, shows the king, with the tall Sumerian and Hittite hat, grasping the forelock of his enemy with the left hand, and with uplifted mace in his right hand preparing to strike his foe, and behind him is his body servant. In front is the Sun-Hawk hooking the captured enemy by the nose; and the six plants are supposed to represent the hieroglyph of 6000, as indicating the number of captives. Behind the captive is the hieroglyph of his name. And in the bottom compartment are two fleeing foes.

### DECIPHERMENT OF NARMAR'S PALETTE INSCRIPTIONS OF HIS VICTORY OVER MAGAN

These critically important historical inscriptions engraved on the labels and standards of the several personages and scenes pictured in Narmar's Palette, are now discovered to be written significantly in Sumerian script and in the Sumerian language. The Sumerian script employed, though largely of the usual standard linear type of the Sargonic period in Mesopotamia, has certain of the pictographs drawn in full realistic form for pictorial effect, such as the Ship-sign (*Ma*) in the name Ma-gan, and the Lion or Wolf sign on the

[1] RV. 2, 13, 8.  [2] Quibell, H. 10.
[3] The picture somewhat resembles the Sumerian pictograph of *Pisan-mat* or *Gur-mat*. B. 272.

PLATE XII.

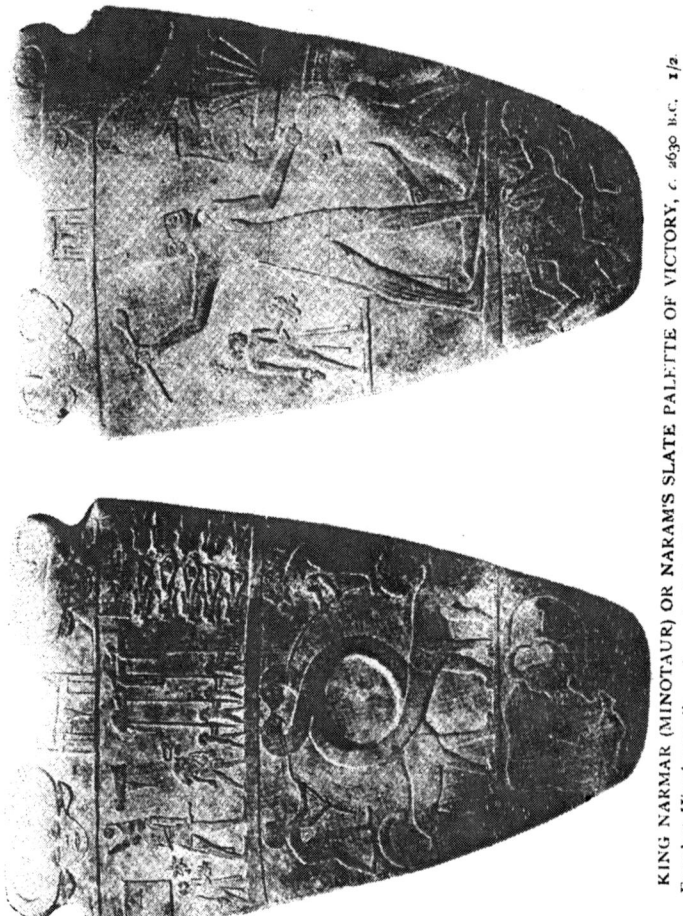

KING NARMAR (MINOTAUR) OR NARAM'S SLATE PALETTE OF VICTORY, c. 2630 B.C. 1/2
Found at Hierakonopolis, and now in Cairo Museum. (After J. E. Quibell and W. F. Petrie.) Both sides are shown, *A*, top with central well, and *B*, reverse. For detailed description and decipherments and translations of the Standard and other inscriptions, see pp. 94 f. For minute details of Standard inscriptions see collotype and pp. 94 f.

## NARMAR'S EGYPT INSCRIPTIONS DECIPHERED 93

second standard, instead of by their usual diagrammatic and abbreviated Sumerian forms for rapid writing.

It is also noteworthy that the Sumerian writing is in the reversed direction, as if intended to be read by a Semitic people accustomed to read in the *lunar* or reversed direction from right to left, instead of in the *solar* or Aryan or Sumerian direction towards the right from the left.

In my decipherments I place, as before, in line 1, the form of each sign as written on the Egyptian monument arranged in the order in which it is read when placed from left to right; in line 2 are the corresponding forms in the diagrammatic linear Sumerian writing of Mesopotamia; in line 3 are the phonetic values of the Sumerian signs in roman letters according to the standard Sumerian lexicons; and in line 4 are the severely literal translations into English all fully attested by the references in the foot-notes from the standard Sumerian lexicons.

Most of the inscriptions or labels are found on the front or face of the Palette. The chief inscriptions, apart from the name of Narmar, are those over the enemy dead and on the standards.

### Inscription over Enemy Dead Deciphered

This Sumerian inscription is at the upper right-hand corner of the Palette face (see Plate XII, A), below the man-faced bull on the right-hand side and immediately above the double row of decapitated dead bodies of the enemy. It is

Palette. Egypt.

Sumer (Mesop.).

Reads : MA[1]- GAN[2] (Hu) BAT[3] -TI[4] -(Hu) WULU[5] -ES.[6]
Transl. : Magan, dead men ("birds").

Fig. 19.—Palette Inscription over Enemy Dead deciphered.

[1] B. 137 ; Br. 3682.      [2] B. 119 ; Br. 3173.
[3] B. 70 ; Br. 1475 ; and see WSAD. 24, for its root in English and other Aryan words, *e.g.* Bad, Fate, Fatal, etc.
[4] B. 76.      [5] B. 289 ; Br. 6398.
[6] B. 432 ; Br. 9990 = " three," sign for plural and source of our English plural affix S, see WASD. 75.

## 94 EGYPTIAN CIVILIZATION OF SUMER ORIGIN

in two lines dovetailed; the uppermost line containing the sign of the ship (*Ma*) and the gridiron-like sign (*gan*) touch with their tops the top line bordering the compartment with the scenes; and the second line is slightly lower down and partly within the ship or boat. And these two lines are read as in Ancient Greek, the first line from right to left and the second line from left to right, or in *boustrephedon* or " ploughwise " fashion, in the alternating direction of the furrows of a ploughed field. The two Hawks facing the left, and related to the signs of this second line, appear to be introduced merely to show the direction in which this second line is to be read, namely from left to right; though they at the same time indicate the victory of the king who was professedly of the Sun-Hawk cult. In the Decipherment Table Fig. 19, the two lines are read as one line; and the silent Hawk sign is placed within brackets.

Thus the inscription actually describes these decapitated and bound enemy dead as " Magan dead and bound men."

### His Standard Inscriptions

The badges borne aloft on the standards in the procession before King Narmar are now discovered to be his Sumerian titles as " world-emperor " and sea-monarch. As some of

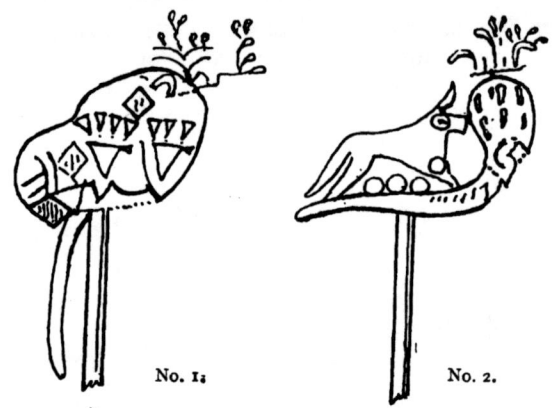

FIG. 20.—Narmar's Standards, Nos. 1 and 2. (Enlarged 3 diameters from Plate XI, A).

## NARMAR'S STANDARD INSCRIPTS. DECIPHERED 95

the signs are small and somewhat faint yet distinct in the Plate when examined under a lens, I give here a drawing of

FIG. 21.—Narmar's Standards, Nos. 3 and 4. (Enlarged 3 diameters).

the first two for reference ; and have numbered them in serial order, that nearest the king being termed No. 1. Full details are only visible in original or its collotype.

The different shapes of the standard emblems are found to be owing to the groups of the word-signs they contain.

### No. 1 Standard Inscription Deciphered

This sausage-like emblem with its tail, which has been variously conjectured to be a liver, a placenta, etc., is now

Palette. Egypt.

Sumer (Mesop.).

Reads : MAD[1]    URI[2] -KI[3] U KISH[4] -TABKI LUGAL[5] -AN.[6]
Transl. : Of the Land of URI (or AKKAD) and KISH City, the One King.

FIG. 22.—Inscription on Narmar's Standard, No. 1 Deciphered.

[1] B. 411 ; Br. 7386.
[2] B. 316 ; Br. 7304-8.
[3] B. 217 ; Br. 9621.
[4] B. 377 ; Br. 8902.
[5] B. 169 ; Br. 4259.
[6] B. 1 ; Br. 17. Literally = " The One," see WSAD. 19.

## 96 EGYPTIAN CIVILIZATION OF SUMER ORIGIN

seen to be a dummy effigy of the Sumerian pictograph sign for " King " with the rest of the inscription within inside it. Its outline minus the tail is obviously a shortened form of the Sumerian head-sign with its crown for " king " ; whilst the tail is the Sumerian sign for " one," defining him as " The One King," *i.e.* Emperor. The signs which are mostly written within the king-sign I read as above.

Here Narmar calls himself " The One King of the Land of Uri," and of Kish City, wherein *Uri* has the Semitic synonym of *Akkad*, which Assyriologists identify with Sargon's and Narām's capital of Agadu. Thus this inscription conclusively identifies Narmar with Narām, the Mesopotamian emperor of Agadu, and grandson of Sargon, who boasts in his Babylonian inscriptions of his conquest of Magan ; and whose title of " The One King " is the equivalent of " Emperor."

### No. 2 Standard Inscription Deciphered

In this inscription, the sign for " king " is given more of its usual early form, but it is bent on itself to accommodate

| | | | | | |
|---|---|---|---|---|---|
| Palette. Egypt. | | | | | |
| Sumer (Mesop.). | | | | | |
| Reads: MAD | -WI[1] | -U[2] | TIANU[3] | LUGAL. | |

Transl. : Of the Western Sunset Land and of Tianu, the King.

Fig. 23.—Inscription on Narmar's Standard, No. 2 Deciphered.

[1] B. 380 ; Br. 8916.  [2] B. 365 ; Br. 8770.
[3] For sign see B. 400 and Menes' Ebony Label ; and Br. 9220-23. The two strokes under the Lion duplicate the sign, which ordinarily reads *Pirig*. The glossaries give its possible phonetic values as Ti-a-nu, Ti-id-nu, Amurru, Martu, Axaru, *Akharu*, etc. ; and cp. MD. 30, 1148. It may possibly be related to the Ikarian Sea Land.

and support the Lion-sign for " Western Land," which latter sign is drawn in full form to render its identity evident from afar, instead of merely the Lion's head, as in the diagrammatic Sumerian, and the lion's head with paw,

## NARMAR'S STANDARD INSCRIPTS. DECIPHERED

as in Menes' ebony label. And the other signs are placed partly within the king-sign as before.

Here Narmar calls himself " King of the Western Sunset Land and of Tianu." This " Western Sunset Land " includes the Mediterranean lands with the Atlantic coast. " Tianu " Land or " Land of the Lions " (variantly read by Assyriologists as *Tidnu* or *Tidanu*) is considered to be Asia Minor or Amorite Land, that is Syria-Phœnicia; and one of its definitions in the glossaries is *Amurru* Land, *i.e.* " Amorite Land." It is probably related to the old Hittite city of Tyana in S. Cappadocia, which was within Amorite Land.

### Nos. 3 & 4 Standard Inscriptions Deciphered

These two standards bear the same general emblematic form. This emblem, which replaces the " King " sign of the first two standards, is apparently the effigy of the

| | Palette. Egypt. | | | | | | |
|---|---|---|---|---|---|---|---|
| | Sumer (Mesop.). | | | | | | |
| Reads : | MAD | -MAD | -U | -A-A[1] | NUN[2] | -HU[3] | -PAR.[4] |

Transl. : Of the Lands and Waters, The Great Sea-Lord, the Hawk(-line) Pharaoh.

FIG. 24.—Inscription on Narmar's Standards, Nos. 3 and 4 Deciphered.

Sumerian pictographic ⌐ sign of the Shepherd's Crook for the title *Bar* or *Par*, " Lord," which Sumerian word-sign we have seen was the source of the Egyptian title of " Pharaoh "; and it has also in Sumerian the angular form of ⌐. And the surmounting Hawk designates him as " Pharaoh of the Sun-Hawk line."

The two inscriptions differ slightly, the first referring to his Land and Sea empire, and the second to his universal Sea-empire.

Here on standard No. 3 Narmar calls himself " The

---

[1] As before.   [2] B. 94; Br. 2622.   [3] B. 82; Br. 2045.
[4] B. 77 a; Br. 1722 and 1752; and WSAD. 33-34; WISD. 31, 40 f.

Great Sea-Lord of The Lands and Waters, the Hawk(-line) Pharaoh," and he uses the same Sumerian sign and title for "Sea-Lord" as we have seen was used by his ancestral Aryan sea-emperors of Uruash's First Phœnician Dynasty for "Sea-Lord," namely, the sign of "the great Fish" or Sea-serpent of the Deep. On his 4th standard he calls himself "The Great Sea Lord of the Lands of The Seven Seas," the earliest occurrence known of the latter title.[1]

Thus, the four Standards of Narmar with their emblems and inscriptions confirm positively the identity of Pharaoh Narmar, "The One King of Akkad, Kish, and of the Western Sunset Land and of Amurru, and Great Sea-Lord (of the Two Seas), the Hawk (-line) Pharaoh, and conqueror of Magan" with the Mesopotamian emperor Narām, grandson of Sargon, King of Agadu and the Four Quarters of the World and conqueror of Magan, as recorded in his own inscriptions in Mesopotamia.

### INSCRIPTION OVER NARMAR'S ATTENDANT

The Sumerian inscription over the attendant behind the king, carrying what appear to be a pair of sandals and a pot reads: *E* or *Kha-du* or *Khal-du*,[2] according to whether the top sign is six-rayed or the eight-rayed Sun pictograph; but both compounds mean the same, namely, the "Runner forth,"[3] and obviously designate his functions.

### NAME OF MAGAN, CAPTIVE CHIEF ON NARMAR'S PALETTE AS "MANUN DAN" AS ON HIS MESOPOTAMIAN INSCRIPTION

The personal name of the captive Magan chief who is pictured on the reverse of the Palette (Plate XII B) in a kneeling posture, with his forelock grasped by King Narmar with uplifted mace, is enclosed within a rectangular panel. Above this panel is the Sumerian sign for "The Man."[4]

The name written in the panel is presumably that of the

---

[1] "The Seven Seas" are not specifically mentioned in the Indian Vedas, but these repeatedly refer to "The Seven Mother Rivers," "The Seven Regions of the Earth," "The Seven Races of Men," "The Seven Horses" of the Sun-God's Car, "The Seven Fiends," "The Seven Days of the Week," "The Seven flames of Fire," and "The Seven Sages."
[2] Br. 7873; and WSAD. 68 f.
[3] B. 2; Br. 78; and B. 207: Br. 4871.    [4] *Wulu*, B. 289.

# NARMAR'S PALETTE INSCRIPTS. DECIPHERED

vanquished king of Magan, who is called in the copies of Narām's Mesopotamian inscriptions "Mannu-(?)Dan." The signs on the palette are here so minute that several cannot be clearly deciphered even by a lens. But the name appears to read " Ma-nun-dan."

### NARĀM ENZU'S VERSION OF HIS CONQUEST OF MANNU DAN IN HIS MESOPOTAMIAN & BABYLONIAN RECORDS

Having thus discovered and deciphered Narām's own original inscription in Egypt as Narmar, on his victory over the king of Magan, it is necessary for us now to compare it with Narām's own accounts of that victory in his Mesopotamian inscriptions, for it further strikingly confirms the identity of Narām with Narmar.

The emperor Narām Enzu in Mesopotamia considered his conquest of the king of Magan as one of his great victories, for he repeatedly refers to it in his records in Mesopotamia, and it is also recorded in the later Babylonian Chronicle copies of his inscriptions. The Babylonian Chronicle states:

" Narām An-Enzu, the son [1] of King Gin (Sharru-Gin) . . . against Magan City he marched and Mannu-Dānnu (?), the king of Magan City [his hand subdued]." [2]

The Omens repeat the same, but using the word " land " instead of " city " and supplying the sentence enclosed above within square brackets. And on the base of a diorite statue of Narām in Elam, the latter claims to have " cast down Manu . . . [(?) Dannu] lord of Magan " on his conquest of that country.[3]

### KING OF MAGAN DEFEATED BY NARMAR OR NARĀM WAS NOT KING MENES OF EGYPT

It is thus rendered abundantly clear by the testimony of King Narmar or Narām himself on his own Egyptian monument that King Manun-(?)Dan (or Mannu-Dannu) of Magan, conquered by him, was not, as has hitherto been supposed, Menes of Egypt, who we have found was his own father.

---

[1] Here " son "=" descendant."
[2] KC. 2, 38 f.
[3] DP. *Mém.* 6 (1905), 25 ; STS. 3, 5 ; TDI. 239.

On the contrary, besides his name and country-name, this king of Magan is pictured by Narmar in this Palette of aboriginal type, with large broad negroid nose, long matted and (?) woolly hair, and like the other aborigines in the scenes, naked except for a loin string.

KING NARMAR OF EGYPT IDENTICAL WITH KING NARĀM ENZU (OR " SIN ") OF MESOPOTAMIA, SON OF MANIS-TUSU (OR MENES) AND GRANDSON OF " SARGON "-THE-GREAT

We have thus established conclusively the identity of King Narmar of Egypt with the Mesopotamian emperor Narām Enzu (or " Sin "), the son of the Mesopotamian emperor Manis-Tusu, who was the son of Sargon-the-Great, by a mass of positive contemporary documentary evidence from their own monuments in Egypt and Mesopotamia, and from the official king-lists of Menes' Dynasty in Egypt and from those of Manis-Tusu's Dynasty in Mesopotamia. The occurrence of his name in some sealings, alternating with *Man*, his father's name, presumes that he was co-regent for a time in his father's old age.

This new evidence also strikingly confirms the previous evidence we have elicited for the *Sumerian or Aryan Origin of Egyptian Civilization.*

The identity of the subsequent kings of Menes' Dynasty in Egypt with those of Manis-Tusu's Dynasty in Mesopotamia is demonstrated in the next chapters.

# VIII

## 3RD KING OF 1ST DYNASTY, GANI, SHAR-GUNI, GUNI OR " KHENT " IDENTICAL WITH GANI, SHAR-GANI OR GUNI OR GAN-ERI, 3RD KING OF MANIS' DYNASTY IN MESOPOTAMIA, *c*. 2584 B.C.

*With his Sumerian Inscriptions in Egypt & Indus Valley deciphered for first time*

THE third king of Menes' dynasty, Gani, Guni or " Khent " is disclosed as the son of Narmar who preceded him and as the grandson of Menes or Manis. His Sumerian inscriptions in Egypt and the Indus Valley are deciphered for the first time. His Indus Valley seals disclose that before his accession to the imperial throne he was as heir-apparent governor of the Indus Colony under his father's suzerainty in accordance with the old Sumerian custom established by the first Sumerian emperor, Uruash or Haryashwa who first founded that colony about 3075 B.C.

This general identity of Menes' Egyptian Dynasty with Manis-Tusu's Mesopotamian Dynasty, I have already established by the Comparative Table of the official kinglists of those two dynasties Egyptian and Mesopotamian, confirmed by the official lists of the Early Aryan kings from the Indian Chronicles—the agreement being absolute except in regard to the 6th and 7th Egyptian Kings, who were presumably local kings in Egypt and not emperors in Mesopotamia. From that Table, it is seen that the third king and successor of Narmar in Menes' dynasty in Egypt is the socalled King " Khent " of Egyptologists, the " Kenkenēs of Manetho's list ; but who writes his name on his own Egyptian monuments, as we shall now find, as *Gani* or *Guni*, *Shar Guni-Rit* and *Sag-Gina*.

## THIRD KING OF MENES' DYNASTY, SHAR-GANI OR SHAR-GUNI-RIT (OR -RI), THE SO-CALLED "KHENT" OR "KENKENES" OR "ZER" IDENTICAL WITH THIRD KING IN MANIS-TUSU'S DYNASTY IN MESOPOTAMIAN & IN INDIAN LISTS

The identity of the third king of Menes' dynasty in Egypt, the so-called King "Khent," or Kenkenēs of Manetho's list, with the third king of Manis-Tusu's dynasty in Mesopotamia has been demonstrated in the above Table.

In Mesopotamia the name of the son and successor of Narām Enzu is conjecturally read by Assyriologists variously as *Shar-gani-shar-ri*, *Shar-gali-sharri*, *Shar-gani-shar-ali* and *Shar-gani-shar-eri* (or *eru*). As, however, he is seen to be a namesake of his great-grandfather Sargon, whose personal name we have seen as Shar-Gani or Shar-Guni is properly "King *Gani* or *Guni*," the front half of his name therefore reads "King *Gani* or *Guni*." The latter half or the special titular portion of his name is not however spelt in Sumerian *Shar-ri* or *Shar-eri*, but is spelt *Lugal-Ri* (or *Eri*),[1] that is "King *Ri*," and the last sign has also the value *Eridu*.[2] Thus this king's name reads in his Mesopotamian records "King *Gani* (or *Guni*), the king *Ri* (or *Eri* or *Eridu*)."

The Indian lists support this reading of his name, as the solar versions give his name variously as *Kunti*-jit and *Ritu*-jit, that is "*Kunti* or *Ritu* the victorious," wherein *Kunti* equates with the Sumerian *Guni* and *Ritu* with *Ri* of the Sumerian.

## INDUS VALLEY SEALS OF KING SHA-GIN II or GAN-ERI

In the second batch of Indus Valley seals I found the following four seals of this king, shown in Plate XI, and give their detailed decipherment in Appendix V. In the first and second he is Under-King Companion in the Indus Valley, presumably under his father Narām. In the others he is emperor. The second seal is especially important in that he calls himself therein by his title of *Dili*, as in his ivory tablet in Egypt and by the Sumerian sign, and also "The

---

[1] B. 39. Br. 889-90.
[2] On *Eridu* value of this sign see HCC. No. 41, p. 39, and Pr. 2645 and 2649.

## THIRD PHARAOH'S NAME AND SEALS 103

King of the Great Khāmaesh Land," that is as we have seen Egypt, thus apparently implying that the Indus Valley was then tributary to Egypt.

The records on these seals read as follows :—

No. 1 Seal (Plate XI, 4 and Fig. 80)

" Under-King Companion SHA-GIN at Edin (or Agdu) Land."

No. 2 Seal (Plate XI, 6 and Fig. 83)

" Under-King Companion GAN, The Great KHĀMAESH King DILI, The Great Khāmaesh (Egypt) King, The Seal of GIN the Gut."

No. 3 Seal (Plate XI, 3 and Fig. 79)

" GAN-ERI, The Ruler of the Lands, The Lord GIN."

No. 4 Seal (Plate XI, 5 and Fig. 82)

" Lord GIN at Edin (or Agdu) Land."

### THIRD KING'S NAME IN EGYPTIAN RECORDS

In Egypt, the name of this third king, which has been read variously as " Khent " and Zer-Ta, is found on several

FIG. 25.—Ivory Label of Third King. (After Sir F. Petrie, PRT. ii. Pl. VI.)

FIG. 26.—Sealing of Third King. (After Sir F. Petrie, PRT. ii. Pl. XV.)

ivory labels and clay sealings impressed by cylinder-seals of Sumerian type from his tomb at Abydos (see Figs. 25 and 26).

The writing on these labels and sealings is seen to be essentially in Sumerian script.

## 104 EGYPTIAN CIVILIZATION OF SUMER ORIGIN

### Third King's Name on Ivory Label in Egypt Deciphered & in Agreement with Mesopotamian & Indian

The inscription on his ivory label (see Fig. 25) is written in reversed direction; and when the signs are arranged to read from left to right they are as follows in Fig. 27, where their equivalent Sumerian signs and values, with translation, are added, as in the other cases. It also discloses the Sumerian origin of more Egyptian hieroglyphs.[1,2]

Here the king calls himself, or is called in his tomb, " King *Gani* (or *Guni*), Man of the (Sun-)Hawk (line), *Rit*, the

Egypt Label.

Sumer (Mesop.).

Reads: SHAR [1]-GA [2]-NI [3] DILI [4]-PA [5] RIT [6] A [7] - SAKH [8] GUN.[9]
Transl.: King GANI, man of the (Sun-)Hawk (House of Pharaoh) RIT, the Lord GUN.

Fig. 27.—Third King's Name on Ivory Label deciphered.

Pharaoh *Sakh-Gun*." And it is of immense critical significance that his title here as " Man of the Sun-Hawk line," which is spelt in this Egypto-Sumerian text *Dili-pa*, is actually given as his solar title in the Indian king-lists as *Dilī-pa*. This is another striking testimony to the remarkable authenticity of the Indian Chronicles, and shows again that the Indian scribes who transcribed the Sumerian syllabic writing into the Indian alphabetic script were familiar with Sumerian, and also that they evidently differentiated this king from his namesake, his great-grandfather Sargon, by selecting for him this more distinctive part of his title, *Dilī-pa*. And the identity is still more striking

---

[1] B. 170; Br. 4297. Sumer source of hieroglyph *Sha*, "garden."
[2] B. 275; Br. 6104. S. source of hieroglyph *Ga, Ka*, "bull."
[3] B. 228; Br. 5310. This sign is between the horns of the cow. The object represented by this Sumerian sign is supposed to be a Teat.
[4] B. 1; Br. 27= "man."
[5] B. 83; Br. 2048. Has also *Hu* value.   [6] Br. 5956.
[7] B. 293; Br. 6542 or *Du* B. 294; Br. 6644.
[8] B. 269; Br. 5928.   [9] B. 307; Br. 6985.

## THIRD PHARAOH'S NAME DECIPHERED

by the Indian lunar versions giving him the title of " *Ritu* the Conqueror," wherein *Ritu* is in series with his *Rit* title in this Egyptian inscription. This presumes that his Mesopotamian affixed title *Ri* is a shortened form of *Rit*.

### THIRD KING'S NAME ON SEALINGS IN EGYPT DECIPHERED

In these clay sealings (Fig. 26) the king's personal name seems spelt *Gin-ti* instead of *Gani*, in series with his *Kunti* title in the Indian lists and *Khent* in the later Egyptian hieroglyphs. In the annexed figure these signs are arranged for decipherment as before:

Egypt Sealing.

Sumer (Mesop.).

Reads: BURU[1] MAR[2] -PA[3] RIT[4] GIN[5]-TI (or NA).[6]

Transl.: Lord (Pharaoh) Son of the (Sun-)Hawk, RIT (or SAG), GIN-TI (or NA).

FIG. 28.—Third King's Name on Sealings deciphered.

Here the king calls himself " The *Buru* (Pharaoh), Son of the (Sun-) Hawk, *Rit*, *Ginti*. And significantly in the next compartment of the sealing (see Fig. 26) it will be noticed that he calls himself again *Dilipa Rit* as his solar title, in agreement with his Indian solar titles of *Dilipa* and *Ritu*.

We thus find that the third king of Menes' Dynasty in Egypt in his Egyptian inscriptions is called by the same name and titles as the third king of Manis-Tusu's Dynasty in Mesopotamia and in the lists of Early Aryan kings in the Indian Chronicles.

[1] B. 365; Br. 8632, 8657-9.
[2] B. 392, and cp. form of this sign *mar* in WSAD. Pl. IV; WPOB. Fig. 36, and in present work, and WMC. 149.
[3] B. 83; Br. 2048.   [4] As before.
[5] B. 283. As before, in Sargon's Egyptian inscription.
[6] B. 76; Br. 1695. This sign seems to be the local Egyptian form of the Sumerian sign *Ti* for a drill, which is defined as " drive away, throw down," and in Egyptian this sign with alphabetic value *T* is considered the picture of a stone-drill cap. GH. 49. But this sign may have been read in Sumerian as *Na*, the Stone-sign.

## IX

FOURTH KING OF MENES' DYNASTY BAGID IDENTICAL WITH
FOURTH KING OF MANIS-TUSU'S DYNASTY, c. 2560 B.C.[1]

*With his name on Egyptian Monuments and Indus Seals deciphered*

THE fourth king in Manis-Tusu's dynasty has his name spelt *Igigi* in the Babylonian lists in Kish Chronicle; but no inscriptions of him have been found in Mesopotamia.

FIG. 29. — Stele of 4th King of Menes' Dynasty. (After Petrie.)

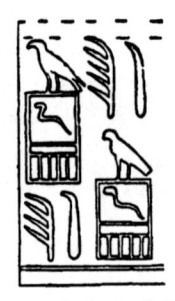

FIG. 30.—Seal of 4th King "Zet" in Egypt. (After Sir F. Petrie. PHE. I, 17.)

He arose and reigned during a brief period of anarchy or revolution on the death of the third king; and he corresponds to the Indian list king, called Bhagī-ratha or "Bhagī-the-charioteer."

This latter name supplies a key to his name on the

[1] WMC. p. 61.

## FOURTH PHARAOH'S NAME DECIPHERED 107

Egyptian monuments, see Figs. 29 and 30. In Egypt the fourth king of Menes' Dynasty wrote his solar name by the Sun-hawk and the sign of the Serpent, which last has a phonetic value of *Gid*. Thus with the *Ba* or *Bag* value of the Hawk-sign followed by *Gid*, we get his name as *Bagid* or *Baggid*, in series with his *Bhagi* name in the Indian Lists, see decipherment table, Fig. 31.

Egypt Seal.

Sumer (Mesop.).

Reads: BAG , GID [1] GI [2] - RU.[3]
Transl.: The (Sun-)Hawk (line) Pharaoh GID, GI- RU.

FIG. 31.—Seal of 4th King of Menes' Dynasty Deciphered.

It thus appears that the *Igigi* name for the Fourth Babylonian King of Manis-Tusu's Dynasty is corrupted from his Egyptian solar title of *Gid-Gi-ru*. It is also somewhat in series with the *Tcha* value read for this Egyptian name by Budge, see p. 78.

### Indus Valley Seal of 4th King of Menes' Dynasty

I find a seal of his from the Indus colony, see Plate XI, 7, and deciphered in Fig. 83, App. V. It reads :— " BAG-ERI of the house of Maru-Ner at Uri-du Land." This seal name thus equates with his Indian name of " Bhagīratha," into which it has been expanded by the Brahmans to give it an Indian meaning.

[1] Br. 7504; B. 325. *Bu* and *Bur* are other values.
[2] B. 283; Br. 6307.
[3] This sign on the seal is a long tapered wand with recurved tip, which in later Egyptian has the value of *Ta* or *Ty*. GH. 62. It is now seen to be the Sumerian sign *Tal* or *Til*="stretched out" (M. 9); and thus disclosed as the Sumerian source of our English word "Tall." But its *Ru* value is obviously intended here.

## X

**5TH KING OF 1ST DYNASTY, DUDU OR DAN OR "DEN" IDENTICAL WITH DUDU OF MANIS' DYNASTY IN MESOPOTAMIA, c. 2557 B.C.**

*With his Sumerian Inscriptions in Egypt & Indus Valley deciphered for first time. His title of "Usaphaidos." His invocation of the Sun-archangel Tasia or Tascio as in Sumerian, Asia Minor, Indus Valley & Ancient Briton inscriptions & his Aryan titles of "Ukus" & "Goth"*

THE fifth king or Pharaoh of Menes' dynasty, Dudu or Dan, the so-called "Den" of Egyptologists (who conjecturally employ *e* for the unexpressed vowel in hieroglyph writing now shown to be *a*) has left in Egypt richer and more splendid cultural remains and more inscriptions and seals than any of the other Pharaohs of the First Dynasty. And his tomb (see Pl. XIII) of astonishing magnificence, paved with blocks of granite, was on a much larger and more developed scale than those of his predecessors. His blood-relationship to the previous Pharaohs, hitherto unknown, is disclosed by his Sumerian inscriptions in Egypt (now read for the first time) and in agreement with his seals in the Indus Valley colony, where he was governor for a time. He was son of the third Pharaoh of Menes' dynasty, Gani or Gan-Eri (or "Khent"), and identical with the emperor Dudu of Mesopotamia, who according to the Kish Chronicle succeeded his father Gani three years after the death of the latter, those three years being described therein as an interregnum with four claimants. His name Dudu, moreover, is in agreement with its nasalized form as "Dhundu" in the Indian lists.

Significantly he calls himself like ancestor "Sargon" a descendant of Ukus (or Ukusi), the first Sumerian or Aryan king, and also Gūt, Got or "Goth." And in one of his

# FIFTH PHARAOH'S NAME DECIPHERED 109

Egyptian tombs' inscription he invokes the Sun-archangel Tasia or Tascio (see Fig. 40) as did the Sumerians in their inscriptions and amulets in Mesopotamia, Asia Minor, Indus Valley and Ancient Britain.

The fifth king of Menes' Dynasty, "Den" of Egyptologists, is now demonstrated to be identical with the fifth chief king of Manis-Tusu's Dynasty, *Dudu* or *Dundu* (see Kish Chronicle list), and the *Dhundu* of the Indian lists.

FIG. 32.—King Dudu or "Den's" Portrait on a label from Abydos. (After Sir F. Petrie.)

### INDUS VALLEY SEALS OF KING DUDU OR DAN

In the second batch of Indus Valley seals I found two seals of King Dudu or Dan, figured in Plate XI, 8 and 9. These are of critical historical importance in giving besides his name *Dudu*, also his synonym of *Dan*, and also his father's name as GANI ERI, who is moreover called GAN-*the-Second*, that is " Sargon-the-Second " ; and he appears also to call himself, like Sargon, a descendant of Ukus or " Ukusi," the first Sumerian or Aryan king.

The detailed decipherment is relegated to Appendix V. The records on the seals read as follows :—

No. 1 SEAL (Plate XI, 8, and Fig. 84)

" DUDU DAN, son of GANI (or SHUKUNNI-)ERI. The seal of the Minister Lord at Agdu Land."

No. 2 SEAL (Plate XI, 9, and Fig. 85)

" DAN, the son of GAN-the-Second of the House of AHA and (Lord) NER-SIN, ruler of (the line of) UKUS, the Gūt (or ' Goth ')."

## EGYPTIAN CIVILIZATION OF SUMER ORIGIN

### KING DUDU'S NAME & INSCRIPTIONS IN EGYPT

He has left several immensely important historical inscriptions besides his seals and signatures, all of which being written in Sumerian script have not been hitherto read, and are now deciphered and translated here for the first time.

### PERSONAL NAME OF 5TH KING AS DUDU OR DUNDU, & DECIPHERMENT OF ITS SIGNS

In Egypt the personal name of the fifth king reads I find in the Sumerian inscriptions of that king as *Dudu* or *Dundu(n)*, that is just as we have seen it so spelt in his inscriptions in Mesopotamia (see Table opposite p. 78).

*a.*     *b.*     *c.*

FIG. 33.—Personal Name of Dudu, Dan or Dundu in 5th King's Inscriptions in Egypt. (After Sir F. Petrie.)

*a.* PAT. 1, pl. 5, 11 ; *b. Ib.*, 1, pl. 5, 12 ; *c. Ib.*, 2, pl. 7, 7.

In Egypt this personal name is written by duplicating the " Desert " sign or hieroglyph of a three-knobbed mound (see Fig. 33 *c*). The phonetic value of this sign in Egyptian has been unknown, but because it is used as a determinative or pictorial index-sign to words meaning " desert," it has been assumed by Egyptologists to have had the phonetic value of the commonest Egyptian word for " desert," namely " *Sem-t* " ; and hence the name of this king has been conjecturally read as " Semty."

But this " desert " hieroglyph, which occurs in the Sumerian inscriptions of this king in Egypt, is now seen to be merely a fuller realistic drawing of the Sumerian pictograph *Du* or *Dun*, meaning " mound, earthwork, hill " (see Fig. 34) ; and it is, as I have shown, the Sumerian origin of our English word *Dune* for " sand-hills," *Downs*, etc., Sanskrit *Dhanu*, " sandbank," and it runs with this sound and meaning throughout

# FIFTH PHARAOH'S NAME DECIPHERED 111

the other Aryan languages.[1] The three knobs in the Egyptian hieroglyph are now seen to be a fuller form of drawing the three strokes inside a circle or triangle, to which the Sumerians in Mesopotamia reduced this picture diagrammatically for speedy writing (see Fig. 34). And the identity of the signs is further confirmed by the interior dots within some versions of the Egyptian hieroglyphs (see Fig. 34), which dots are also found in this sign in some Sumerian documents (see Fig. 34)—these dots presumably picturing grains of sand, earth or pebbles on the mound sign.

THE MOUND-SIGN DU OR DUN IN EGYPTIAN HIEROGLYPHS DECIPHERED THROUGH THE SUMERIAN & IDENTICAL IN SUMERIAN & EGYPTIAN

The Egyptian phonetic value of this mound sign is discovered through the Sumerian in the following figure, in which the Egyptian forms of the sign are given in the first

Egypt.

Sumer (Mesop.).

Reads: DU (or DUN),[1] DU (or DUN).[1]

FIG. 34.—The Sumerian Mound sign in Egyptian=DU or DUN as in Sumerian.

[1] B. 417, pls. 108 and 171; Br. 9577. On the *Dun* value for this sign see WSAD. 63, and cp. Br. 4861 and Br. 9577.

line, the Sumerian diagrammatic forms in the second line, and the phonetic value of the latter in the third line.

This *Du* value for this Mound sign was later preserved also in Egyptian, as the phonetic value of *Du* is occasionally attached to the two-peaked Mound sign;[2] and in some of this king's inscriptions the sign is two-peaked.[3]

It is thus seen that the personal name of the fifth king of Menes' Dynasty in Egypt, written by the duplicated Mound

[1] WSAD. 63.   [2] GH. 31.   [3] PRT. 2, pl. 7, etc.

sign, in his inscriptions which are in the Sumerian writing and language, reads *Du-du* or *Dun-du* (*n*). And it is thus in strict literal agreement with his name as the fifth chief king in Manis-Tusu's Dynasty in Mesopotamia.

We now proceed to his solar title or name.

### SOLAR TITLE OF 5TH KING, DUDU, OF MENES' DYNASTY "DEN" DECIPHERED AS DAN

The usual solar title of the fifth king of Menes' Dynasty is written as in Fig. 35, by the hieroglyphs of a Hand and the Negation sign; and it is read by Egyptologists as D-N or conventionally " Den," that is as we have seen properly *Dan*, as the unexpressed vowel in alphabetic Egyptian and Indian and Phœnician writing is *a* and not *e*.

Now both of these hieroglyphs, the Hand and the Negation signs, are derived with their form, sound and meaning from the Sumerian. The Hand sign with its value *Da* I have already demonstrated to be of Sumerian origin.[1] Similarly so is this *Nu* or negative hieroglyph, which in Egyptian means " No " or " Not."[2] It is the Sumerian *Nu* or *No* or *Na*,[3] which is now disclosed as the source of the English " No," " Not," and all the negative N words in the Aryan family of languages. In Sumerian its sign pictures a line cancelled by a wavy or straight stroke through it (see Fig. 36 line 2); and in Egyptian it is a wavy cancelling line (see Fig. 36 line 1) as in modern conventional cancelling of a written word by a wavy line. These are therefore other striking instances of the derivation of the Egyptian language and writing from the Sumerian.

Thus his solar title as seen in Fig 34, reads *Da-na*[4] or *Du-nu*,[5] or as one syllable *Dan* or *Dun*. *Dan* in Sumerian as in Egyptian and other Aryan languages means " mighty, powerful ";[6] or if its value was *Dun*, it had the same form as his personal name.

[1] See Pl. XVIII and cp. WSAD. 44, Pl. II. [2] BD. 339 a.
[3] B. 79; Br. 1958. The Sumer *u* has frequently an *o* value (WAOA. 38 f.), but Akkadian words ending in *u* have *a* in Sumerian.
[4] B. 294; *Da*, Br. 6643; on *Du* value, Br. 6644.
[5] See foot-note 3. [6] WSAD. 49.

## Dudu's or "Den's" Title of "Usaphaidos" in Sumero-Egyptian

This fifth king of Menes' Dynasty is called by Manetho "Usaphaid-os," a title which Egyptologists have failed to find on the monuments or explain, though an inscription has been read as "Den-Setui." This inscription is here given in Fig. 35.

FIG. 35.—Inscription of Dudu or "Den" from Lid of a Seal-box. (After Petrie. PHE. 1, 20; PRT. 1, pl. 7, 12.)

This inscription through the Sumerian reads as follows :—

Egypt.

Sumer (Mesop.).

Reads :    DA (or DU)-NU    BU [1]    - SA [2] - HAP.[3]

FIG. 36.—Inscription of Dundu with title "Busahap" deciphered.

This *Busahap* title in his own inscription in Egypt clearly discloses the Sumerian source of Dudu's Egyptian title of Usaphaid-os of the later scribes. It is moreover incidentally of considerable historical importance, in that it supplies *in all three of its signs* additional evidence to what I have demonstrated in my *Sumer-Aryan Dictionary* of the deri-

[1] B. 325.   [2] B. 118; Br. 3083.   A Net.
[3] Br. 10159; B. 443. This square conventionally=a circle.

vation of the Egyptian hieroglyphs from the Sumerian in form, sound and meaning. The first sign *Bu* figured in Sumerian by a Serpent is seen to be the Sumerian source of the Egyptian value of *Fau* for Serpent and its sign.[1] The second sign *sa*, "a net," and pictured by a net in Sumerian is seen to be the Sumerian source of the Egyptian hieroglyph *skha(t)* or *sha(t)*[2] "a net," and its sign. And the third sign picturing a loop of cord, with the meaning in Egyptian of "loop, circle, ring," and secondarily through its sense of enclosure " great multitude,"[3] is now disclosed as the Sumerian sign *Hap* (the source of the English " Heap ") which possesses all these meanings and also that of "Heap"[4] and its Akkadian value of *Shinu*[5] is now discovered to be obviously the source of the Egyptian name and phonetic value of *Shenu* for the cartouche or surround for royal names.

INSCRIPTIONS FROM EGYPTIAN TOMB OF KING DUDU OR DUNDU DECIPHERED, DISCLOSING HIS WORLD-EMPERORSHIP IN WEST, MESOPOTAMIA, & EAST, HIS PARENTAGE & INVOCATION OF SUN-ARCHANGEL TASIA AS IN SUMERIAN, TROJAN & INDUS VALLEY SEALS & IN PREHISTORIC MONUMENTS & COINS OF THE ANCIENT BRITONS

The immensely important historical inscriptions of this king from his tomb in Egypt are written in Sumerian, and are now deciphered here for the first time.[6] In these he designates himself, or is designated, besides " King of Upper and Lower Egypt," also " King of the Lands from the Rising Sun to the Setting Sun in the West " and " King of the West " and " son of King Gana or Gin-Ri," that is the third king and grandson of Menes or Manis-Tusu ; and thus identifying him absolutely with the Mesopotamian emperor Dudu or Dundu. He moreover invokes for his Resurrection the Sun-archangel Tasia, and in the same general formulas as in the Sumerian, Trojan, Indus Valley seals and in the " prehistoric monuments of the 3rd millennium B.C. in Ancient

[1] Cp. WSAD. 76.   [2] BD. 618, 695.
[3] GH. 47.   [4] B. 443; Br. 10198 f.   [5] M. 7695.
[6] The proposed interpretations of some of the signs by Mr Griffiths, PRT. 1, 40 f., were admittedly " tentative " and conjectural.

PLATE XIII.

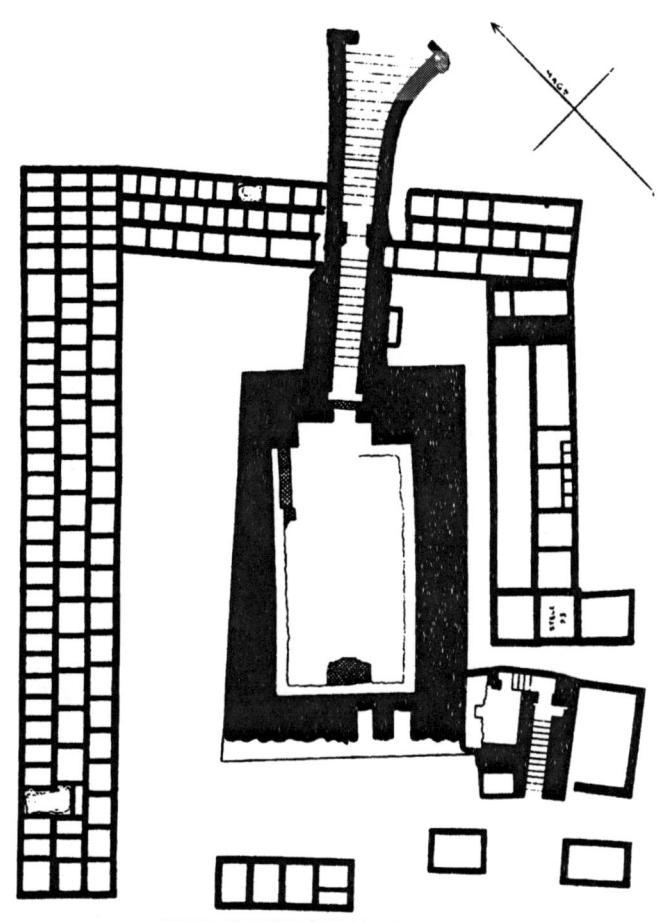

TOMB OF KING DUDU AT ABYDOS.

(After Sir F. Petrie, PRT. II, Pl. LXII.)   Note the enormous development
of the tomb with surrounding chambers to accommodate the abundant food and
other offerings to minister to the supposed comfort of the spirit of the deceased
king and his retinue.

## 115    DUDU'S EGYPTIAN INSCRIPTS. DECIPHERED

Britain.[1] This discovery of the active prevalence of this Tasia cult (the " Tascio " of the Ancient Briton pre-Roman coins) in Egypt in this Sargonic or Menes' Dynasty in the early part of the third millennium B.C., appears to indicate the route by which that cult reached Ancient Britain about that period (as I have shown that it did), through the seafaring, colonial and mining trade activities of this enterprising Egypto-Sumerian world-empire.

These tomb inscriptions are mostly engraved on ivory and ebony tablets, some of them with portraits of the king. Those selected here for examination and decipherment are the best preserved of the larger of those many fragmentary records (Plate XIV).

### DECIPHERMENT OF EGYPTIAN INSCRIPTIONS OF KING DUDU OR DUNDU

The writing in the inscriptions from the tomb of King Dudu or Dundu in Egypt is seen to be unequivocally of Sumerian type in the linear cursive kind, written with pen and ink, and ink inscriptions are found on some of those tomb objects) as found engraved in the earlier Sumerian period in Mesopotamia and in the Indus Valley seals, as opposed to the more angular diagrammatic form in the lapidary and cuneiform style latterly current in Mesopotamia. Some of the signs are already becoming conventionalized into their local Egyptian forms as found in the Egyptian hieroglyphs; and this well illustrates the derivation of the latter from the Sumerian writing.

In this pioneer decipherment of this writing in its transition stage from the Sumerian to the conventionalized Egyptian hieroglyphs and hieratic writing, the readings and translations are made as before through the Sumerian keys of the lapidary script of Mesopotamia. The freely cursive form of the writing in these Egyptian inscriptions, as in the Indus Valley, somewhat modifies the forms of the Sumerian signs occasionally. But although a few signs are thus somewhat doubtful, it is believed that these in no material way alter

[1] WPOB. 243 f.; 249 f.; 254 f.; 261 f.; 335 f.; and *passim*; WISD. 37 f.; 79 f.; WSAD. 53.

PLATE XIV.

KING DUDU'S ("DEN-SETUI'S") TOMB EBONY LABELS
AT ABYDOS, c. 2536.
(From photographs by Sir F. Petrie, PRI. I, Pl. XI.) For decipherment and
translation, see pp. 115 f.

## 116 EGYPTIAN CIVILIZATION OF SUMER ORIGIN

the sense of the records and their immense historical and religious significance. For convenience of reference I have marked the two chief inscriptions of King Dudu here deciphered as Nos. 1 and 2 on the next and following pages.

### KING DUDU OR DUNDU'S TOMB INSCRIPTION NO. 1, DISCLOSING HIS WORLD-EMPIRE TITLES, PARENTAGE & PRAYER TO SUN-ANGEL TASIA FOR RESURRECTION

This ebony label inscription (Plate XI,[1] facing p. 88) is incomplete in its lower edge—the lower fragment in the

Egypt

Sumer (Mesop.).

Reads: BATU [1] LUGAL [2]-DU-DU [3]-GE [4] TUR [5] ENE [6] BARA.

Transl.: Of the dead [1] King DUDU the tomb. The (enthroned) Lord the Pharaoh.

FIG. 37.—Line 1 of column 1, of Dudu's Tomb Ebony Label No. 1 deciphered.

[1] This sign *Batu* or *Bat* (B. 432; Br. 9971) is, as I have shown, synonymous with *Bat* "Dead" (Br. 1578; WPOB. 243 f.; WSAD. 24); and is the usual sign for "Dead" on Sumerian funereal monuments, with the phonetic variant of *Matu* (WPOB. 255 f.; WISD. 89 f.). It is also defined as "crushed, beat out" (M. 7543). And it is, as I have shown, the Sumerian source of the English Bad, Fate, Fatal, and their compounds (WSAD. 24).
[2] This sign for "king" in Sumerian is a diagram of the King's bust and crowned head; without legs.
[3] The prominence given to the legs of the king in the pictograph suggests that they are to be read separately as 2 legs, which have the Sumerian sign value of *Du-du*: especially as this king wrote his name Du-du in Mesopotamia always by the sign of 2 legs with the meaning of "run" as here pictured. The Leg-sign=*Du* in Sumerian. B. 207; Br. 4860.
[4] *Ge* or *Gi* "of" (Br. 7313; and cp. WAOA. *Gi* in pl. 1).
[5] This is evidently a pictograph of a tomb (B. 57 and 95), with definitions "dig, dwelling, cave, fold," etc.
[6] Throne sign *Ene* (B. 112) with meaning "enthroned" or "lord," 2810, etc.

---

[1] From PRT. 1, pl. XI, 14.

## DUDU'S EGYPTIAN INSCRIPTS. DECIPHERED 117

plate is part of another ebony tablet which was evidently more or less a duplicate of the upper one. This ebony label was found crusted over and varnished with hard resin, which had been poured over it in a melted state, and had to be cleaned off by a needle, " so that it is possible that some points may not have been fully cleaned out."

The writing, which is in two columns, is in cursive Sumerian linear script with syllabic and not alphabetic values, and the

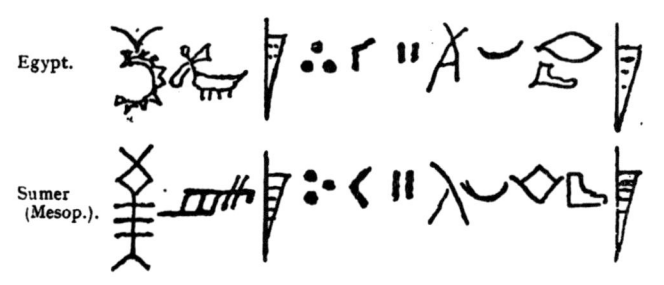

Egypt.

Sumer (Mesop.).

Reads: MUSH [1]-SUR [2]-TAG [3]-MAD [4]-GI-TAB [5] KUD [6]-U [7] E [8] TAG.[9]

Transl. : of MUSHSUR (Egypt) Land, the Two Lands. The One Judge. And of the Sunrise Land.

FIG. 38.—Line 2 of column 1 of Dudu's Ebony Label No. 1 deciphered.

language is Sumerian. The writing is again in the retrograde direction ; but for decipherment, the signs are arranged in their usual Sumerian or Aryan direction to read from the left hand towards the right. The first and second lines or registers of column 1 are bracketed together and contain the king's imperial titles. The third and fourth lines are funereal and contain a prayer for the dead king's resurrection. No reference numbers are attached to those Sumerian signs

[1] B. 328 ; Br. 7637-8.
[2] B. 364 a ; M. 6536-7. The cross-bands of the sign are seen in the lower duplicate fragment.
[3] B. 146, M. 2490.  [4] B. 322 ; Br. 7386.
[5] *Tab* or *Dab*="two" B. 144 ; M. 2463 ; and it is source of English " Two, Twain, Double," etc. WSAD. 46.
[6] B. 12 ; Br. 364.  [7] As before.
[8] E or *Khadu* pictured by Sun + Foot or " Sunrise." Br. 7869.
[9] B. 146=" Land." M. 2470.

## 118 EGYPTIAN CIVILIZATION OF SUMER ORIGIN

which have previously been duly attested. It is significant that his name *Dudu* is spelt three times in the labels by the same duplicated Foot-sign by which he spells his name in Mesopotamia.

The first line of column 1 is as Fig. 37.

The second line of column 1, which is bracketed in the text with the first line by a curved line on its right border, is a continuation of the first line. It significantly contains amongst his territorial titles the word-sign for " Egypt " in the form of *Mush-sur* or *Mush-sir*, written by the two signs

Egypt.

Sumer (Mesop.).

Reads: EGIR [1]-SHU [2]-USHU [3]-WI [4]-MAD-GI TIL [5] LUGAL DU-DU-U [6] PARA AN.

Transl.: back to the Setting Sun of the West-Land, the complete king, DUDU, and One Lord or Pharaoh.

FIG. 39.—Line 2 continued of Dudu's Ebony Label No. 1 deciphered.

[1] B. 212 ; 5001.
[2] B. 365 ; Br. 8675.
[3] B. 403 ; Br. 9250.
[4] B. 380 ; Br. 8919 and Pinches, JRAS. 1917, 102=*Wis* " West."
[5] B. 70 ; Br. 1500-1.    [6] B. 365.

of the great Serpent (*Mush* or *Sir*) [1] and an Insect (*Mush* or *Sur*).[2] And that land is given also the title of the " Great " or " mighty," as well as " The Two Lands," *i.e.* Upper and Lower Egypt.

The third and fourth lines, which are not bracketed with the above, contain the stereotyped prayer for resurrection from the dead. This significantly is in series with those which I have demonstrated are engraved on the Sumerian burial amulets and tablets of Mesopotamia, the Indus

[1] B. 328 ; Br. 7637-8.
[2] B. 364 a ; M. 6536-7. The cross-bands of the sign are seen in the lower duplicate fragment.

## DUDU'S EGYPTIAN INSCRIPTS. DECIPHERED 119

Valley, Troy and the " prehistoric " monuments of Ancient Britain.[1]

The fourth line is wanting except its last sign.

Egypt.

Sumer (Mesop.).

Reads : BAR [1]-U [2] MAD-MAD TAX [3] GIN [4] -SHU-DU [5] . . . (? SHU)-KHA [6] . . .

Transl. : O (Sun-)Lord of the Lands, TAX (Tasia) The Helper, descend ! . . . O (Sun-)Fish-Lord. . . .

FIG. 40.—Line 3 of column 1 of Dudu's Ebony Label No. 1 deciphered.

[1] B. 77 ; Br. 1802, 1752.  [2] B. 365 ; Br. 8659.
[3] B. 182 ; *Tax* or *Dax.* Br. 4537. On this title for the Sun-archangel Tasia, see WSAD. 53 and WPOB. 258 f.
[4] B. 92.  [5] Br. 227.
[6] This appears to be a diagram of the great Sun-Fish or the " Resurrecting " Sun (Shu-Kha) which the Sumerians invoked for resurrection from the dead. WISD. 88 f.

The second column of this ebony label continues King Dudu's inscription, with his territorial, imperial and solar titles, and his paternity, disclosing him to be the son of the

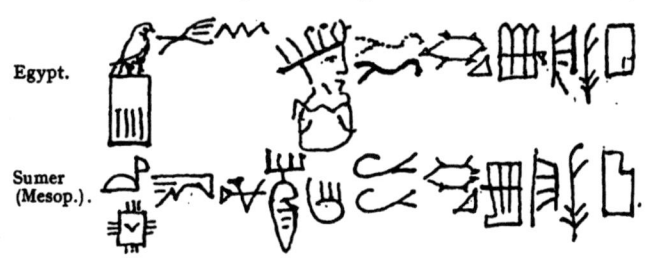

Egypt.

Sumer (Mesop.).

Reads :  PA DA-NU LUGAL KAD [1] (DU)-DU [2] MAR [3]-GI GANA [4] RIT [5] GIN ERI.[6]

Transl. : The (Sun-)Hawk (line) DANU, the King the *Kad* DU-DU son of GANA, RIT, GIN-ERI.

FIG. 41.—Line 1 of column 2 of Dudu's Ebony Label deciphered.

[1] B. 311 ; Br. 7063.   [2] B. 207, pl. 50.   [3] B. 392.
[4] B. 160 ; Br. 4036.   [5] B. 270 ; Br. 5956.   [6] B. 39.

---

[1] WPOB. 255 f.

120    EGYPTIAN CIVILIZATION OF SUMER ORIGIN

third king of Menes' Dynasty, namely King Gana, Rit or " Khent," that is the *Kunti* or *Ritu* of the Indian lists. The first line reads as Fig. 41.

The prefix here of *Shu* (which is a synonym of *Kad*) to Dudu's name perhaps accounts for his " Sudyumna " name in the Indian lunar lists. The second line continues with a prayer to the Twin Sun-god Min or Man for Resurrection of the King who is called " The Ruler of the Western Lands." The rest of the lower portion of this label is missing.

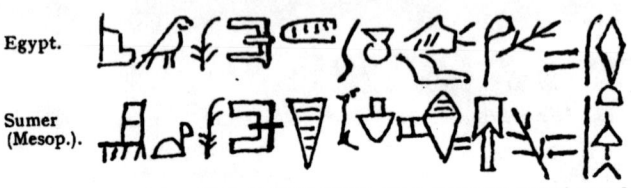

Egypt.

Sumer (Mesop.).

Reads :     ENE PA -GIN-RA [1] KU [2] SHU [3] -TA [4] -TIANU [5] QUM [6] XAL [7] MIN TIL-TI.

Transl. : Unto the enthroned Hawk(-line) ruler, the perished one (hasten) ! Unto the fallen one of the Western Land, the crushed one hasten, O Min (to) Life !

FIG. 42.—Line 2, column 2, of Dudu's Ebony Label deciphered.

## SUMMARY OF KING DUDU'S OR DUNDU'S TOMB INSCRIPTIONS

This fragmentary inscription from the tomb of King Dudu or Dundu thus reads as follows :—

" Of the dead King DUDU (this is) the tomb. The (enthroned) Lord the King of MUSHSUR (Egypt) Land, the Two Lands. The One Judge of the Sunrise Land back to the Setting Sun of the West Land, the complete king, DUDU, One Lord. O Sun-Lord of the Lands, TAX, the

[1] B. 287 ; Br. 6365.     [2] B. 481 (not 229).     [3] B. 490.
[4] B. 158. "Unto, to."
[5] On this title as Tianu, etc., see before. The two strokes which double this Lion-head or *Pirig* sign are seen in front of its head. Compare these doubling strokes with those in Menes' ebony label and in the label from " King Zet's " tomb in PRT. 1, Pl. XI, in which last the doubling two strokes are placed inside the neck of the Lion. On the location of this land as Asia Minor, also the Western Lands generally, including Europe, as the Greater Amorite Land, see before.
[6] B. 193, the Flail sign.     [7] B. 2.

# DUDU'S EGYPTIAN INSCRIPTS. DECIPHERED 121

Helper, descend! . . . O (Sun-)Fish-Lord . . . [resurrect him] . . . The (Sun-)Hawk (line) DANU, the King, the *Kad* DUDU, son of GANA RIT, GIN-ERI. Unto the enthroned Hawk(-line) ruler, the perished one (hasten)! Unto the fallen one of The Western Land, the crushed one hasten O Min (the) Life!"

FIG. 42A.—Tasia or Tax, *Taš-Mikal* of Phœnicians, the deified second Aryan king as Sun-archangel Michael in Egypt, as "Lord of Corn" (Resep). Invoked in First Egyptian Dynasty tomb inscriptions and in prehistoric Briton monuments and figured freely on pre-Roman Briton coins. (After Renan.)

Note his Goat's head chaplet and his handled Sun-Cross or "Key of Life." For details and numerous representations from Asia Minor, Phœnicia, Mesopotamia and Ancient Britains, see WPOB. *passim*.

## XI

### 6TH & 7TH KINGS OF 1ST DYNASTY, BIDI OR "MIE-BIDOS" & "SAMPATI" AS TRIBUTARY LOCAL KINGS OF EGYPT

The sixth and seventh Pharaohs of Menes' dynasty in Manetho's and Sety's lists (see Table opposite p. 78) were not Mesopotamian emperors, being absent in the Kish Chronicle and Isin King-Lists, as well as in the solar version of the Indo-Aryan King-Lists. They are shown, however, in the lunar versions of the latter (see Table cited).

Both kings were presumably tributary to King Dudu and were his contemporaries.

### SIXTH KING OF MENES' DYNASTY, NOT A MESOPOTAMIAN EMPEROR & ONLY A TEMPORARY KING

The sixth king of Menes' dynasty, in the king-lists of Manetho and Sety I, is now clearly seen by our Comparative Table at p. 78 to have not been a Mesopotamian

FIG. 43.—Clay sealing of 6th King of 1st Dynasty of Egypt.

emperor; but was evidently merely a local king and presumably tributary to King Dudu. In keeping with this, seems the statement by Prof. Petrie that "This tomb is

# 6TH & 7TH PHARAOHS' NAMES DECIPHERED 123

the poorest in contents and in remains of all those of the first dynasty."[1]

His name is read by Egyptologists as *Azab Merpaba*—the latter half of which is his title in the Egyptian lists; whilst Manetho calls him *Miebidos*, which is in series with his lunar title in the Indian lists of *Bahu-bida*. His signature on his clay sealings is seen in Fig. 43.

This inscription reads through the Sumerian as in Fig. 44.

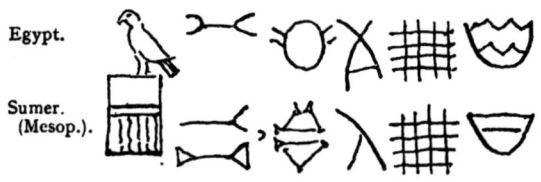

Egypt.

Sumer. (Mesop.).

Reads: PA-RIN-BARA[1]   BI[2]   -DI[3]   KUD   -U   -MAR.[4]
Transl.: The Hawk-line Pharaoh BIDI, Lord MAR.

FIG. 44.—Name of 6th King of 1st Dynasty of Egypt deciphered.

[1] As before.   [2] B. 70; Br. 1477.   [3] B. 415.   [4] B. 532; Br. 11982.

Here his *Bidi* solar name equates with his *Bida* name in the Indian Lists, and explains his *Miebidos* name in Manetho; whilst the *Mar* in his personal name seems related to the readings of it as *Mer-paba* by Egyptologists.

## SEVENTH KING OF MENES' DYNASTY, A TEMPORARY OR TRIBUTARY KING & NOT AN EMPEROR

The seventh king of Menes' dynasty likewise is not shown by the Babylonian lists as an emperor of Mesopotamia, and was presumably tributary to King Dudu. His name is variously read with " some uncertainty " by Egyptologists as Semerkhet Shemsu, etc., see Table opposite p. 78. He corresponds to *Sampati* in the Indian Lists cited in that Table.[2]

[1] PHE. 1, 20.   [2] And in fuller detail in WMC. 524 f.

## XII

### 8TH & LAST KING OF IST DYNASTY, SHUDUR KIB, "QA" OR "QEBH" IDENTICAL WITH SHUDUR KIB OR QA, LAST KING OF MANIS' DYNASTY IN MESOPOTAMIA, c. 2536–2527 B.C.

*With his Sumerian Inscriptions in Egypt & Indus Valley deciphered for first time & his Aryan title of " Ukush " & " Goth "*

THE absolute identity of the eighth or last king of Menes' dynasty with the last king and emperor of Manis-Tusu's or Sargon's dynasty in Mesopotamia (see Kish Chronicle, p. 77) *strikingly completes and establishes the identity of the dynasty of Menes with that of Manis-Tusu and the identity of these two personages themselves.*

His name has been read by Egyptologists as *Qa* or *Qa-Sen*, and a seal of his period has been read by them as *Qebhu*, see Comparative Table opposite p. 78. But it is now found by the new keys to the Sumerian script used by the First Egyptian Dynasty that his name reads in one of his Egyptian inscriptions *Shudur Kib*, that is precisely as he spelt his name and by the same Sumerian signs as in his own inscriptions as Sargonic emperor in Mesopotamia. And he is also called on other objects curtly, *Kib, Kibbu* and *Qa*.

I have, moreover, found several of his official seals in the Indus Valley collection, attesting his long rule of that Sumerian colony on the Indus.

### INDUS VALLEY SEALS OF KING KIB OR QA

In the second batch of the Indus Valley seals, I found no fewer than seven seals of King Kib, the last member of the Sargon-Menes' Dynasty, as shown in Plates XI and XV. They are of especial historical importance in that, while

PLATE XV.

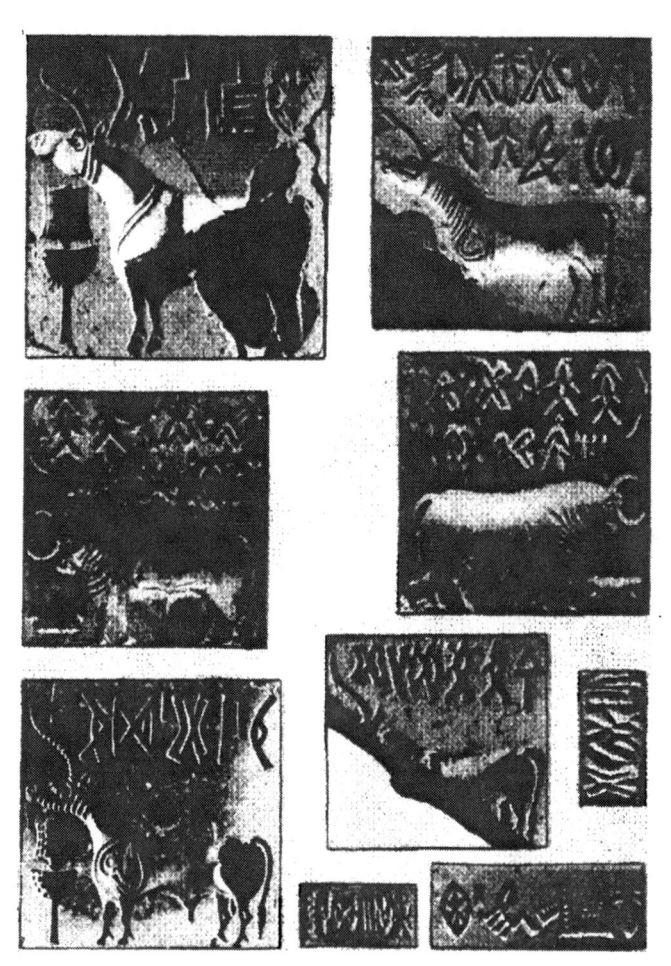

INDUS VALLEY SEALS OF PHARAOH SHUDUR-KIB, OR
QA, AND HIS SON, AND URI-MUSH.

(From photographs after Sir J. Marshall.)  For decipherments and
translations, see pp. 124 f., 196 f.

# 8TH PHARAOH'S INDUS SEALS DECIPHERED

attesting his rule on the Indus and in Egypt, they give his genealogy from " Sargon-the-Great " and Aha Menes as well as his title of *Qa*. Their detailed decipherment is displayed in Appendix V. Their inscribed records read literally as follows :—

### No. 1 (Plate XI, 10, and Fig. 113)

" Kib-bu Shuha, son of the House of Aha at Agdu Land."

### No. 2 (Plate XV, 1, and Fig. 114)

" Kib, the *Pharaoh*, the seal of the Lord at Agdu Land."

### No. 3 (Plate XV, 2, and Figs. 115 and 116)

" Kib-bu, *devotee of Fire*, Kib the Gut, Kibbu (of line of) Shar-Gin the Gut (son of) Dan, the son of Gin of the House of Ner (?-Mar) at Uriki (Akkad) Land."

### No. 4 (Plate XV, 3-4, and Figs. 117 and 118)

" For the Life of Suhahatur-Kib Qa, Turn the Evil from the Gut of the House of Gin ! KIB of the House of Ner at Magan Land."

### No. 5 (Plate XV, 5, and Fig. 119)

" Shuhadur Kib, the Pharaoh (son of) Gan at Agdu Land."

### No. 5A (Plate XV, 5A, and Fig. 119A)

" Kibbu, the Deep-Water Lord, son of Aha-Men."

### No. 6 (Plate XV, 6, and Fig. 120)

" King Qa of Ma(-ash)-Gan, Mushsir (Egypt)."

In addition there is a seal of a son of Kib (Plate XV, 10) which reads " The Gut Shu son of Pharaoh Kib."

## Name of the King in Egypt, Mesopotamia & Indian Chronicles

Fortunately there are several of this king's Egyptian labels and sealings extant, giving his name and titles in fairly full detail. All are written in Sumerian script and in the Sumerian language; and in one of these *he writes his name with the self-same Sumerian signs as he writes it as Sumerian emperor in his Mesopotamian inscriptions; and in his Indus seals.*

In his Mesopotamian inscriptions he writes his personal name and title as *Shu-dur-Kib*;[1] and similarly it is written in the Kish Chronicle lists (p. 77), where he is called the "son of Dudu." And this name of *Shudur* (or *Shutur*)-Kib, or "*Shudur* or *Shutur* of the Mighty Flood-tides or Oceans,"[2] is seen to equate substantially with the form of his name as *Suhotra, Shruta*, or *Xattra* in our Indian Chronicle key-lists.

Similarly in Egypt, he spells his name Shudur Kib by the self-same signs as in his Mesopotamian inscriptions; and also by the phonetic variants of *Shudaru-Kib, Shudaru-Quibi* and *Shudur-Gibi*, thus giving the equations:—

| Egyptian. | Indian Lists. | Mesop. Monuments & Lists. |
|---|---|---|
| Shudur (or Shutur) Kib | = Suhotra | = Shudur (or Shutur)-Kib |
| Shudaru Kib | = Shruta | — |
| Shuduru Qibi | = Xattra | = Xudaraur Kib |
| Shudur Gibi. | | |

And he gives amongst his titles on the objects in his Egyptian tomb, besides that of " King of the Two Lands of Upper and Lower Egypt," also those of " The One Lord of Uruki (*i.e.* Ur or Erech) " and " The King of Tianu (*i.e.* The Western or Amorite Land)." This absolutely fixes his identity with the last Pharaoh of Menes' dynasty and the last ruler of Manis-Tusu's dynasty in the Mesopotamian empire.

His solar title in Egypt reads " Kia " or " Qia "—the so-called " King Qa " of Egyptologists.[3]

---

[1] See tablets published by Pognon (AOT. b. 69, rev. 1 and 420) and Craig (*Relig. Texts*, I, pl. 57), and TDC. 63; on the attested values of the signs, see Kish Chronicle (p. 61) and below. His name is disguised in *Cambridge Anc. History* (I. 669) and elsewhere as " Gimilduril "—another of the innumerable instances of how students of history are misled by the fantastic conjectures of Assyriologists unpossessed of any keys to the form of the names!

[2] B. 223; MD. 244.

[3] The surname " Sen " given him by Egyptologists is a conjectural alphabetic misreading of the Sumerian signs for Shudur Kib.

PLATE XVI.

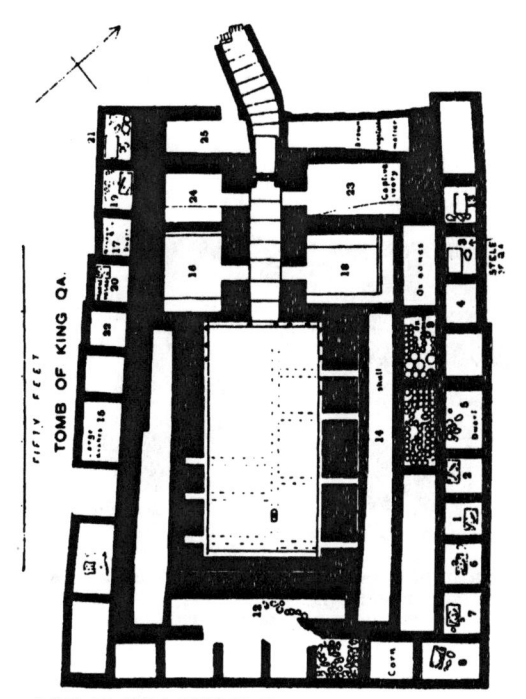

TOMB OF KING SHUDUR-KIB, OR QA, AT ABYDOS.
(After Sir F. Petrie, PRT. II, Pl. LX.)
Note the contents of the various chambers with provisions for
the spirit of the dead king and his retinue.

PLATE XVII.

*A*  *B*

SHUDUR-KIB'S (QA'S) TOMB IVORY LABELS AT ABYDOS.
(From Sir F. Petrie's photographs, PRI. II, Pl. VIII, 2, and I, Pl. XII, 2.)
For decipherments and translations, see pp. 127 f.

# 8TH PHARAOH'S NAME IN EGYPT DECIPHERED 127

His Inscriptions on his Tomb in Egypt deciphered through the Sumerian & disclosing his World-Empire Titles

The inscriptions of this king on his tomb, upon votive articles, stone vases, ebony and ivory labels and clay sealings are numerous. The three chief ones are seen in Plate XVII, and they are here deciphered and read through the Sumerian as in the previous cases.

In the first of these, on a weathered ivory label [1] (Plate XVII A) his name is seen on the right-hand column to be written by the same sign as in his Mesopotamian inscriptions, and in his Indus seals. It reads as follows :—

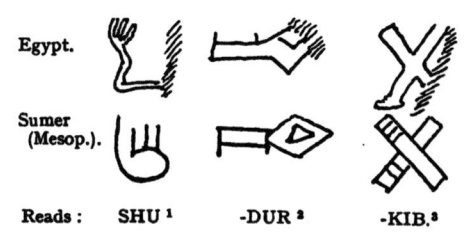

Fig. 45.—Name of last King of Menes' Dynasty, Shudur Kib, on Ivory Label A, deciphered.

[1] B. 311; Br. 7065. The sign of the Uplifted Hand.
[2] Or *Tur*, B. 122; Br. 3331.   [3] B. 223; Br. 5217.

The other columns on this label are somewhat defaced, but the second contains his title as " King of Tianu (Western or Amorite Land)," which title is repeated on others of his labels.

On another ivory label (Plate XVII, B),[2] broken but with well-preserved inscription as far as it goes, his solar title of *Kia* or *Qia* occurs within the rectangle under the large Sun-Hawk on the left side. Significantly in the last column his name is spelt by other signs of the same phonetic values, to introduce other meanings, and it is recorded that he is " *of the* Ukush Line "—that is the same as claimed by his dynastic ancestor Sargon-the-Great, namely, descent for

[1] PRT. II, Pl. VIII, No. 2.   [2] PRT. I, Pl. XII, 2.

## 128 EGYPTIAN CIVILIZATION OF SUMER ORIGIN

*Ukusi*, the first king of the First Sumerian Dynasty of the Kish Chronicle.

This inscription in the last column reads :—

Egypt.

Sumer (Mesop.).

Reads : PA KI-A [1] SHU [2]-DU [3]-U -UR [4] UKUSH [5] -GI-TIL-GE.

Transl.: The (Sun-)Hawk (line) KIA (or QIA) SHUDUUR, the overthrown one of the UKUSH line.

FIG. 46.—Inscription of Shudur Kib on Label B, cols. 4 and 5, deciphered.

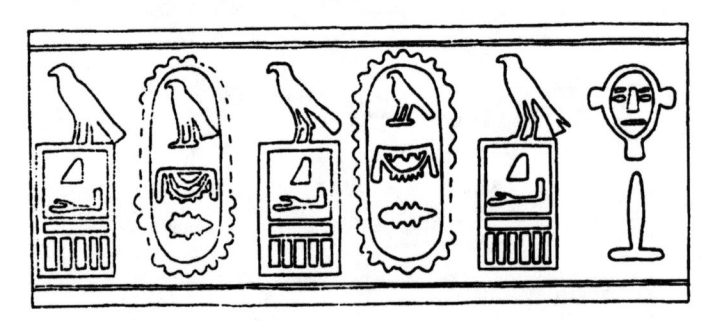

FIG. 47.—Clay Sealing of King Shudur Kib in Egypt (after Sir F. Petrie).

On his Egyptian sealings (Fig. 47) [6] his name and titles are stamped to read in the Sumerian or Aryan, towards the right. His solar title is given first place and it is followed by his personal name written within an oval cartouche; in the other two it is followed by his title Kib variantly spelt. It is noteworthy that in the first sealing the first syllable of his name is spelt *Xu*, in place of *Shu*, and has the added syllable of *ur;* this coupled with the variations in

[1] This may be either *Ki* or *Qia* (B. 419) + A.
[2] The Island sign, B. 481.
[3] B. 417.
[4] The spiked Club-sign, B. 529.
[5] B. 495; Br. 10882. The Harp-sign.
[6] From Mr Griffiths' drawings in PRT. 1, Pl. XXIX. The end signs, the mask and inverted T, read in Sumerian *Dim-me* or " Official messenger."

# SHUDUR KIB'S EGYPTIAN INSCRIPTIONS

the spelling of *Kib* in the other sealings suggests that the scribes were Egyptian born and not Mesopotamians.

The decipherment of these sealings through the Sumerian is given in the following Table (Fig. 48). The Net-sign with value of *Dara* used in spelling the second syllable of his name, is seen in its fuller form as the second hieroglyph within the oval cartouche. In other sealings, it is seen that the *Kib* title following his solar name is variantly spelt phonetically *Qibi* and *Qibbi*.

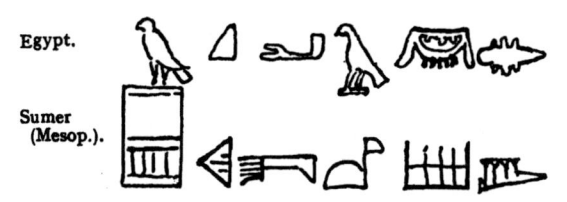

Egypt.

Sumer (Mesop.).

Reads: PA (or XU) KI-A (or QI-A) XU [1]   -DARA [2]-UR.[3]
Transl.: The Hawk (line) KIA, XUDARAUR.

FIG. 48.—Name on Sealing A. deciphered.

INSCRIPTIONS OF SHUDUR KIB, LAST KING OF MENES' DYNASTY, IN HIS TOMB IN EGYPT, IDENTIFY HIM WITH SHUDUR KIB, LAST EMPEROR OF MANIS-TUSU'S DYNASTY IN MESOPOTAMIA

We thus find that the inscriptions in his tomb in Egypt identify Shudur Kib, the last king of Menes' dynasty in Egypt, with Shudur Kib, the last emperor of Manis-Tusu's dynasty of Mesopotamia. These inscriptions now deciphered spell his solar name as *Kia* or *Qia*, and his ordinary name as *Shudur Kib*, and describe him as king of Tianu, *i.e.* The Western or Amorite or *Muru* or *Martu* Land, a land which included the Mediterranean coast-lands and embracing Mauretania.[4]

[1] B. 83; Br. 2045.
[2] The Net-sign, B. 480, is drawn in fuller form in the Egyptian.
[3] The spiked Club-sign, as before.
[4] WMC. 18, 27, 161.

## XIII

### Complete Identity of Menes' Dynasty in Egypt with Manis' Imperial Dynasty in Mesopotamia & in the Indo-Aryan King-Lists & the Sumerian or Aryan Origin of Egyptian Civilization

Thus we have demonstrated by actual concrete contemporary documentary evidence the identity of Menes' First Dynasty of Egypt with Manis-Tusu's Dynasty of "World emperors" of Mesopotamia. And at the same time we have demonstrated the identity of the individual kings of these respective dynasties and in their identical order of succession.

This identity is established not only by the contemporary records of the kings themselves in Egypt and Mesopotamia, and in their official signets and seals in their Indus Colony, but also by the identity in their names and chronological order in both the Babylonian, Egyptian and Indian Chronicle king-lists—the sixth and seventh kings of Menes' Dynasty in the local Egyptian lists proving to be local or tributary kings of the Sumerian empire.

### Menes' Date discovered by newly-found Synchronism between Ancient Egypt & Mesopotamia as no earlier than about 2704 b.c.

This additional concrete contemporary evidence now adduced, by proving that the whole of Pharaoh Menes' dynasty is identical with the whole imperial dynasty of Manis-Tusu, the son of Sargon of Mesopotamia, thus fully establishes for the first time a synchronism between Ancient Egyptian and Babylonian History which definitely fixes by the identification of Menes, the founder of the First Dynasty of Egypt with Manis-Tusu, the son of Sargon, the date of Menes at a period no earlier than about 2704 b.c., and the end of his dynasty under King Shudur Kib at about 2522 b.c., as detailed in the chapter on Chronology.

### Aryan Origin of Egyptian Civilization Established

Through this identification of Menes and his dynasty with

# ARYAN ORIGIN OF EGYPTIAN CIVILIZATION

Manis-Tusu, the son of Sargon, and his dynasty, coupled with our discovery of Sargon-the-Great as the leading Predynastic king of Egypt, with proved Aryan descent continuously back to the first Sumerian or Aryan king of the First Sumerian or Aryan Dynasty, and the fact that both Sargon and his son's dynasty in Egypt wrote their inscriptions there in the Sumerian script and in the Sumerian language, we have demonstrated by unequivocal contemporary inscriptional evidence the Aryan or Sumerian Origin of Egyptian Civilization, as well as the Aryan Racial Origin of the Sumerians. And we have seen that the Aryan or Sumerian Civilization was spread abroad more largely over the world, and especially the Western World, including Crete by the "world-empire" and colonial rule of Sargon and his son Menes' dynasty, a dynasty disclosed to be Aryan-Phœnician. At the same time we have also established still further the remarkable historical authenticity of the official Indian Chronicles as an unique and independent source of Sumerian, Babylonian and Ancient Egyptian History.

FIG. 49.—Foreign Captive on Ivory gaming-reed of King Shudur Kib or Kia's period. (After Sir F. Petrie, PHE. i. 25.)
The inscription above the man reads in Sumerian *Na-rim* or *Na-ri* (B. 386, 443; Br. 8990, 10169); and *Narima* is the name for Upper Syria in the Amarna Letters of the Egyptian archives.

## XIV

### SECOND EGYPTIAN DYNASTY WITH RISE OF INDEPENDENT KINGDOM OF EGYPT

*Disclosing the Aryan Race of the 2nd Dynasty of Egypt from Indian Lists*

WITH the end of Sargon's mighty dynasty of World Emperors, with its dual centres East and West, in Mesopotamia and Egypt respectively, about 2522 B.C., we reach one of the most momentous epochs in the History of the Ancient World, especially as regards Europe. For with this disruption began the definite cleavage of Civilization into Western and Eastern branches and types. The centre of the most progressive elements in the Sumerian or Aryan Civilization shifted permanently westwards from Mesopotamia to Egypt on the basin of the cool Mediterranean, which Sargon and his dynasty of Caucasians and their clansmen had deliberately selected as their future homeland. And from Egypt the Higher Civilization now radiated back to Asia Minor and westwards to Europe. For this period of transition, the Babylonian records do not help us much, as it is one of the darkest periods in Mesopotamian history. Apart from the bare list in the Kish Chronicle of the names and chronology of a short-lived weak dynasty, the "Fifth" Dynasty of that chronicle, which immediately succeeding Sargon's dynasty in Mesopotamia, reigned only for twenty-six years, and of which no monuments have been found, there is no reference whatever to this crisis in Babylonian history with the loss of the Western Section of the empire.

But from what we have elicited regarding Sargon in Egypt, and his son Menes' dynasty, with their tombs in that more favoured western part of their empire, coupled with our existing knowledge of the Second and subsequent early dynasties of the Egyptian empire, and their relationships with Asia Minor, the Levant and Europe, and some references in the Indian Chronicle, we gain considerable light on the happenings at this epoch.

### DISINTEGRATION OF SARGON'S "WORLD EMPIRE" ON THE FALL OF HIS DYNASTY IN MESOPOTAMIA

It is clear that on the fall of Sargon's dynasty in Mesopotamia, that is the " Fourth " Dynasty of the Kish Chronicle, after a glorious reign for 197 years, as that chronicle records, the vast unwieldly world empire which its founder had built up completely collapsed and broke into pieces, and was never afterwards regained by any Mesopotamian or other king.

Sargon's mighty dynasty had perhaps fulfilled its useful mission in propagating by its world-wide sway the most advanced civilization of that period much more widely over the world than ever had been done before its day. And its far-flung colonies, especially in Egypt and the West, by this time had doubtless become sufficiently developed into separate civilized nations, with experience of ordered government, to undertake their own independence, with ability to defend themselves against the impositions and aggressions of such a remote central government, nominally, if not altogether actually, in distant Mesopotamia, and which no doubt, with its hosts of bureaucratic officials, must have tended to develop an intolerable tyranny. Such movements for independence from the yoke of their parent empire would only be in agreement with those made latterly by the colonies of the Phœnician, Greek and Roman empires in the Mediterranean, Asia Minor and on the European Continent, and with those of certain British colonies, " dependencies " or " dominions " in modern times. The time was evidently ripe for the rise of a crop of new independent, self-governing, civilized nationalities and states within Sargon's old empire.

Amongst the chief independent new states which now emerged are seen to be those of the Guti or Goths in Asia Minor[1] in the old Gothic province whence we have seen a branch of their stock had originally descended as the

[1] See WMC. 357 f.

"Sumerians" into Mesopotamia, of the Amorites of Syria-Phœnicia and of the Egyptian empire. In Mesopotamia itself we find now only a weak and short-lived dynasty, which within two and a half decades was absorbed by the Guti. But the later Sumerian kings of Mesopotamia although still occasionally carving out small empires, and sometimes assuming the imperial title when dominating the greater part of the city-states within Mesopotamia or Babylonia, with at times the adjoining Elam province of Southern Persia and the Indus Valley colony on the East, never appear to have succeeded in extending their empire to Egypt and the Mediterranean or to Central and Western Asia Minor—though an occasional raid on Sinai or Magan and Kimash is mentioned a few centuries later.

### Rise of Independent Egypt as the chief Centre of "Sumerian" or Aryan Civilization

The main centre of Sumerian Civilization appears to have been definitely and deliberately shifted from Mesopotamia to Egypt when Sargon and his son Menes, following the practice of their immediate ancestral Pharaohs, and followed by their dynasty, made their mausoleums and those of their families in that more temperate and central portion of their empire on the banks of the Nile, outflowing into the cool basin of the Mediterranean. Egypt was climatically a land much more naturally fitted for the scions of that great ruling branch of the Caucasic Race, which from the exigencies of their over-lordship had been forced for many centuries to live in exile in tropical Mesopotamia. On the extension of their empire westward to include Egypt and the Mediterranean and Southern Europe, Egypt became a suitable centre for their Western empire. And the fact that Sargon and his dynasty selected that land for their tombs and the residences of their families, presumes that they regarded it as their new adopted home-land.

We have seen how Sargon's son Menes made Egypt his own especial home-land, and the centre for the western half of his " world empire." And the last two kings of his dynasty, Dudu and Shudur Kib, evidently resided largely in Egypt with their families and staff of state officials, as attested by the tombs of their families and officials there, and their lavish monumental remains and the profusion of written documents, especially in the reign of the last king or emperor. And this absence in Egypt from Mesopotamia doubtless contributed to the downfall of the dynasty.

On the revolt of Mesopotamia, on the death of this last king or emperor of Menes' dynasty, Egypt with its body of imperial officials and their families, and doubtless possessing the Western armies and fleets, would automatically become an independent empire and centre for the western half of the old world empire, and all the more so as it was practically secure against attack from Babylonia by the great impassable Arabian desert on its eastern border, which had doubtless tended largely to the disruption of the vast empire.

### The Second Dynasty of Egypt as the First Independent Dynasty of Egypt & as (?) Sargonid

Although Egypt, as we have seen, had been held for a time by Menes independently of his father Sargon, on Menes' accession to the imperial Mesopotamian throne, however, Egypt again became an integral part of the Sargonic empire and practically a colony of the latter. But on the fall of Sargon's dynasty in Mesopotamia, Egypt now obtained complete independence; so that the dynasty which succeeded that of Menes, namely the Second Dynasty of Egypt, was practically the first independent dynasty of Egypt.

Nothing is known to Egyptologists regarding the origin of the Second Dynasty of Egypt, nor of the circumstances which led to the fall of the First Dynasty. And unfortunately the Egyptian lists of the Second Dynasty kings are confused and corrupt, and few of the names and titles of the kings of this dynasty from their own monuments have been equated by Egyptologists with the form of the names on the lists.[1] Hence, I cannot at present give a full comparison of the names with those in the Indian lists, such as I have done with the First Dynasty, until the decipherment of their monumental names is revised in detail.

[1] PHE. I, 28.

### Indian Version of Second Dynasty Kings of Egypt

But here it is noteworthy, that in the Indian list of kings given in the Puru version of the Indian Aryan King-Lists—that is in that version which preserves especially full details of Menes' dynasty as Manasyu of Gopta—we find that *the immediate successors of Manasyu's dynasty are Nine kings, whose names equate to a considerable extent with those of the Nine kings forming the Second Dynasty in the lists of Manetho and the others.* And these nine kings were clearly the *local* successors of Manasyu's dynasty in Egypt and not in Mesopotamia, for they are absent in all the main-line lists of the Early Aryan kings, who, we have found, were kings of Mesopotamia.[1]

In this Indian Puru version of the kings who immediately succeeded Manasyu's dynasty, is given a string of nine names of which the holders are described as the " sons " or descendants of Raudrāshwa, a personage who is therein (MBt. I. 94) called a " brother " of Sargon (or Pra-Vīra, see p. 4); and who is stated to have married " the nymph " Misri-Keshi, whose name *Misri* is suggestive of the old name *Misr* for Egypt.[2] And Sargon's father was, as we have seen, a Predynastic Pharaoh of Egypt. This presumes that Raudrāshwa was an *elder* brother of Sargon and was resident in Egypt. And the fact that he did not succeed his deposed father in the kingship in Mesopotamia could be explained by his having died before the reign of the usurper Zaggisi, *i.e.* before Sargon had attained manhood and recovered his father's empire; for Sargon being a posthumous son could not have had a younger brother. In this view therefore, there were resident in Egypt, contemporary with and during the reign of Sargon's or Menes'

---

[1] This list of nine kings is found at the very end of the dislocated Manasyu Dynasty, which we have seen had been transferred by the later Puru scribes *en bloc* back to the fifth place from the first Aryan king, through confusing the later king Puru, the father of Sargon, with Puru I. See WMC. App. I, col. 4.

[2] This Raudrāshwa, although specified as Pra-Vīra's brother, is arbitrarily made by the later Puru scribes to be the " son " of the last king of Manasyu's Dynasty, as they were in the habit of gratuitously making each king the " son " of the preceding king, which we have found by the monuments was often not a fact. Similarly they made, as we have seen, mere titles of the kings into names of different contemporary kings or " brothers " of the king whose name preceded.

## 2ND EGYPTIAN DYNASTY & INDIAN LISTS

dynasty, the descendants of an older brother of Sargon, who overthrew Menes' dynasty and founded the Second Dynasty of Egypt. And apparently confirming this is the fact that the Son of Pharaoh Shudur Kib, whose seal is found in the Indus Valley (see p. 125), did not succeed either to the Egyptian or Mesopotamian throne.

Be this as it may, the fact remains that the names of Raudrāshwa's nine " sons " or descendants present a striking general agreement with those of the nine kings in the lists of the Second Dynasty of Egypt. And their divergences from what is admittedly a confused Egyptian list may be explained or removed when the names of the kings of the Second Dynasty of Egypt on their own monuments are duly revised and compared with those of the Indian lists.

### SECOND DYNASTY OF EGYPTIAN LISTS COMPARED WITH INDIAN

In the following Table, I compare the names or titles of those nine [1] kings of the Indian lists with those of the Egyptian lists for the Second Dynasty.[2] It will be noticed that the names of the first three kings are practically identical in both lists, Egyptian and Indian, except for the initial of the first name, which has $B$ in the Egyptian as read by Egyptologists instead of $R$ in the Indian, and the third name which has the initial $B$ for *Sth*. But in the former name the Indian form with $R$ is clearly the correct one; for its initial is the Foot or Leg sign used as the initial of his name in the Egyptian, which has the Sumerian value of *Ra*; whereas it is only in later Egyptian that the Foot or Leg sign has the value of $B$. And similarly the other differences may doubtless be explained on revision of their signs or hieroglyphs. Moreover, as there is no $L$ in the later Egyptian hieroglyphs, the old $L$ words being spelt therein by an $R$ sign, I have accordingly altered the $R$ in the Egyptian lists, as transliterated by Egyptologists in Nos. 3 and 6, into $L$, when the Indian lists show it to be $L$. And the Indian name *Prasanneyu* closely resembles the name *Perabsen* found on the tomb of one of the kings of this dynasty.

[1] In the Indian texts, whilst their number is stated to be " ten," only nine names are specified. WVP. 4, 128 f.
[2] From PHE. 1, 28.

## 138 EGYPTIAN CIVILIZATION OF SUMER ORIGIN

Second Dynasty of Egyptian Lists Compared with Indian:

| Egyptian Lists | Indian Lists |
|---|---|
| 1. Razau or Roetho(s) ["Bezau" or Boētho(s)]. | Rajeyu, Riceyu or Riteyu, " son " of Raudrāshwa. |
| 2. Kakau or Kaiekhos. | Kaksheyu. |
| 3. Banetelen, or Binothlis. | Sthandileyu. |
| 4. Uaznes or Tlas. | Vriteyu or Ghriteyu. |
| 5. Senda or Sethenes. | Jaleyu, Ganeyu (or Santateyu) |
| 6. Khailes or Ka. . . . | Sthaleyu (or Jaleyu). |
| 7. Neferkara. | Santateyu. |
| 8. Sesokhris or Neferka. | Dhaneyu, Varpeyu. |
| 9. Kheneres or Hezefa. | Vaneyu or Prasanneyu. |

This comparison establishes a presumption that the Indian list of nine post-Manasyu kings preserves the names or titles of the nine kings of the Second Dynasty of Egypt; and thus presumes that this second dynasty consisted of kinsmen of Menes and his dynasty. In the Indian lists, where the order of succession of the later kings varies in different MSS., the kings are "brothers," which if true would greatly reduce the total regnal years for this dynasty.

FIG. 50.—Egyptian Cross Button-Amulets of Sumerian and Hittite type of VIIth-VIIIth (Amorite) Dynasties. (After Sir F. Petrie, PHE. i. 120.)
*A*. As from Bism'ya, Mesopotamia. *B*. As swastika from Bismiya. *C*. As from Abeppo and Cilicia. *D*. "Turtle" type. *E*. "Hathor" head and serpent over enemy. *F*. Hawks and *Ankh* over enemy. *G*. From Abydos. *H*. Prism. For great collection of Sun-Crosses of Sumer type from Egypt, Troy, Phœnicia and Ancient Britain, see WPOB. 294 f.

## XV

### REAL CHRONOLOGY OF EARLY EGYPT & ITS CIVILIZATION & KINGS RECOVERED

*With fixed Dates for Predynastic & First Dynasty Kings & basic Date of Menes as c. 2704 B.C.*

> "Egyptian Chronology is either a very inexact science or very little is known about it."—Sir E. W. BUDGE, *Book of Kings*, I, lii.

THE real chronology of Early Egypt and its Civilization is now recovered, in place of the vastly divergent conjectural chronologies of Egyptologists hitherto current and all of them very wide of the actual dates. This has been elicited, as we have seen, by the discovery for the first time of a long string of synchronisms and identities of the First Dynasty and Predynastic kings or Pharaohs of Egypt with the Sumerian kings or emperors of contemporary Mesopotamia.

Although Mesopotamian chronology as conjectured at present by modern Assyriologists is equally conjectural and divergent *for the earlier periods*, fortunately Assyriologists generally are agreed, to within a latitude of about one century, in respect to the dates of "Sargon-the-Great" and his son Manis-Tusu and their so-called "Akkad Dynasty" with which are concerned the synchronisms now established.

As, however, the *real* chronology of the Early Sumerian period in Mesopotamia, as well as that of this "Akkad Dynasty" (as Assyriologists arbitrarily term it) has now been definitely discovered and fixed by my new Indo-Aryan keys, it is necessary for us here to see how this recovery of the exact dates of Sumerian chronology continuously back to the first king of the First Sumerian Dynasty has been effected. This is all the more necessary as both the predynastic Pharaoh "Sargon-the-Great," his son Manis-the-Warrior and several of his descendants in his dynasty claim to be descended from this first Sumerian or Aryan king; and this descent is also repeatedly ascribed to them in the epic chronicles of the Early Aryan Kings, the historicity of which has now been established.

### Failure of All Previous Attempts at Estimating the Chronology of the Early Sumerian & Egyptian Periods from Babylonian & Egyptian King-Lists, and by Archæology & Astronomy

All previous attempts at solving the great outstanding problem of the Chronology of the Early Sumerians, now demonstrated to be the Early Aryans, on which depends the real dates for all the Ancient World Civilizations, have up till now proved abortive.

All the hitherto known legendary and traditional Babylonian chronological lists purporting to give a continuous line of the kings from the first dynasty of the civilized period down to the modern periods, which have been used as a basis for the attempted recovery of dated Ancient History, have been compiled by late oriental priests, a class admittedly unhistorically minded. They make the earliest kings to be generations of gods and demi-gods and legendary heroes, with fabulously vast superhuman ages and reigns, and in regard to none of these could any remains ever be found. This inveterate defect exists in the lists hitherto used for Mesopotamia, namely those of Berosos and the Isin priests, and in respect of Egypt in Manetho's lists. Added to this is the further defect that dynasties purporting to be successive were in reality sometimes more or less contemporary. And the archæological and palæographic arguments employed by historians to control the vagaries of their texts are in themselves necessarily vaguely relative and incapable of fixing any dates with any approach to historical precision. The astronomical data also for Mesopotamia, while fixing with comparative exactitude the end of the First Babylonian Dynasty still left the latter dynasty separated by gaps at either end of unmeasured width, from the Second and Third Babylonian Dynasties below, and from the Sumerian of Ur-Isin above, and so failed to connect with the Early Sumerian period and recover the earlier Sumerian Chronology.

## PREVIOUS ATTEMPTS AT SUMER CHRONOLOGY 141

In illustration of the conflicting chronological inferences which result from the archæological and palæographic arguments—not to mention the discrepancy of 2246 years between the estimates for the date of Menes by the two different schools of present-day Egyptologists, each claiming support by an appeal largely to archæological arguments, and the date of 4000 B.C. for Minos of Crete arrived at also by the same means—numerous instances of their misleading results may be found in regard to Mesopotamian chronology in Radau's *Early Babylonian History* of 1900. Thus on archæological and palæographic grounds Manis-Tusu, before it was known that he was the son of Sargon I, was placed very considerably earlier than the latter.[1] Similarly, to come down to present-day beliefs, Udu, now disclosed to be the fourth king, is placed after the thirty-eighth king of the "postdiluvians" in the very latest text-book [2] by these two classes of arguments. Similarly the Sumerian king Medi, No. 20 in our list (whom by the way they call Semitic and Semitize his name into "Me-silim") is placed conjecturally c. 3638 B.C., whilst the first and earlier king of his dynasty (No. 15 in our list) is placed arbitrarily several centuries later at c. 3100 B.C.[3] Such misplacements show how very inexact and misleading these two classes of arguments may prove in estimating chronology.

This confused condition of early Mesopotamian chronology has recently become acutely intensified by the unscientific and credulous acceptance by Assyriologists of the long string of purported dynasties, with absurdly fabulous ages, which the superstitious and ill-informed later Isin priests prefixed to the First Dynasty of the Kish Chronicle, which latter we have demonstrated to be the first of all Sumerian dynasties and the first of all historical dynasties in the Ancient World. As we have already in a previous work [4] exposed the fictitious character of all this prefixed Isin chronology, with its prefixed dynasties purporting to extend for geological (241,200 years) ages "before the Flood," and downwards for some 35,000 years after "the Flood," with reigns of individual kings for 43,200 to 1500 years for each king—an average of several centuries for each postdiluvian

[1] RB. 28.   [2] CAH. 1924, I, 667.   [3] *Ib.*, 668.   [4] WMC., Chapter VII.

king, none of whom could be traced,¹ and all of them before the First Dynasty of the Kish Chronicle, it would be a mere waste of our time to refer further to it. And yet it is made the basis of the present-day Early pre-Sargonic Mesopotamian Chronology of Assyriologists!

## Failure of Traditional Babylonian "Synchronisms" to solve the Problem of Sumerian Chronology

The Babylonian "Synchronistic Tables," compiled by later Babylonian and Assyrian scribes, relate merely to kings and dynasties subsequent to about 1400 B.C., and do not connect with the Early and Middle Sumerian periods at all.

The chief Babylonian traditional "Synchronism," which has been used in the endeavour to fix a date in the earlier period, is that which relates to Sargon's dynasty. It is an isolated reference given solely by the last king of Babylon, Nabonidus who reigned 555-538 B.C., and nowhere else. In repairing the Sun-temple at Sippara, this king recorded on a clay cylinder, now preserved in the British Museum,² that he found in the foundations the foundation-tablet of "Narām Sin, the son of Shar-Gena," which that founder had deposited there " 3200 years previously." Now as Narām Sin was the grandson of Sargon I (the "Shar Gena" of King Nabonidus' Babylonian record) it was hoped that this figure would fix the date of the latter. But Nabonidus does not specify either his own regnal year in which he made the discovery nor the regnal year in which Narām Sin deposited the tablet in his long reign of 56 years, thus leaving an uncertainty of 56+18, or 74 years, even supposing that his figure of 3200 years was correct; though it is obviously a mere rough estimate.

Yet, despite these uncertainties it was arbitrarily assumed that the date of Narām Sin was "approximately 3750 B.C." and that of his grandfather Sargon " 3800 B.C." ; ³ and mainly on the basis of these early dates the beginning of Sumerian history has been set back as far as 5000 B.C. and even 10,000 B.C.

¹ The fictitious chronology and misplacement of "Mesannipada" has been explained in WMC., Chapter VII.
² CIWA. V. pl. 64, 2, 2, ll. 54-65. For a literal translation of this inscription, see RB. 5.
³ KHS. 1920, 60. Narām Sin was then believed to be the "son" of Sargon.

## PREVIOUS ATTEMPTS AT SUMER CHRONOLOGY 143

It was then found, however, that such an early date for Sargon at about 3800 B.C., and based on an isolated statement by the last Babylonian king and a Semite, and unsupported by any other reference in either early or late Babylonian texts, was entirely incompatible with all the known archæological facts which had been elicited regarding the short interval of time which separated the well-known Sumerian king Gudia from Sargon's dynasty. The buildings, culture, art and form of writing and shape of the clay tablets of Gudia are so very similar to those of Sargon's dynasty as to show that the two ages followed each other without any considerable break. The date of Gudia had become relatively fixed at "about 2450 B.C.," not only by his art, business documents, etc., but also by local synchronisms with the equally well-known Ur Dynasty, including Dungi, and the actual buildings of Gudia and Dungi were found to be almost directly on the top of the foundations of Sargon's dynasty, with practically no intervening stratum separating them. It was therefore supposed that Nabonidus had made a mistake of 1000 years in his inscription, and that the date of Sargon was "about 2800 B.C." This date, thus arbitrarily arrived at, is nevertheless that which is now generally adopted as the date of Sargon, and it has been further arbitrarily extended to "circa 2872 B.C." in the latest text-book [1]—a figure which by its semblance of exactitude misleads historians and other readers into believing that Sargon's date has been definitely ascertained, whereas it merely rests, as we have seen, on a chain of more or less doubtful suppositions of the most vague and indefinite kind. Yet it is upon this admittedly concocted and unsolid basis that all the dates of the Sumerian period above and immediately below Sargon's epoch have hitherto been placed.

NEW SOLID BASIS FOR THE CHRONOLOGY OF THE SUMERIANS OR EARLY ARYAN PERIOD, FROM FIRST SUMERIAN DYNASTY DOWNWARDS, DISCOVERED BY THE OFFICIAL INDO-ARYAN KING-LISTS

The chief obstacle hitherto encountered in all the attempts at solving the problem of Sumerian Chronology and at

[1] CAH. 1, 669; but since altered in 2nd edition to *c.* 2752 B.C.

placing that chronology on a solid scientific basis, has been the want of any complete chronological list of the Sumerian kings from the First Sumerian Dynasty continuously down to the Babylonian dynastic period which connects with our modern era ; and apart from the non-recognition of that First Dynasty, not even the name of the first king of the First Sumerian Dynasty has hitherto been known, through Semitic misreading of its polyphonous Sumerian writing.

This fundamental want is now supplied by our official King-Lists of the Early Aryans which have been uniquely preserved in the Indian Epic Chronicles by the eastern branch of the Aryans, and the marvellous authenticity of which has been fully demonstrated in the preceding chapters, which also establish the identity of the Sumerians with the Early Aryans. And these king-lists, it was seen, are not compilations by priests, but are the official copies of the original official records of the old archives scrupulously preserved by the ruling kingly caste and jealously treasured as sacred heirlooms by their royal Indian descendants.

These uniquely complete Indian copies of the king-lists by preserving for us the traditional forms of the names of the Aryan or Sumerian kings in due chronological order, from the first king of the First Sumerian Dynasty continuously downwards to the modern period, and bridging over all the gaps left in the Kish Chronicle and its supplementary Nippur and Isin Chronicles and the late Babylonian dynastic king-lists, enable us for the first time to reconstruct *a complete dated chronology* of the Sumerian period on a solid basis, by means of the regnal years for individual kings and dynasties preserved in the Kish Chronicle and its supplements.

The Indian lists themselves preserve no *dated* chronology whatsoever, as the Indian scribes and Brahmans have always been notoriously lacking in the historical sense, presumably because in their dreamy oriental fatalism in India the passage of time was of little consequence to them. The unique value of the Indian King-Lists consists in their scrupulous preservation of the complete official lists of the kings' names in their traditional forms, and in the strict chronological order of their succession, by which they record for us the traditional

NEW SOLID BASIS FOR SUMER CHRONOLOGY 145

forms of the names of the Sumerian kings, and by bridging the gaps left in the Kish and Babylonian lists complete the chronology of the latter for the first time.

### AUTHENTICITY OF THE DATED CHRONOLOGY OF THE KISH CHRONICLE & ITS SUPPLEMENTS

The authenticity of the years of reign of kings and dynasties preserved in the Kish Chronicle and its Nippur, Isin and Babylonian supplements is evidenced by their recorded years being generally found to be strictly in agreement with those recorded in the contemporary monuments of the respective kings, wherever the latter have been found available for testing. The regnal and dynastic years of the Kish Chronicle and its supplements were presumably copied from the original contemporary records of the dynasties, or from their official copies from the First Dynasty downwards. For the Sumerians are found to have been an essentially scientific people, and had always since their emergence the historical sense highly developed; and they were already familiar with writing very many centuries before the founding of their First Dynasty of Kings. This is evident from the form of the writing in the contemporary inscription of that First Dynasty (Udu's Bowl), in which the pictographs are already reduced to conventionalized diagrams, showing very long practice in their picture-writing, which must have been in vogue for many centuries before the epoch of their First Dynasty. And one of the most striking traits of the Sumerians from their earliest known period is their remarkably developed historical sense, manifested by their free recording of genealogies, and their profuse use of dated and attested business documents, contract tablets, etc.—as they were great traders—and their practice of recording the names of the kings in the foundations and walls of their buildings, and even on the individual bricks; and their ancestor-worship led them to preserve especially the names and regnal years of their earliest kings of their First Dynasty.

### THE SUMERIAN TIME-RECKONING BY YEARS

Time-reckoning by years must have been early prevalent amongst the Sumerians, and very long before the foundation

146    EGYPTIAN CIVILIZATION OF SUMER ORIGIN

of their First Dynasty of Kings. The Sumerians were the most advanced Sun-worshippers and were the first systematic agriculturists, for whom a yearly system of reckoning was indispensable. They are admitted to have evolved the system of the calendar year of 360 days, which was borrowed by the Ancient Egyptians,[1] divided into three seasons of four months each, thus forming twelve calendar months, with the expedient of adjusting it to the solar year by intercalary additions of a month at the end of a specified number of years, which the Egyptians modified to an annual addition of five days, thus making the year 365 days.

Full years are employed in the Kish Chronicle for recording the regnal years of the kings and dynasties. And the scientific precision of these Sumerian records is seen in their giving not merely the regnal years for each individual king in each dynasty and his relationship to the preceding king, if any, with the name of his capital city ; but they also give at the end of each dynasty the total number of years for each dynasty. They are in fact models of terse, scientific, historical chronology for the periods they cover (see, for example, p. 77 and the complete Kish Chronicle, WMC. pp. 59 f.).

### MATERIALS FROM WHICH THE DATED CHRONOLOGY OF THE SUMERIAN PERIOD IS RECOVERED & RECONSTRUCTED

The materials from which we are now enabled to recover and reconstruct the *dated* Chronology of the Sumerian Period back to the First Sumerian Dynasty are (*a*) the complete unbroken List of the Sumerian kings from the First Sumerian or Early Aryan Dynasty on the Rise of Civilization continuously down to the modern period which has been preserved by our Indian key-lists ; (*b*) the regnal years for each king and dynasty preserved in the Kish Chronicle and its supplements ; and (*c*) a fixed date in the later or Babylonian period which connects with the anterior and unbroken Sumerian period above and with our modern Christian era below.

From these materials the reconstruction of a complete *dated* Chronology of the Sumerian Period back to the first

[1] F. Hömmel, ERE. 3, 73.

# NEW SOLID BASIS FOR SUMER CHRONOLOGY 147

king of the First Sumerian Dynasty now becomes a mere matter of arithmetical calculation by "dead-reckoning" from the fixed point below.

### FIXED DATE OF FIRST BABYLONIAN DYNASTY BY ASTRONOMICAL COMPUTATION

This fixed date below from which our reckonings are now made is that of the Foundation of the First Babylonian Dynasty. Previously, this date was approximately estimated variously by complicated calculations from various different sources, from the "Babylonian Dynastic Chronicles," "Babylonian List of Kings," several local synchronisms, the "Synchronous History" of about 1400 B.C. to 800 B.C., and controlled by Ptolemy's Canon from 747 B.C. down to the last Babylonian king Nabonidus, and by the contemporary monumental records of many of the kings of those later dynasties themselves.

Now, however, the date of the Foundation of the First Babylonian Dynasty has lately been definitely fixed by astronomical data with remarkable precision. The astronomical observations which now fortunately fix for us this date are an admirably exact series made at Babylon on the morning and evening disappearances of the planet Venus, recorded by the orders of Ammi-"Zadugga," the tenth king of this dynasty, for the twenty-one years of his reign. Of these observations, the most critical of all for the exact fixation of the date, are those taken in the sixth year of his reign. The original calculations made by Father Kugler, S.J., who was the first to recognize the unique importance of these observations for dating purposes for this king and his dynasty, have now been revised by other astronomical experts, Schoch and others, with better values for the apparent acceleration of the Sun and Moon in relation to the Gregorian calendar. The results of these revised calculations have been published,[1] and show that the date of the Foundation of the First Babylonian Dynasty, which satisfies alike astronomy, the Babylonian seasonal calendar and history, is the year 2105 B.C., with a possible alternative

[1] F. T. Dangin, RA. 1927, 181 f.; and still remaining the most authoritative.

of 2113 B.C., being one eight-year period of Venus;[1] but that the former date is the more probable. In any case, it is stated that the actual date must be either the one or the other. I have therefore adopted in our reckonings the former date, namely the year 2105 B.C., as the fixed date for the Foundation of the First Babylonian Dynasty, though it must be remembered that the actual date may possibly be eight years earlier.

### Dated Chronology of the Sumerian or Early Aryan Kings, from the First King at Rise of Civilization to the Kassi Dynasty, c. 3378 B.C. to 1200 B.C.

With this fixed date for the Foundation of the First Babylonian Dynasty, along with our recovery of the other two classes of fundamental data above cited, it now becomes merely a matter of arithmetical calculation by "dead-reckoning" backwards to recover all the dates of the Sumerian kings and dynasties back to the first Sumerian or Aryan king on the Rise of Civilization. The results of this reconstructed Chronology are shown in the accompanying Table, pp. 150 f.

The connecting link between the First Babylonian Dynasty and the imperial Sumerian or Aryan main-line list of imperial kings we have already found[2] was the capture of Isin City by "Sin Mubalit" (the father of Khammu-Rabi), the fifth king of the First Babylonian Dynasty in the seventeenth year of his reign, and who reigned as emperor three years. From this point the imperial line of kings goes continuously back to the first king of the First Sumerian Dynasty. The omission from our Indian key-lists of the imperial line of the name of Sargon's immediate predecessor, the "usurper" Zaggisi, does not in any way affect the other dates, as in addition to the length of his reign being known, we know also the total regnal years for the preceding dynasty, the Second Dynasty of the Kish Chronicle. The exact duration of the overlapping of the First and Second Dynasties of the Kish Chronicle has already been examined and fixed.[3]

[1] F. T. Dangin, RA. 1927, 181 f. These dates were calculated by Schoch, who, however, abandoned them, presumably under the influence of the school which tends to further reduce the date of this Babylonian Dynasty. But these dates are shown by Dangin to be the only ones which satisfy the calendar references of history; and they remain the most authoritative.
[2] WMC. 432 f.     [3] WMC. Chap. IV.

## DATES FROM 1st SUMERIAN KING RECOVERED 149

The omission of the individual regnal years for the 27 kings of the Great Gap of the Kish Chronicle [1] and of its supplementary Isin and Nippur Chronicles, namely kings Nos. 10 to 36 in the main-line list, does not in any way affect the exactitude of the dating of the kings above and below this gap, because the total duration of this gap is definitely specified as 430 years. The Ur Dynasty in the Isin Chronicle gives King Dungi a reign of only 46 years, but his own date-years in his monuments and business documents specify 58 years of reign, which is the figure here adopted.

Regarding the Babylonian Dynasties we have seen that the Second Babylonian Dynasty contained one king of the contemporary Sea-land Dynasty who held imperial rule, namely, the fourth king of that dynasty, therefore the date for the beginning of the Kassi Dynasty is 1790 B.C. The new date for Menes resulting from this chronology is more conveniently examined after our Table has been studied.

Here it is to be remembered that as different versions of the Nippur and Isin Chronicle tablets give slight variations in the total length of reign of Narām Sin and some others and in the total reign of the Guti Dynasty, although we have adopted the generally accepted versions in such cases, the results are thus only approximate to within a few years. But in this regard it will be recalled that even so relatively recent an event as the birth of Christ has not yet been definitely fixed, and its estimate ranges from 6 B.C. to 6 A.D. It is also to be noted that the uneven date for the accession to the throne of the first Sumerian-Aryan or Gothic king results from the process of dead-reckoning of regnal years from below upwards.

From the Kassi Dynasty (which I have not detailed in the Table beyond the 5th king for the reasons in WMC. 458) the chronological connections downwards are fixed with comparative exactness through their contemporary inscriptions and synchronisms, and the later Babylonian and Assyrian King-Lists and "Synchronous Tables" and the Ptolemaic Code, down to the Persian occupation or so-called 27th Dynasty in 527 B.C., and onwards through Alexander's empire to the Ptolemaic period of 305-50 B.C. and through this to our Christian era.

[1] On this Great Gap filled by the Indian Lists, see WMC. 63 f.

## Dated Chronological List of Sumerian or Early Aryan Kings from Rise of Civilization to Kassi Dynasty, c. 1200 B.C.

(The years of Reign are within brackets—s. = Son)

| Date B.C. (approximate). | Sumerian Names in King Lists and Monuments. | Dynasty. | Indian List Names. | No. |
|---|---|---|---|---|
| 3378–3349 | Ukusi of Ukhu City or Udu, Uduin or Odin, Indar, Induru, Dur, Pur, Sakh, Sagaga, Zagg, Gaur or Adar (30) | 1st Dynasty | Ikshvāku or Indra or Sakko or Purū (-ravas) | 1 |
| 3348–3337 | Azag Ama Basam or Bakus, Tasia Mukhla, Gin, Gan or Kan or Nimmirud (12) | — | Ayus, Ama-Basu or Bikukshi-Nimi | 2 |
| 3336–3273 | Azag Bakus or Gan at Unuk, Enoch or Erech City (64) | 2nd Dynasty | (As above) | |
| 3272–3248 | Naksha, Enuzu, Anenzu, Unnusha, In, Enu, s. (25) | — | Nahusha, Anenas or Janak | 3 |
| 3247–3242 | Udu, Uduk, s. (6) | — | Udā-vasu, Yadu, Yayati, ((?) Puru) | 4 |
| 3241–3312 | Zimugun, Dumuzi (30) | — | Janamejaya or Jina | 5 |
| 3211–3206 | Uziwitar, s. (6) | — | Vishtara or Wishtara | 6 |
| 3205–3195 | Mutin Ugun (11) | — | Matinara | 7 |
| 3194–3184 | Imuashshu or Pishmana (11) | — | Vishamsu or Tamsu | 8 |
| 3183–3181 | Naili (or Nandu) Iaxa Sumaddi or Duag, s. (3) | — | Anila, (?) Ucchaya, Dushyanta or (?) Sun-anta | 9 |
| 3180— (or 27) Kings | Baratutu, Bardō, Barti Pirtu | | Burata, Brihad, Prithu | 10 |
| | Gaudumu or Dodumunu | | Gautama, Dhundhumara | 11 |
| | Dutu-Gindara | | Dwat, Candra-ashva | 12 |
| | Azag, or Ashita-ab | | Aja-midha or Siteshu | 13 |
| | Ishaax or Gishax Gamesh | Uruash's Dyn. of "Panch." | Chaxus, Riksha, Rucaka or Ruk-meshu | 14 |
| | Uruash-Khād, Urusag-Khaddu Barama'hasha or Arwasag [c. 3100 B.C.]. s. (30) | | Haryashva or Barmyashva | 15 |
| | Madgal, A-Madgal, Mukh, s. | | Mudgala or Mogallo | 16 |
| | Bi(d)ashnadi, Bi(d)sar, Biugun or Biguaxu, s. | | Badhryashva, Pasenadi or B'ujyu | 17 |

## DATED SUMERIAN & ARYAN CHRONOLOGY

| Date | Sumerian | | Aryan | # |
|---|---|---|---|---|
| | | | Yuvanashwa | 18 |
| | | | Dāsa (Divo- or "divine") or Trasa-Dasyu I | 19 |
| | | | Mettiyo or Mitrayu | 20 |
| | | | Cyavana or Muckunda | 21 |
| | | | Su-Dāsa, Dussaha or Trasa Dasyu II | 22 |
| | | | Somaka, Sambhuta | 23 |
| | | | Jantu | 23a |
| | | | Prishada or Suvarna Roman | 24 |
| | Enun-nad Enash-nadi | | | |
| | Tarsi (Ene- or "divine") or Dixxi (Di- or "divine") | | Drupada I, Hrashva Roman or Rohida-ashva | 25 |
| | Medi or Meti, s. | | Vyoman, Vasumanas | 26 |
| | Kinga, Mukuda, s. | | Jimūta | 27 |
| | Tarsi, Dix-saax or (?) Shu-Dix, s. | | Bhanu or Ban-kirti | 28 |
| | Tizama or Tiz-kar, s. | | Satya-brata | 29 |
| | [(?) Anda ] | | Harish-candra II | 30 |
| | Rumau or Pashipadda ("Mesanni-padda") | | Harita or Rohit-ashwa II | 31 |
| | Uruduki Raman Duruashi-padda or Rut-assa Rāma ("Anni-padda") [c. 2900 B.C.], s. | | Cuncu or Dhundu | 32 |
| | (?) Eama . . . | | Vijaya | 33 |
| | . . . Biama | | B'aruka or Ruruki | 34 |
| | (?) Paunukha (" ? Meshkalamdug ") | | Vri-Taka or Dhri-Taka | 35 |
| | (Illegible) | | Pra-Cinvat, B'arad-Vaja, Bāhu or Bahuka or Puru II | 36 |
| −2751 | " | | | 36a |
| | Gungun, Kingubi-Dudu | | Kuni Sha-Kuni or Sagara | 37 |
| | Mama-gal | "ERECH DYN." | — | 37a |
| | Kalbu-(?) ru | | | |
| | Tuke | | Asa-Manja, Manasyu | 38 |
| | Bara-Gina, Puru-gin, Pardui-Bazum or Urudu-Gina, or Uruka-Gina (25) | | Anjana, Ansu-mat or Karamba ba, s. | 39 |
| 2750–2726 | Zaggisi or Saggisi (55) | "SARGON'S" DYN. | | |
| 2725–2671 | Guni, Shar-Guni, Kin or "Sargon" (15 or 9) | | | |
| 2670–2656 | Mūsh (Uru-), s. (15) | | | |
| 2655–2641 | Manis-Tissu (in Mesop.), s. of Kin | | | |
| 2640–2585 | Narām-Anenzu (or "Sin") or Narām-ba, s. (56 or 38) | | | |
| 2584–2561 | Shar-Gani Shar-Ri or Dilipa (24) | | Kunti-jit Khatwanga Dilīpa | 40 |
| 2560–2558 | Nigigi, Imi, Nanum, Iama (in inter-regnum) four kings (3) | | Bhagī-ratha | |
| 2557–2537 | Dudu (21) | | Dhundu | 41 |

The Great Gap of 430 years with 26

## 152 EGYPTIAN CIVILIZATION OF SUMER ORIGIN

| Date B.C. (approximate). | Sumerian Names in King-Lists and Monuments. | Dynasty. | Indian List Names. | No. |
|---|---|---|---|---|
| 2536–2522 | Shādur-kib, s. (15) | | Suhotra II, Shruta Shrutāyus | 42 |
| 2521–2519 | Uru-Nigin (?Nikin Uru of seal WSC. 390) (3) | 2ND ERECH DYN. | Nabhin, Nābhāga | 43 |
| 2518–2513 | Urish-Ginar, s. (6) | | Harish-Candra or (?) Ambarisha | 44 |
| 2512–2507 | Tardu (or Kudda) (6) | | ((?) RathiTara 'g.g. son" of Ambarūshu) | 44a |
| 2506–2502 | Ba-Sha-nini (or -ama) (5) | | Sindhu-dhipa, Sanjaya | 45 |
| 2501–2494 | Uru-ash (or -an)-uta (6) | | | |
| 2493–2452 | Guti occupation without kings (44 or 42) | GUTI DYN. | [KUSHA DYN.] Ayutāyus (or ? Dutha- liyās, k. of Khatti) | 46 |
| 2451–2449 | Muruta (3) | | [Mūrtaya] Ritu-parna | 47 |
| 2448–2443 | In Kishu or Gishu (6) | | [Kusha] | |
| 2442–2437 | Irilla Tax [or Warla Gaba] (6) | | | |
| 2436–2431 | Dug-me or Ug-me (6) | | [Kushāmba] Sarva-Kāma | 48 |
| 2430–2425 | Eamamesh or Kashushamama (6) | | [Basu II or (?) Bhaji] | |
| 2424–2420 | Inima Bakies, Baesies, Bakus or Basam (5) | | | |
| 2419–2414 | Iziaush (6) | | | Su Dāsa II 49 |
| 2413–2399 | Iārla Tax or Dax (15) | | | |
| 2398–2396 | Ibate (3) | | [Kushāmba (2nd term)] | |
| 2395–2393 | Iārla ((?) Gash) or Kashushamama (?) 2nd term) (3) | | [Basu II or Bhaji (2nd term)] | |
| 2392– — | Basium, Basam or Bakus (2nd term) (3) | | (?) Sarva-bhauma | |
| 2391–2389 | ... Nikin (or Nigin) (2) | | | |
| 2388–2387 | [Lasi]-rubūm or La-Sirab (2) | | | |
| 2386–2385 | Irarum (1) | | | |
| 2384– — | Darranūm (2) | | | Kalmāshu-pāda 50 |
| 2383–2382 | Khâblum or Khab-Kalamu (7) | | | (Sruta, Upa-Gupta) |
| 2381–2375 | Suratâsh Sin or Sarati Gubi Sin (7) | | | |
| 2374–2368 | Iârla Gu(ash)da [? Gudia] (7) | | [Gādhi] | |
| 2367–2361 | [En-Ridi-Pizir] Pisha Ruddu (7) | | Vishva-Ratha, s. of Gādhi | |
| 2360– — | [Tiri]-gan (40 days) | | [Trishanku, contemp. of above] | |
| 2360–2353 | Ashukhamukh or Utukhe-gal (7½) | 3RD ERECH DYN. | Ashmaka | 51 |

## DATED SUMERIAN & ARYAN CHRONOLOGY 153

| Dates | Name | (n) | Dynasty | Aryan | No. |
|---|---|---|---|---|---|
| 2352–2335 | Uruash-Zikum | (18) | Ur Dyn. | [Uru Branch Dyn. Uru-Ricika] Mūlaka | 52 |
| 2334–2277 | Dungi or Duk-gin (Shamu-), s. | (58) | — | [Dagni (Jama-)] | |
| 2276–2268 | Purash-Sin (" Bur-Sin "), s. | (9) | — | [Parashu-Rāma and his massacre] Dasha- | |
| | | | | ratha or (?) | |
| 2267–2259 | Suash-Sin (" Gimil Sin "), s. | (9) | | [Sushena] Shata-ratha | 53 |
| 2258–2233 | Il-Ibil-Sin, s. | (26) | | Il-Ibila or Ilivila | 54 |
| 2232–2200 | Ishbi-Ashurra | (33) | Isin Dyn. | Vishva-saha | 55 |
| 2199–2190 | Katnini-Kat (or Shu-lilishu), s. | (10) | | Khatvanga or Diltpa | 56 |
| 2189–2169 | Itiash-Dakhu, s. | (21) | | Dirgha-bahu | 57 |
| 2168–2149 | Ishshibash-Dakhu, s. | (20) | | Raghu | 58 |
| 2148–2138 | Libiash Ugun, s. | (11) | | Aja | 59 |
| 2137–2110 | Dashashi-urash, Muru | (28) | | Dasha-ratha | 60 |
| 2109–2089 | Amar-Sin (" Bur-Sin II "), s. | (21) | | Rāma (-Chandra) | 61 |
| 2088–2084 | Libi (Insakh), s. | (5) | | Lava and Kusha | 62 |
| 2083–2076 | (Ash-)urra Iwiti | (8) | | | |
| 2075–2052 | Insakh-bani | (24) | | Atithi or Suhotra IV | 63 |
| 2051– — | Zāmbi (3), Tenirpisha (4), Urdukuga (4), Sin Mapish (11) | | | Nishadha | 64 |
| —2007 | Damiq-ilushu | | | | |
| 2023–2004 | Anuha-Muballit (" Sin Muballit " (20), of which four as emperor) | (23) | | Nala | 65 |
| | | | | Nabha or Nabhas | 66 |
| 2003–1961 | Khammu-Rabi or " Great Lotus ", s. | (43) | 1st Babylon Dyn. as Emperors | Pundarīka or " Great Lotus " | 67 |
| 1960–1923 | Sāmsui-Uduna, s. | (38) | | Kshema-Dhanvan | 68 |
| 1922–1895 | Abieshu'a, s. | (28) | | Devānīka | 69 |
| 1894–1858 | Ammi-Satana (or -Ditana), s. | (37) | | Ruru or (?) Suto-rusta | 70 |
| 1857–1837 | Ammi-Saraga (or -Saduga), s. | (21) | | Ahi-nagu | 71 |
| 1836–1806 | Sāmsu-Satana | (31) | | Sudhanvan or Pariyatra | 72 |
| 1805–1791 | Saharki-Bal | (15) | Sea-Land Dyn. | Sahasra Bala or Bala (with separate line) | 73 |
| 1790–1775 | Xatal (" Gandash ") | (16) | Kassi Dyn. | Sthala or Gaya | 74 |
| 1774–1753 | Agu-um, s. | (22) | | Auka or Uktha | 75 |
| 1752–1745 | Bizuiru (" Kashtiliash ") | (8) | | Vajra-nābha | 76 |
| 1744–1737 | Ushigu | (8) | | Shankha | 77 |
| 1736– — | Abisuttash | | | Ab'yutthit-ashva or Dhyushit-ashva | 78 |

## Date of the First "Sumerian," Aryan or Gothic King Ukusi of Ukhu, Iksh-vāku or Oku Thor or Ygg of the Gothic Edda, c. 3378 B.C.

By this Table we now gain at last the fixed date for the greatest of all kings and culture heroes, the first traditional civilized king in the Ancient World at the Rise of Civilization, the immortal Aryan, "Sumerian" or Gothic king who first established Civilization and Agriculture and built the first town or city; and he is disclosed as a historical personage, whose inscribed sacred stone-bowl or "holy grail" still exists. And his date is seen to be fixed at c. 3378 B.C., with approximate exactitude to within a few years of the actual epoch.

This unsuspected relatively recent date of 3378 B.C. for the advent of the first civilized king and the first establishment of Civilization, whilst now explaining the surprising "Modernness" of all the ancient civilizations from their earliest known period and their essential one-ness in character, at the same time exposes the grossly exaggerated chronology which has been conjecturally thrust upon Civilization, that is Civilization properly so-called, and not the mere primitive Neolithic culture with which it is so often loosely confounded.

His world-wide immortal fame as the greatest of all culture heroes amongst all civilized peoples, ancient and modern, under either his personal name or one or other of his "Sumerian" titles confirms his identity as the establisher of Civilization. Thus we have seen he was early canonized and latterly deified by grateful mankind. As the greatest man known to the civilized world, he was made the basis of the first conception of God as a king and father, thus making God in the image of Man. And as such, most of the names and titles of God are coined from his human personal name or titles. Thus we have seen that under his Sumerian title of *Asaru*, he is the historical human original of the Egyptian father-god *Asar*, the "Osiris" of the Greek writers.[1]

---

[1] On his Egyptian titles derived from the Sumerian, see WSAD. 20 f. and WBE. 25 f. And on his Gothic titles derived from the Sumerian, see footnote, pp. 165 f., and numerous representations from Egyptian and Sumerian sources in WBE.

## New Date for Menes of Egypt at
### c. 2704 B.C.–2641 B.C.

The other most critically important date emerging from our Table is the new fixed date for Menes, the founder of the First Dynasty of Egypt. The date of Menes in Egypt, which hitherto has been the most widely disputed of all dates in Ancient History, although one of the most critically important of dates, in that it is the basis for those of the ancient civilizations of the Mediterranean and the West, including Europe, is now recovered for the first time with approximate exactitude by our new historical keys.

Hitherto that date was estimated by accepting the traditional lists of the Egyptian dynasties as given in the surviving mutilated copies of the lists compiled by the late priest Manetho of the Ptolemaic period, which contained the traditional regnal and dynastic years, and purported to be consecutive dynasties. When those lists were compared with other fragmentary ones and with the known reigns of certain kings, the variations proved so great that different Egyptologists made Menes' date vastly different, ranging from 5869 B.C. of Champollion to 4400 B.C. or less;[1] and at present the "long-date" school of Egyptologists still places his date "about 5546 B.C." which, with the other dates, give the misleading impression of well-ascertained chronology. On the other hand, the "short date" Egyptologists under Meyer, recognizing the relatively late or developed stage in the culture of Menes and his dynasty, including the use of metals and systematic writing, have dismissed the early chronology of Manetho, and have arbitrarily reduced the date to "about 3300 B.C.," and attempted to support it by astronomical arguments based on some late references to the Sothic cycles—the heliacal risings of the Dog-star Sirius or Sothis; although there seems no evidence that the Egyptians ever used the Sothic cycle as an era; nor is it probable that any Sothic æon was observed in Egypt before that of 2781 B.C., if even that one were really observed there, which is doubtful.

[1] BKI. I, LIV. f.

## 156   EGYPTIAN CIVILIZATION OF SUMER ORIGIN

But now his real date is fixed at about six centuries still lower than that hypothetical "short date."

Our recovery of the real date of Menes is now made possible by our discovery of the identity of Menes or Manj with the great Mesopotamian emperor Manis Tusu, the son of Sargon, as demonstrated in the previous chapters, through our new Indian keys; and fully confirmed by the actual contemporary inscriptions of Menes himself and his dynasty in their Egyptian records and in their Indus Valley official signets.

The regnal dates of Manis Tusu preserved in the Kish Chronicle and its Isin and Nippur supplements refer only to his emperorship in Mesopotamia, which began, according to those chronicles (see Table, p. 77 [1]) fifteen years after the death of his father Sargon, by whom we have found through the Indian Chronicles that he was disinherited for his revolt against his father through his declaration of independence in Egypt; and thus did not immediately succeed the latter on the Mesopotamian throne. In order to ascertain, therefore, the date of Menes' founding of his dynasty in Egypt we have to calculate on the basis of the Egyptian circumstantial tradition that he reigned in Egypt for sixty-two years, and that the last year of his reign as emperor of Mesopotamia was the year of his death. This reckoning yields us from our Table the following date for his founding of the First Dynasty in Egypt thus:

|   |   |
|---|---|
| Death of Menes or Manis Tusu | = 2641 B.C. |
| Reign in Egypt | = 62 years |
| Date of Founding First Dynasty in Egypt (completed year) | = 2703 B.C. |

That is to say, Menes ascended the throne in Egypt in the year 2704 B.C.

And this date of 2704 B.C.–2641 B.C. for Menes is quite in keeping with his culture, which we have seen was that of the Sargonic period, to which he and his dynasty belonged.

This date of 2704 B.C. for the founding of the First Dynasty in Egypt by Menes or Manis Tusu implies that the latter

[1] For full Kish Chronicle, see WMC. 61 f.

## REAL DATE FOR MENES RECOVERED 157

established his independence there in the twenty-second year of the reign of his father Sargon, who commenced to reign in 2725 B.C. (see table), thus 2725–2703 = twenty-two years. The Indian Epic chronicles emphasize that Prince Asa Manja or Manjas revolted from his father in his early youth. Our figures suggest that the age of Menes when he declared his independence in Egypt against his father was probably about twenty-one, if his father did not marry till he recovered his patrimonial empire. But as we have found that the young Sargon is described as having recovered Kish before he dethroned the Emperor Zaggisi of Erech, he may have been married before the latter event, and thus Menes might be a few years older, say twenty-five years old, when he established his independence in Egypt. This would make Menes, when he died about twenty-one plus sixty-two, or eighty-three years old, or about twenty-five plus sixty-two or eighty-seven years old; and all Egyptian tradition credits Menes with having reached a very old age when he met his tragic death; and the vast works which he performed in the Delta in reclaiming Memphis from the sea imply a very long reign.

It may be objected at first sight by Egyptologists, accustomed to placing the date of Menes so very much earlier, that the new date does not allow sufficient space for the long string of twenty-six dynasties down to the Persian period of 525 B.C. But it is now well recognized that some of these traditional dynasties were not consecutive but more or less contemporary; that the lengths of several dynasties, especially the eleventh, twelfth and the Hyksos (15th and 16th) dynasties are largely conjectural, and the allowance by Brugsch of an average of thirty years' reign for each king is considerably above a normal average.

Thus the average length of the recorded reigns of the 77 main-line Sumerian or Early Aryan kings over the long period from the 1st Sumerian or Aryan king about 3378 B.C. down to 1737 B.C. is $21\frac{1}{3}$ years, which number significantly is in general agreement with the average of individual reigns in modern historical times, and affords striking confirmation of the historicity of the official Sumerian records preserved in Mesopotamia.

Indeed, as a fact, we have found that the length of reign

## 158  EGYPTIAN CIVILIZATION OF SUMER ORIGIN

of the First Dynasty is grossly exaggerated in Manetho's lists. The period from the accession of Menes to the last king of this dynasty, Shudur-kib, we have found by the precise and authentic records of Mesopotamia was only 182 years (2703–2522), and with six kings, of whom one reigned less than three years, as opposed to the eight kings with a reign of 253 years, as given in Manetho's lists, that is an excess of dynastic years of no less than seventy-one years for this one dynasty. Such exaggerations are probably inherent in many of the other dynasties; and it may be that some of even the long dynasties may prove to have short individual reigns, like the Guti Dynasty of Mesopotamia, which had twenty kings reigning for only eighty-one years.

In any case, this newly-found date for Menes of 2704 B.C. is obviously the real date, and it is well established by the mass of new concrete facts and is consistent with the leading facts of contemporary history. And the intervening dynasties between his dynasty and the eighteenth dynasty of c. 1550, with which the more solid dated Egyptian history begins, will doubtless be capable of automatic adjustment within the new limits thus imposed by our discoveries.

### Dates of the Intervening Aryan Kings of Imperial Line from First King of First Aryan Dynasty at Rise of Civilization continuously down to the end of the Kassi Dynasty, about 1175 B.C.

All the dates for the individual kings of the imperial or main line of the Sumerians or Early Aryans, from the first king of the First Dynasty continuously down to the end of the Kassi Dynasty, about 1175 B.C., and including the First Dynasty of Egypt, and through Menes for Minos of Crete, follow as a matter of mere calculation by " dead-reckoning " from the official lists of their regnal years as preserved in the Sumerian and Babylonian records, once the continuous main-line succession is established and a fixed date in our era obtained for one of the kings in the continuously dated Sumerian or Early Aryan series.

PLATE XVIII.  SUMERIAN.                                   EGYPTIAN.

| | Sumerian | | Egyptian |
|---|---|---|---|
| | **ASARU,** "Lord or God Asar," titled "Son of the Sun" = Pict. eye under a throne. Br. 913. 924.  B. 44. | | **ASAR, ASIR,** "God Osiris," Father-god of Sun-cult. Pict. eye under a throne. BD. 83ᵃ. |
| | **BAK,** "Bird of Lord Bel, Lord of the Winds"—the Hawk. Br. 2047, 2051, 5933.  B. 83. | | **BAK,** "The Sun-Hawk", word-sign for Horus Sun-god as "Soarer." G. 20. |
| | **BAN,** "Child creating, nourish." = Pict. pair of breasts. Br. 4105, M. 2726, 2723, MD. 1150.  B. 161. | | **BAN(-T),** "Breast." Pict. pair of breasts. BD. 203ᵃ. |
| | **BAR,** "House, palace, temple. = Pict. house with ?stockade. Br. 6878, 6881, M. 4908.  B. 301. | | **PAR,** "House." Plan of house or hall. G. 35. fig. 193. |
| | **BUZ,** "Vegetation-goddess," "The Lady of the Earth" = Pict. a sprout or ?serpent. Br. 7516, WPOB. 242.  B. 325. | | **UAZ, WAZ,** Vegetation-goddess. Pict. ?conventional papyrus G. 28, fig. 188. |
| | **DA, TA** "Hand" (right hand) = Br. 6647. M. 4757. WPOB.251.B. 294. | | **DA, DA(-T), TAT** "Hand" (right). G. 12., fig. 172. |
| | **DA,** "Put, set, place, peg, plug" = Pict. peg or wedge. Br. 6643-5, 6647. M. 4757.  B. 294. | | **DA,** "Put, set, place." Pict. of a ?wedge. G. 64. figs. 18, 123. |
| | **DAG, TAG,** "Dagger, wound, strike." = Br. 3786, 3798.  B. 146. | | **DAS,** "Knife, sharp, point, cut." G. 50. |
| | **DE, DI,** "Heat, smith." Pict. furnace with flames. Br. 6714-15, 6723 f.  B. 227. | | **TA,** "Fervent heat." Pict. a kiln with flame. G. 42. fig. 145. |

L.A.W. del.

SUMERIAN ORIGIN OF EGYPTIAN HIEROGLYPHS (B).
(Continued from Plate II.)

# XVI

SUMERIAN ORIGIN OF EGYPTIAN HIEROGLYPHS & OF RADICAL, CULTURAL & OFFICIAL WORDS IN THE EGYPTIAN LANGUAGE

THE earliest of all forms of civilized writing known is that of the Sumerians by picture-signs or pictographic word-signs. This Early Sumerian pictographic writing I have shown in my *Sumer-Aryan Dictionary* was all unsuspectedly the source of the Egyptian hieroglyph writing; and in my *Aryan Origin of the Alphabet* I have demonstrated that it was also the source of all the chief forms of alphabetic writing, ancient and modern.

In the earliest known specimen of historical Sumerian writing, namely the votive inscription on the trophy stone-bowl or " Holy Grail " captured from the Serpent-Dragon worshippers by the first Sumerian king Zagg, Ukusi or Tur (Ar-Thur) and engraved by his great-grandson King Udu of Kish about 3245 B.C. (all conjectured dates for inscriptions before this date being merely imaginary, as shown in the preceding chapter), the picture-writing has already become diagrammatic, in order to permit of its being written more rapidly by pen and ink on wood or parchment. This implies the long antecedent use of pictographic writing by the ancestors of the Sumerians in the Neolithic Age, even before the rise of civilization itself in the Metal Age, with ordered city-life. And I suggested that the Hittite hieroglyphs of Asia Minor and Syria, with their elaborately drawn realistic and naturalistic pictorial signs, represented probably the original or earlier form of writing the chief Sumerian pictographic signs. This is confirmed by the fuller and naturalistic form given to many of the Sumerian signs in the official Sumerian seals in Mesopotamia and the Indus Valley colony, and in most of the predynastic and First Dynasty inscriptions in Egypt, being in general agreement with the Hittite hieroglyphs.

The antecedent use of Sumerian pictographic writing in Egypt before the appearance of conventionalized Egyptian hieroglyphs is fully established in the preceding chapters. The writing used by Menes and his dynasty as well as by his predynastic ancestors for their records in Egypt is seen to be essentially Sumerian script, that is syllabic and non-alphabetic writing, and its language is Sumerian.

The local Egyptian conventional form of writing the Sumerian pictographs, which gradually came into use towards the end of the First Dynasty, is now generally known by the Greek term of " hieroglyphs " or " sacred writing," as that script continued to be used by the priests for sacred as well as official writing long after it had become obsolete for general purposes. The early Sumerian writing may also be called " hieroglyphic," as it continued to be used not infrequently in its earlier pictographic form in the seals of priests and priest-kings and on amulets, long after the ordinary writing had become cuneiform for writing rapidly by dabbing with a wedge-shaped or cuneiform wooden style on moist clay-tablets, which were afterwards hard-baked and so rendered imperishable.

The Egyptian hieroglyphic writing is now seen to be a local reversion to the earliest style of Sumerian picture-writing by giving most of the signs their fully and elaborately drawn objective and naturalistic pictorial forms. This is well seen in my decipherment tables of the Egyptian writing in the preceding pages and appendices, showing alongside the corresponding diagrammatic Sumerian signs for reference, and more especially in the plates illustrating the present chapter. For instance the finely proportioned and elaborately drawn signs of the bull, Sun-Hawk, king, boat, vases, etc. etc., in the Egyptian script, which could only be drawn by trained artists with considerable time and care, are represented in the Sumerian by rough conventional diagrams of those animals, figures, etc., adapted for rapid writing by business men. Thus the seeming archaism of Egyptian hieroglyphic writing is seen to be merely a neo-archaism or a pseudo-archaism.

PLATE XIX.   SUMERIAN.                                    EGYPTIAN.

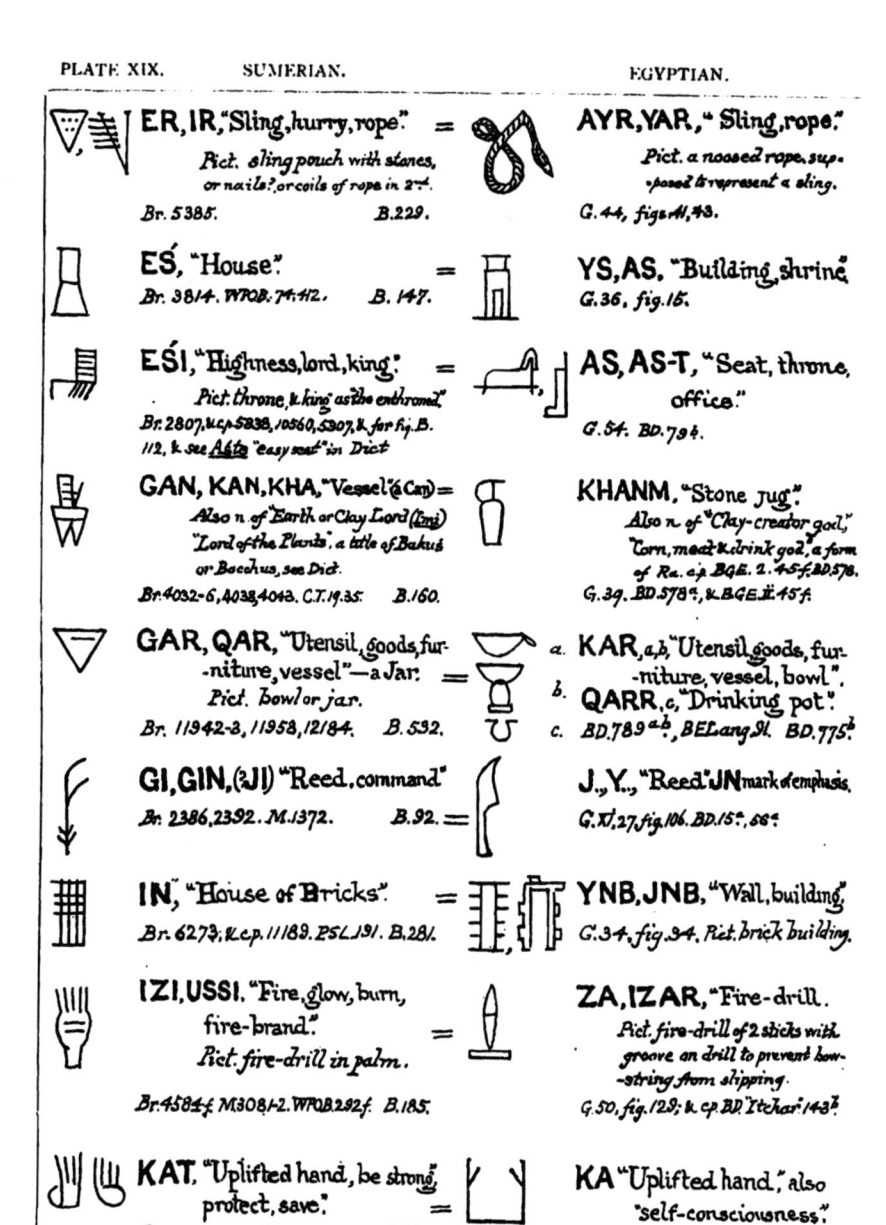

| | Sumerian | Egyptian |
|---|---|---|
| | **ER, IR,** "Sling, hurry, rope." Pict. sling pouch with stones, or nails? or coils of rope in 2ⁿᵈ. Br. 5385.   B.229. | **AYR, YAR,** "Sling, rope." Pict. a noosed rope, supposed to represent a sling. G.44, figs A1, 43. |
| | **ES,** "House." Br. 3814. WROB. 74.112.   B.147. | **YS, AS.** "Building, shrine" G.36, fig.15. |
| | **ESI,** "Highness, lord, king." Pict. throne, & king as the enthroned. Br.2807, & cp.5838, 10560, 5307, & for fig. B. 112, & see Akta "easy seat" in Dict | **AS, AS-T,** "Seat, throne, office." G.54. BD.794. |
| | **GAN, KAN, KHA,** "Vessel (a Can) = Also n. of Earth or Clay Lord (Enj) "Lord of the Plants", a title of Bakus or Bacchus, see Dict. Br.4032-6, 4038, 4043. C.T.19.35.   B.160. | **KHANM.** "Stone jug." Also n. of "Clay-creator god," "Corn, meat & drink god", a form of Ra. cp BGE. 2. 45 f; BD.578. G.39. BD.578ᵃ, & BGE.II.45 f. |
| | **GAR, QAR,** "Utensil, goods, furniture, vessel"—a Jar. Pict. bowl or jar. Br. 11942-3, 11958, 12184.  B.532. | a. **KAR,** a,b, "Utensil, goods, furniture, vessel, bowl". b. **QARR,** c, "Drinking pot". c. BD.789ᵃ⁻ᵇ, BELang II. BD.775ᵇ. |
| | **GI, GIN, (JI)** "Reed, command" Br. 2386, 2392. M.1372.   B.92. | **J., Y.,** "Reed," JN mark of emphasis. G.XI, 27, fig.106. BD.15ᵃ, 56ᵃ. |
| | **IN,** "House of Bricks." Br. 6273; & cp. 11189. PSL.191. B.281. | **YNB, JNB,** "Wall, building" G.34, fig.34. Pict. brick building. |
| | **IZI, USSI.** "Fire, glow, burn, fire-brand." Pict. fire-drill in palm. Br.4584f; M308 f-2. WROB.292 f.  B.185. | **ZA, IZAR,** "Fire-drill. Pict. fire-drill of 2 sticks with groove on drill to prevent bow-string from slipping. G.50, fig.129; & cp. BD. Ytchar 143ᵇ |
| | **KAT.** "Uplifted hand, be strong, protect, save." Br. 7068, 7070. M.5058.   B.311. | **KA** "Uplifted hand," also "self-consciousness." G.14. |
| | **KHA, KU, KUA,** "Fish." Br.11817-19. WROB.285 f; WISD.31 f. B.525. | **KHU,** "Fish." BD.537ᵇ; & cp. Kha "dead fish" c. |

SUMERIAN ORIGIN OF EGYPTIAN HIEROGLYPHS (C).   L.A.W. del.

PLATE XX.    SUMERIAN.                                EGYPTIAN.

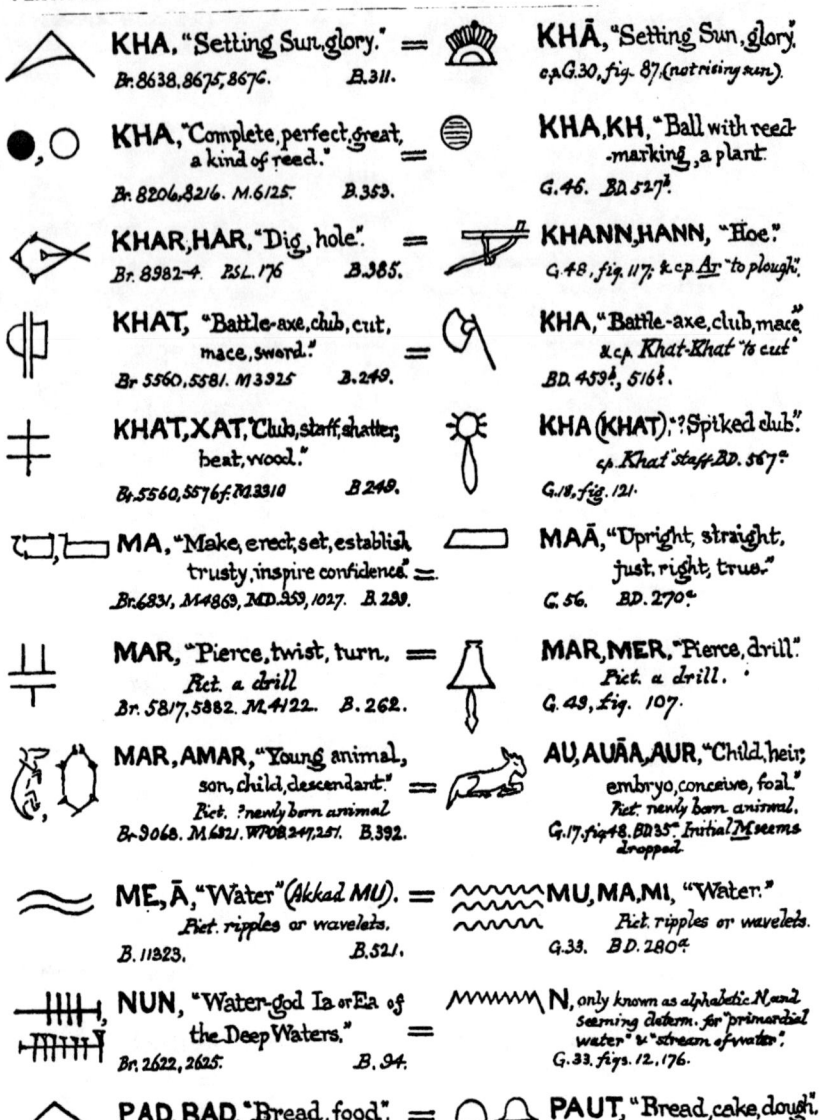

| Sumerian | Egyptian |
|---|---|
| KHA, "Setting Sun, glory." Br. 8638, 8675, 8676. B.311. | KHĀ, "Setting Sun, glory." cp. G.30, fig. 87 (not rising sun). |
| KHA, "Complete, perfect, great, a kind of reed." Br. 8206, 8216. M.6125. B.353. | KHA, KH, "Ball with reed-marking, a plant." G.46. BD.527ª. |
| KHAR, HAR, "Dig, hole." Br. 8982-4. PSL.176. B.385. | KHANN, HANN, "Hoe." G.48, fig. 117; & cp. Ar "to plough". |
| KHAT, "Battle-axe, club, cut, mace, sword." Br. 5560, 5581. M.3925. B.249. | KHA, "Battle-axe, club, mace" & cp. Khat-Khat "to cut". BD. 459ª, 516ª. |
| KHAT, XAT, "Club, staff, shatter, beat, wood." Br. 5560, 5576f. M.3910 B.249. | KHA (KHAT): "?Spiked club." cp. Khat staff BD. 567ª. G.18, fig. 121. |
| MA, "Make, erect, set, establish, trusty, inspire confidence." Br.6831, M.4869, MD.259, 1027. B.239. | MAĀ, "Upright, straight, just, right, true." G.56. BD.270ª. |
| MAR, "Pierce, twist, turn. Pict. a drill. Br. 5817, 5882. M.4122. B.262. | MAR, MER, "Pierce, drill." Pict. a drill. G.49, fig. 107. |
| MAR, AMAR, "Young animal, son, child, descendant." Pict. ? newly born animal. Br.9068. M.6321. WPOB.247, 251. B.392. | AU, AUĀA, AUR, "Child, heir, embryo, conceive, foal." Pict. newly born animal. G.17, fig.48. BD.35ª. Initial M seems dropped. |
| ME, Ā, "Water" (Akkad MU). Pict. ripples or wavelets. B. 11323. B.521. | MU, MA, MI, "Water." Pict. ripples or wavelets. G.33. BD.280ª. |
| NUN, "Water-god Ia or Ea of the Deep Waters." Br. 2622, 2625. B.94. | N, only known as alphabetic N and seeming determ. for "primordial water" & "stream of water". G.33, figs. 12, 176. |
| PAD, BAD, "Bread, food." Pict. a loaf of bread. Br. 9925, 9928-30. B.429. | PAUT, "Bread, cake, dough." Pict. a loaf of bread. BD. 230ª, & cp. At "bread." G.55. |

L.A.W. del.

SUMERIAN ORIGIN OF EGYPTIAN HIEROGLYPHS (D).

## SUMER ORIGIN OF EGYPTIAN HIEROGLYPHS 161

In order to demonstrate further the Sumerian origin of the Egyptian hieroglyphs, already seen in the decipherment tables, I give in the accompanying Plates (II, XVIII-XXI) forty-eight of the commoner Egyptian hieroglyphs with their phonetic values or sounds and their meanings, on the right hand, and alongside each on the left hand the corresponding Sumerian diagrammatic pictographic word-sign with its phonetic value and meaning. It will be noticed that each sign is identical in Sumerian and Egyptian in sound and meaning. The form also of the objects represented by the Egyptian hieroglyphs is essentially the same as in the diagrammatic Sumerian pictographs, the differences being merely in the modification of shape which the object has undergone or possessed in the local environments of Egypt. Thus are seen to be the differences in form of the brazier, shield and plough in Pl. II, opp. p. 8; the throne, knife and kiln in Pl. XVIII; the house, jug, bowl or basket, reed, fire-drill and fish in Pl. XIX; the hoe, battle-axe, club, drill, foal and cake in Pl. XX; and the garden, serpent and dog in Pl. XXI.

Additional Egyptian hieroglyphs, demonstrated to be of Sumerian origin, in pictographic form, sound and meaning, have been given in the preceding pages. They include the *Du* or Mound-sign (p. 111); *Fau* or Viper-sign (p. 114); *Ga* or *Ka* or Bull-sign (p. 104, from the Sumerian *Ga* or *Gu* and cp. BD. 785); *Sha(t)*, the Net-sign (p. 114 and cp. BD. 618); *Ti*, the Drill-sign (p. 120) and others.[1]

The language also of the Ancient Egyptians, although in its idiom latterly Semitic, is found in its chief cultural and official root-words or word-stems to be radically of Sumerian origin, as demonstrated in full detail in my comparative *Sumer-Aryan Dictionary*. Of the six hundred or so root-words and verbal roots in the Sumerian language (compared with about 461 Aryan roots in the English language as estimated by Skeat), practically all of them are found in Ancient Egyptian, as well as throughout the Aryan family of languages; and they possess the same sound and meaning or shade of meaning in Ancient Egyptian as in the

---

[1] Several others are given in my *Aryan Origin of the Alphabet*, and in *Makers of Civilization*, pp. 602-3.

Sumerian language. This confirms Sir Flinders Petrie's observation that "the later Egyptian [language] comprised much Semitic in structure, though most of the words were from other sources"[1]—sources presumably hitherto unknown.

This Sumerian or Early Aryan origin of the Egyptian hieroglyphs and of the chief cultural and official root-words in the Ancient Egyptian language supplies further evidence of the Sumerian or Early Aryan origin of Egyptian civilization.

[1] *Migrations*, Huxley Lect. for 1906, *Jour. Anthrop. Inst.*, xxxvi [6].

PLATE XXI.     SUMERIAN.                                    EGYPTIAN.

| | SUMERIAN | | EGYPTIAN |
|---|---|---|---|
| ▭ | **PIR, PIUR.** "Base, foundation, floor, platform." —(?Pier) = Br. 5480, 5483, MD. 415. B. 234. On Pi value cp. Br. 7506. | ▭, ▢ | **P.** "Base, stand, block of wood or stone." (word unknown in Egypt, only initial known.) G. 47, fig. 95. BD. 229ª. |
| ◇, ◇ | **RA,** "Sun, bright, Sun-god." Pict. winged disc or circle. M. 5741, 5785, 5807. WPOB 242f. B. 337. | ◉, ⊙ | **RĀ,** "Sun, Sun-god." G. 30, fig. 10. |
| ⋀, △△ | **SAT,** "Land, country, mountain." Pict. of three hills. Br. 7392, 7396. B. 322. | ⌒⌒⌒ | **SAT, SAMT,** "Foreign land, hilly desert." Pict. 3 hills—M in neighborhood of S seems unfixable. G. 31. |
| ⊖, ▽ | **SAB,** "Heart, interior, midst." Pict. diag. of heart with valves. B. 7388. B. 340. | ⏝ | **AB,** "Heart, interior, middle." Pict. heart with vessels & valves. G. 18, fig. 46. |
| 🌿🌿 | **SAR,** "Garden, plantation, park, grove, marshland, green." Pict. garden with plants. Br. 4237, 4303, 4315f. M. 2865. B. 170. | 🌱🌱🌱 | **SA,** "Garden, plants, orchard, grove, meadow, green." Pict. pool with lotuses. G. 28. BD. 721ª. The final R is? dropped. |
| ⋉⫝̸ | **SIR, ṢIR,** "Serpent." Pict. serpent with coils. Br. 7638-39. B. 328. And see Ar "serpent" & Fi "Viper" in Dict. | 𓆙 a.  𓆚 b. | **YĀR, AĀR,** "Serpent (uraeus) a. **ZE-T, SYA-T,** "Snake (cerastes) b. BD. 29ª, 583ª, 641ª; G. 24, figs. 16, 173. S initial seems dropped out in a. |
| ⅃⅃ | **-U,** "Go, come, bring." Pict. a pair of feet & legs. Br. 4933-34. M. 3369. B. 208. | 𓂻 | **AU,** "Go, come, visit, return." Pict. a pair of feet & legs. G. 16, fig. 156. BD. 30ª-31ª. |
| △ | **KI, GI, QI,** "Earth, land, ground." Pict. a mound of earth. Br. 9621, 9635. B. 419. | ◿, ▷ | **QAY, KHI, KHUI,** "Earth, land, high ground." G. 32; BD. 537ª. |
| ▦ | **NA,** "Stone." Pict. a stone with strokes for solidity. Br. 1632. B. 71; & cp. Na "jewel", M. 249. | ▦ | **NA,** "A kind of Stone, a gem, determinative of stones." BD 344ª & cxxvi. 69. |
| ⌐ | **UR, URU,** "Dog." Diagram of dog's head & neck. Br. 11260. M. 8642. B. 516. | 🐕 | **UHR,** "Dog." Pict. of mastiff. BD. 147ª. 177ª. |

L.A.W. del.

SUMERIAN ORIGIN OF EGYPTIAN HIEROGLYPHS (E).

## XVII

### MYTHOLOGY OF EARLY DYNASTIC EGYPT ESSENTIALLY IDENTICAL WITH SUMERIAN, ARYAN & GOTHIC

THE exalting Sun-worship introduced into Egypt by the Predynastic and First Dynasty kings, in place of the blighting primitive aboriginal cult of the Serpent, Wolf (Set) and Mother-Cow of the Moon worshippers with their cruel animal sacrifices, was characteristically Sumerian of the earlier period and of the Early Aryans. It was also the religion of the Goths—a people of whom the Sumerian kings and the Predynastic and First Dynasty Egyptian Pharaohs claimed to be members. This identity in mythology is demonstrated in detail in my former works, *The Makers of Civilization, Sumer-Aryan Dictionary* and *The British Edda* epic of the Western Goths, as literally translated for the first time.

Whilst the Sun itself, as the Light of the World and scientifically recognized as the source of mundane Life, continued to be adored or worshipped more or less by the Sumerians and Early Aryans—a fairly rational and scientific cult reintroduced into Egypt in later times by the semi-Hittite king Akhen-Aten, who nevertheless is, strange to say, stigmatized by modern Egyptologists as a " heretic " instead of acclaimed as a reformer—there had arisen amongst the priests before the Sargonic period, which includes Menes, an anthropomorphism which had deified the first Aryan or Sumerian king as the Father-god and as personifying the Sun and Heaven, and with him were associated his deified queen, *As'zu* or *As'tu* (*Aset* or " Isis " of Egypt) and their son, forming a heavenly triad or trinity. The conservative later Goths, who were essentially monotheists and even in the Christian era maintained monotheism as Arians, whilst recognizing his human origin, continued to give the chief place to their solar Father-god, the *Asa* Thor, Sig or Odin, who I have demonstrated in previous works was the *Ash* Tur, Ukusi, Sagg or Odoin of the Sumerians and their deified first king.

One of the Sumerian titles for this solar Father-god Ash Tur is *Asari* or *Asaru*, disclosing the source of the name of the Egyptian solar Father-god *Asar*, the " Osiris " of the Greeks ; and significantly the Egyptian hieroglyph for that name is written, as we have seen, by the self-same pictographic sign as in the Sumerian. Besides this Sumerian source for the name and solar functions of the Egyptian Father-god Osiris, the Egyptian tradition of the origin of that god locates the homeland of his human original vaguely in the direction of Northern Syria. This location it is to be noted is in agreement with the Sumerian and Gothic traditions which definitely place the historical capital of this deified first king in Asia Minor, the ancient Sumerian name for which, as we have seen, was Kur or " Syria " ; and Asia Minor was still called *Suria* or " Syria " by the Seleucids.

This loose Sumerian solar triad is thus disclosed as the source of the well-known later Egyptian solar triad or trinity of " Osiris-Isis-Horus," the Father-Mother-Son, the Egyptian spelling of whose names is *Asar-Ase(t)* or *Isi(t)-Hor* (or *H-r* or *Haru*). The Sumerian origin of the Egyptian names *Asar* (" Osiris ") and Aset (" Isis ") has already been demonstrated above. The Egyptian name for the deified son, the Horus of the Greeks, if not deriving from the Sumerian *Har* or *Harri* or " warrior " title of the solar Sumerian son-god Mar-duk, is probably I think derived from the Sumerian *Sur* (or *As's'ur*) the Sun-god,[1] who is called *Sūra* (or *Asura*) in Sanskrit, and *Hor* (or *Ahura*) in Old Persian, as seen in the familiar compound Zoroastrian title of the Sun-god as " *Hor*-mazd," or " *Ahura*-mazda "—wherein significantly the original S of the Sanskrit and Sumerian becomes, as is usual in Old Persian, H. If this latter be the source of the Egyptian name " Hor " or " Horus," as seems probable,[2] it would indicate strong Elamite or Persian dialectic influence in early dynastic Egypt.

[1] Br. 8209, 8211.
[2] *Haru* or *Hru* in Egyptian=Hawk, the bird symbolizing the Sun and Horus. Cp. GE. 20.

# EGYPTIAN MYTHOLOGY OF SUMER ORIGIN

The representations in art also of this triad of Sumerian solar deities are essentially identical in Sumerian, Gothic and Egyptian as shown in detail in *The British Edda*. The functions also of this solar triad in Sumerian and Egyptian are essentially identical as demonstrated in the same work. Especially noteworthy is the similarity in functions of the son-god, the Egyptian Horus, with his original in Sumerian and Gothic. In all three he is under one or more manifestations or reflexes the warrior-champion of his Father-god in overcoming evil, especially in the person of the Wolf-demon Set (or Sut), the prototype of Satan; and is the resurrector from the dead, and also the patron of agricultural life as the corn-god or angel. In Sumerian he exercises these three capacities under his title of *Tasia* or *Tax Mukla* and *Daxa;* and is the *Dias*, *Daks* or *Dashup-Mikal* of the Phœnicians (the Sumero-Phœnician source of St Michael-the archangel of Christian mythology as I have fully demonstrated), the *Daxa* of the Indian Brahmans, wearing a goat's head (analogous to his Sumerian, Egyptian and Phœnician Goat or Ibex symbol), the *Thiazi* of the Goths, and the *Tas*, *Dias* or *Tascio* carrying weapons, ears of corn and cross symbols in the pre-Roman coins of the Ancient Britons.[1] In later Egypt he is called *Reseph* or *Reshpu*, defining him as "the Corn-god" but representing him as an invincible armed warrior wearing a goat-head chaplet and carrying the cross symbol of Life (Ankh), see Fig. 42A, p. 121. This latter name for him is obviously coined upon his Hittite title of *Tashup* and his Phœnician title of *Dashup*-Mikal. And it is significant, as we have seen, that he is invoked as the solar archangel in King Dudu's tomb tablet for the resurrection of that First Dynasty king just as was done by the Sumerians, Phœnicians and Ancient Britons. And the Egyptian name *Ra* for the Sun-god I have shown to be derived from the Sumerian *Ra* name for "The Sun" and "The Sun-god."[2]

The names and titles of these chief Egyptian solar deities, as well as of the chief aboriginal serpent-cult demons whom

---

[1] See for many representations and details WPOB. xv f., 249 f., 338 f., 353 f.; and WSAD. 53.
[2] See Pl. XXI; and WPOB. 242, 246.

they opposed, are found to be essentially identical in the Sumerian and Gothic.[1]

In symbolism also is to be noted the prominence in all three, Egyptian, Sumerian and Gothic of the solar Hawk as the winged sun, the Sun-Goose, Goat and Bull and the Sun-Cross (latterly given usually the form of the " handled Cross or *Ankh*, but represented on Menes' tomb-label as a red rectangular cross and elsewhere as a pedestalled cross) ; and the abhorrence in Sumerian and Gothic of the aboriginal Serpent and Wolf demonist totems of the Moon-cult, which the later Egyptians exalted into the position of gods. In all three is the Sumerian or Aryan and non-Semitic solar rite of baptism.[2] And even the hitherto unknown meaning of " The Hidden Hand " in Egyptian mythology finds its explanation through the new Gothic and Sumerian keys ;[3] as well as the meaning and usage of the ancient name " Rom " or " Rom-t " for ancient Egypt and pre-Sumerian Syria.[4]

[1] In the following alphabetic list of Sumerian and Gothic prototypes of the chief Egyptian solar gods and their opposing Egyptian demons, the numbers refer to pages of *The British Edda*, where most of them are illustrated from all three sources. *Asar* or Osiris, father Sun-god, 40. *Asari* or *Asaru* of Sumers, 40, 241, 243, 261. *Atmu* or *Atum*, form of Osiris, father Sun-god of Sumers. *Adamu* and Eddic *Ad*, 25, 40, 66, 196, 222, 261. *Bal*, *Balu*, form of aboriginal Set-wolf demon, 12, 104. *Hathor* or *Hether*, aboriginal mother-cow-goddess, 4, 8. *Hemi*(*t*), form of Hathor, 4. *Heru*, form of Horus-Osiris, 222. Horus, 86, 184 f., 250, and see Heru. *Isis* or *Ase-t*, goddess-queen of Osiris, 75 f. *Khan*(m), form of Horus, 232. *Khonsu*, form of Horus, 84, 88, 232. *Makhi*, god of Fire-altar and *Makhi-ar*, harvest-god, 84. *Ptah* or properly *Patah*, aboriginal father-demon, 7, 8, 104. *Ra*, the Sun and Sun-god, 271. *Rann-t*, form of Serpent-mother, 8. *Reshpu*, warrior- and corn-god, form of Tasia or Tascio, 87. *Set*, wolf-demon, 12 f., 119 f., 121, 135, 165, 186, 213, 241. *Tann* or *Tannen*, form of Osiris or Atmu and *Dann* or *Thann* of Edda, 40, 44. *Shehtu*, wind-demon, 121, 242. *Uas*(*t*), aboriginal Serpent-goddess, 324, No. 249.
[2] WBE. 66 f.   [3] Ib. 199 f.   [4] Ib. 277 f.

# XVIII

## Diffusion of Sumerian Culture by Sea-going Aryan Phœnicians, so-called "Hamites" v. Egyptians

> "The able *Panch* (Phœnicians) setting out to invade the Earth, brought the whole World under their sway."—*Mahā-Bhārata*, Epic I, 94, sloka 3738.

THE great Sumerian cities in the Indus Valley colony were founded and already centres of Sumerian civilization, as we have seen, about 3100 B.C., that is about three centuries before civilization reached Egypt. And it was from this Indus Valley Sumerian colony that Menes with his sea-going fleet annexed Upper Egypt and established the First Dynasty in a united and independent Egypt.

The Sumerian emperor of Mesopotamia who founded as sea-king the Indus colony was, as I have conclusively demonstrated in former works, the traditional Aryan founder of the famous clan of sea-going merchant princes, the "Phœnicians," the "Phoinik-es" of the Greeks, the "Phœnic-es" or "Punici" of the Romans, and the "Fankha, Panag or Panasa" of the Egyptians.[1] That Sumerian dynasty of sea-kings who established this early civilization in the rich pastoral, agricultural and gold-bearing Indus Valley is called in the official Indian epic chronicles and in the Vedas "The able *Panch*" dynasty of Early Aryans, a title now disclosed as obviously the origin of the name "Phœnician," Panag, or Fankha. And Menes and his Aryan dynasty are shown therein to be the lineal descendants of that Panch or Phœnician dynasty of Aryans, thus explaining how the Hebrew legend calls the Phœnicians "The sons of Ham," that is "The Sons of Egypt"; and how an ancient Greek name for Egypt as well as Crete was *Aeria* or *Herié*, that is obviously "Land of the Ara, Ari, Harri, Her or Aryans."[2]

[1] WPOB. 12 f., 188 f.; WMC. 19 f., 110 f.    [2] WSAD. 15.

## 168  EGYPTIAN CIVILIZATION OF SUMER ORIGIN

These Early Aryan "Phœnician" sea-faring merchant-princes, who are disclosed as the remote Aryan ancestors of the later somewhat semitized Phœnicians of the classic Greco-Roman period, are described in the Vedas as exploring the wide seas for merchandise and suffering repeatedly shipwreck in the ocean, and "a ship of one hundred oars" is mentioned in connexion with them. They, along with their Aryan kinsmen the Maruts (or "Amorites" who are pictured by the earlier Egyptian paintings as blue-eyed), were the greatest colonizing branch of the Early Aryans. And as cited in the heading, the great Indian epic, the Mahā-Bhārata, records that they "brought the whole World under their sway"; and the Vedas call them "the leaders of the Earth."[1]

After the Fall of the Sixth city of Troy, the Homeric Troy, there ensued for several centuries a period of sea-activity in the Mediterranean by the highly civilized and sea-faring Achaians, Ionians, Dorians, Cretans, and especially the industrial adventurous Amorite and Phœnician sea-rover Aryans. It was a period also subsequent to civilized colonization of Britain by King Brutus the Trojan about 1103 B.C.;[2] and several centuries after the period of the blue glazed beads found at Stonehenge, the date of which is fixed between about 1400 to 1250 B.C.;[3] and these beads are now generally regarded as having been manufactured in a British factory under Phœnician workmanship, implying the existence of high industrial civilization in a part at least of Britain. But Egypt at this period, it is to be specially noted, was not a sea-power. That country had then finally ceased to be imperial and had sunk to the position of a decayed and impoverished petty state under the petty kinglets of the 21st and 22nd Dynasties, "insignificant kings" and "of no historical importance whatever."[4] It had lost its coastal ports in Palestine and Phœnicia, and had lost the Sinaitic peninsula with presumably its Red Sea trade, and was harassed on its isthmus border by the Assyrians and on the south by the Ethiopians. Any spread of civilization therefore along the Mediterranean coastlands and beyond at this period is to be credited presumably to those civilized mari-

[1] RV. I, 7, 1-10.  [2] WPOB. 142 f.
[3] Ib. 219.  [4] HNE. 391, 439.

# WORLD DIFFUSION OF CIVILIZ. BY ARYANS 169

time people, especially the Amorites and Phœnicians and not to the Egyptians.

In India, at the late period presently in question, we find this ruling and sea-faring clan of the Panch Aryans, at the end of the 8th century B.C. and beginning of the 7th century B.C., as the ruling Aryan race in the Ganges Valley in association with their kindred Aryan clan of the Kurus of Kur or Syria-Asia Minor as the Kuru-Panchala rulers of India.[1] These conjoint Aryan clans had at that date freshly migrated from Northern Syria and Asia Minor for the colonization of the Ganges Valley, and had suddenly introduced there a fully fledged civilization of the late Sumerian and Asia Minor Hittite type, which formed the so-called " Indian Civilization " of the Ganges Valley, extending to the Deccan and Ceylon, with which the historical period opens in Eastern India, and which civilization has continued in India with little alteration down to the present day.[2]

On Indo-China, the civilizing effect of this vigorous young Indian civilization became almost immediately evident. We find that in 680 B.C. a powerful trading colony of sea-merchants under Hindu leaders established themselves on the coast of China, in the Gulf of Kia-tchou with trade relations as far as Shantung. They named their station on the south side of that gulf Lang-ga, after the Indian name Lanka for Ceylon ; and their mart and mint-station on the north was Tsih-miah, afterwards Tsih-moh. In 675 B.C. they introduced for the first time the system of coinage into China ; and latterly they established monetary unions for the issue of a joint currency with the names of themselves and inland Chinese cities. And they held a monopoly of the Chinese sea-trade for several centuries.[3] The fact of this early introduction by them of a coinage system into China shows that they were in very close commercial relations with Asia Minor ; for the system of coinage first arose with the merchants of Lydia on the west coast of Asia Minor, according to Herodotus and confirmed by modern authorities, who place the invention of coinage there in the 8th century B.C. or at latest in the 7th century B.C.[4] Now the kinsmen of the

[1] WMC. 42 f.      [2] *Ib.* 40 f.
[3] *Western Origin of Chinese Civilization,* T. de Lacouperie, 89.
[4] *History of Ancient Coinage,* P. Gardner, 1918, 67 f.

Panch, namely the Kurus, who were conjoint rulers of India at this time, were the descendants of the Hittite ruling race of Asia Minor (Kur), from which land they had only recently migrated to colonize Eastern India. And this coinage episode incidentally confirms my recovery of the prehistory of the sudden colonization and civilization of Gangetic and Eastern India by the great migration at this period of Kuru-Panchalas from Syria-Asia Minor.

This Indian sea-trade with China or Cathay necessarily entailed a chain of ports of call along the Malay peninsula and Indo-Chinese archipelago. And it is generally admitted that Aryan India was the civilizer of that peninsula and archipelago, from Burma through Malaya and Siam to Cambodia, with the great outlying islands of Sumatra, Java, Borneo (in part) and the Philippines in the Indo-Chinese archipelago, lands which with their islands are appropriately called " Further India." Of the concrete proofs for their civilization by India, one is the fact that the present day writing on all of these lands and isles is in alphabetic letters derived from the Indo-Aryan alphabet. The writing also is in the Aryan direction of left to right as in English and other Aryan script, and is *not in the reversed direction from right to left as in Semitic Phœnician and Egyptian.* The Religion also in most of these countries is Buddhism of the old Indian form of about the 6th century B.C., and its sacred language is the old Indian Pali dialect of Indo-Aryan speech of that period. And Canon Taylor shows in his classic work on " The Alphabet " that *the old alphabets of Corea and Japan before the adoption of Chinese script were of Indian origin.*[1]

The Art and Architecture of Indo-China and the Malay archipelago also exhibit the profound influence of Indian civilization. The Indian style of art is seen not only in the fine sculptures and their symbolism in the great dead cities and temples from Anaradhapura in Ceylon of the 3rd century B.C. to Borobudur in Java and Cambodia in Indo-China ; but it is seen also in the present-day ceremonial native dress of the people of those lands. The latter is generally reminiscent of the old Indian style of costume, turbans and coiffure found on the magnificent sculptures of the Indian Buddhist

[1] *The Alphabet*, II, 348 f.

emperor Asoka of the 3rd century B.C., and in the ancient sculptures of Bengal, Orissa (Kalinga) and the Deccan, including the Amaravati sculptured marbles of the 1st or 2nd centuries A.D. now adorning the grand staircase at the British Museum, and in the Ajanta cave frescoes of the 6th century A.D. The architecture with colossal stone masonry of the great Buddhist temples and palaces in Cambodia of about the 4th century A.D., for example, has its Indian prototype in the temples and palaces of the Indian emperor Asoka at his capital at Pataliputra on the Ganges, the vast size of the sculptured stones of which (some of which were excavated by me) so excited the admiration of the Greeks that they declared that the city had been built by Hercules.[1] And his monuments and those of his successors at Bharut, etc., are so full of solar symbols that he was thought to be a Sun-worshipper.

The dates of some others of these colonizing and civilizing invasions of the Indo-China archipelago by Indo-Aryans have been historically elicited. Thus Java, the latest to be civilized, was first colonized in 75 A.D. by Hindu navigators from Kalinga, south of the Hughli. And the Chinese Buddhist pilgrim Fa Hian at the beginning of the 4th century A.D. found that island entirely populated by Brahmanist Hindus (the " Children of the Sun " of later writers) who were in maritime relations with the Ganges, Ceylon, Cambodia and China. Then in 603 A.D., Java received a fresh colony of Indian Buddhists from Gujerat in Western India who built the great temple of Borobudur, adorned with magnificent sculptures picturing their fleets of Indian ships and their deep-sea commerce with Malaya and China.[2] But significantly throughout these regions the art and architecture and civilization of Indo-China and its archipelago are Indian, and there is no trace of any Egyptian influence.[3]

[1] *Report on the Excavations at Pataliputra (Palibothra)*, L. A. Waddell, Calcutta, 1903, 7 f. With plates of some of the sculptured stones of the Asokan period unearthed.
[2] *History of Indian Shipping*, R. Mookerji, 1912, 148 f.
[3] Whilst the civilized Burmese, Malayans, Siamese and Cambodians destroy their dead bodies by cremation according to the Indian custom and do not attempt to preserve the body, there is a widespread custom amongst the uncivilized Indonesians of desiccating the corpse without embalmment, by exposing it to the sun or smoke or fire, and thereafter keeping it on a platform or in an empty hut unburied for long periods. This practice,

In America also, the influence of this Indo-Aryan civilization in the Pacific is evidenced in the mighty civilization, monuments and ruined cities with colossal architecture of the Mayas in Mexico and Central America discovered by Cortes in his filibustering expedition, and of the Incas of Peru. The sculpturings there with their solar symbolisms, dress of the people, exotic elephants, etc., are portrayed generally in the conventional Indian style as found not only in India, but also in the Indian colonies of Cambodia, Java, etc., in Further India, indicating that the Indo-Aryan civilization, essentially of Sumerian type, had reached the New World through the Pacific, from the Far East to the Far West, at least a thousand years before Columbus. And here also there is no evidence of Egyptian influence.[1]

Thus, we find that the uncritical theory of the Egyptian Origin of the World's Civilization, whilst failing to supply a single fact in support of its main issue, also entirely fails in its attempt to side-track and obscure that issue by the allegation of a very late diffusion of an Egyptian heterogeneous primitive "culture-complex" over the world. As showing the desperate straits of the latter attempt, the decayed Egypt of that period was apparently recognized as hopelessly incapable of making any such diffusion herself, not even of a belated primitive culture-complex, so the late Semitic Phœnicians are invoked as the vicarious agents of this alleged Egyptian diffusion in India, Indo-China and Oceania, and at a period when Egypt had no suzerainty whatever over Phœnicia. But unfortunately for that theory the "Phœnicians" who were associated with other Indo-Aryans in the diffusion of civilization in India, the Indian Ocean and Pacific are found to have been *not Semitic Phœni-*

---

says E. S. Hartland (ERE. 4, 423), "originated in a rude archaic condition of society and is frequently abandoned in favour of temporary or permanent burial." The custom is supposed to have arisen from affection and reverence for the dead and lothness to part with the corpse, and is in the direction of ancestor-worship, and had no such motive as in the Egyptian embalming.

[1] The desiccation of the dead body practised to some extent amongst the ancient American Indians seems explicable as in previous note. The occasional occurrence of a certain amount of more or less rude embalmment in cases of deferred inhumation, appears to have been no more associated with the peculiar Egyptian motive for mummification than the modes of burial in family vaults and in the catacombs of Rome and Malta, desiccation and partial embalming being occasionally practised for sanitary reasons.

*cians* but Aryans, descendants of the original Aryan "Phœnicians," and in civilization and race descendants of the Sumerians or Early Aryans.

---

In short, the solid and unassailable facts of history conclusively prove :—

(1) That Civilization did *not* first arise in Egypt, but arose amongst the Sumerians, who were *not* of the "Mediterranean" or "Iberian" dark narrow-browed long-heads, but of the fair long-headed, broad-browed and blue- or grey-eyed Aryan race ; and of the same type as the classic Greeks, whose heroes and heroines are described as tall, fair and golden haired and blue- or "glaucous" grey-eyed, and who are represented in their sculptures as broad-browed.

(2) That Civilization was introduced into Egypt in a fully fledged form by the Sumerians or Early Aryans about six hundred years after its origin by Sumerian emperors from Mesopotamia, the so-called "Predynastic kings" of Egypt about 2780 B.C., or possibly a little earlier.

(3) That Egypt for some centuries subsequent to Menes' establishment of the united kingdom of Egypt about 2704 B.C. was a chief centre for the diffusion of Civilization in the Mediterranean and beyond the Pillars of Hercules to the Tin-land of Britain.

(4) That Civilization in the closed rich land of the Nile Valley acquired a distinctive stereotyped local complexion in many of its customs, beliefs, arts and crafts and in the form of writing the Sumerian script, which was the source of the Egyptian hieroglyphs.

(5) That Egypt took little part in the diffusion of Civilization to the East.

(6) That in particular Egypt appears to have taken no part in the diffusion of Civilization to India, Indo-China and Oceania of "The Children of the Sun," and America.

# XIX

## Historical Effects of the Discoveries

The effects of these discoveries on Egyptian History are seen to be profound and far-reaching. Basic blanks in our knowledge of Early Egyptian History and on the unknown history and race of the founders of Egyptian Civilization are filled up, enabling us to reconstruct for the first time the Origin of Egyptian Civilization, Predynastic and Proto-dynastic on a solid historical foundation. The repercussions also momentously react upon Early European, Cretan, Mediterranean, Aegean, Indian and World History.

Egyptian civilization itself is demonstrated to be of Sumerian or Early Aryan origin and invention. It was introduced as a fully fledged Sumerian civilization by Menes and his ancestral " predynastic " Pharaohs, who were at one and the same time kings of Egypt as a Sumerian colony and also Sumerian world-emperors in Mesopotamia, who were not of the " Mediterranean " but of the Aryan race, and regularly called themselves " Goths " and boasted in their inscriptions in Egypt and in the Indus Valley of being lineal descendants from the first Sumerian or Early Aryan king, who was also the first traditional king of the Goths. The intrusive Sumerian civilization latterly acquiring in the closed Nile Valley a distinctive stereotyped local complexion has become known as " Egyptian " Civilization. The official records of these earliest Pharaohs in Egypt are written in Sumerian script and in the Sumerian or Early Aryan language, the root-words of which form the basis of the cultural and official words in the Ancient Egyptian language. The Egyptian hieroglyphic writing also is demonstrated to be derived from the picture-writing of the Sumerians or Early Aryans. And King Minos of Crete, the founder of Cretan or " Minoan " Civilization is proved to be identical with King

# HISTORICAL EFFECTS OF THE DISCOVERIES 175

Menes or Min of Mesopotamia, Egypt, Elam and the Indus Valley and no earlier than about 2704 B.C.

Apart from the flood of new light upon the origin of Egyptian Civilization and its authors, the new comparative method of research is of great service to scientific history by the more accurate Chronology which it introduces. Through the recovery by our new keys of the complete list of the Sumerian or Early Aryan kings continuously back to the first king of the First Sumerian or Early Aryan Dynasty, and bridging over the blanks hitherto existing, we are enabled for the first time to recover the real and exact dates, to within a few years of the actual dates, for the entire main line of Sumerian or Early Aryan kings back to the first king at the rise of civilization, and disclosing Menes' dynasty and the predynastic Pharaohs all in their due chronological positions and sequence.

Thus the real date for the first Aryan or Sumerian king and founder of the World's Civilization becomes about 3378 B.C.; and the real date for Menes, the founder of the First Dynasty of Egypt and the most basic date in Egyptian History, becomes no earlier than about 2704 B.C. And the great confusion that arises from the enormous discrepancies in the extravagantly conjectural dates for these epochs by the rival schools of Egyptologists, none of which are anywhere near the mark, will soon, it may be hoped, disappear from our research records and text-books. The determination of the real date for Menes will not only bring due order into Egyptian Chronology, but must react beneficially on inquiries into the history of the countries with which Egypt was connected during the period covered by its earlier dynasties, including Crete, Greece and Ancient Britain.

The Unity, thus demonstrated, of the three greatest of the ancient civilizations of the world, namely the Sumerian or "Babylonian," Egyptian and Indian, not to mention the Cretan, and the relatively rapid diffusion of the civilization by the same Aryan race as a military aristocracy through their colonizing world-empire, significantly attests the essential Unity of the World's Civilization and its diffusion from one original centre.

The discovery also that the royal tombs at Abydos in

## 176   EGYPTIAN CIVILIZATION OF SUMER ORIGIN

Upper Egypt are the mausoleums of the mighty world-emperors of Mesopotamia who propagated civilization over the old world, east and west, in their far-flung imperial colonizing sway, and selected the more alluring Nile Valley as their last resting place, is also of first-class historical interest and importance for the history of European and Mediterranean Civilization, as indicating that the Sumerian world-emperors had already at that early period deliberately transferred their home residence and centre of their affections and energies from the East to the West on the cool basin of the Mediterranean.

The leading part played by the Early Goths in the civilization not only of Egypt but of the World at large is of great historical importance. The Gothic race of Menes and Sargon and their dynasty, as well as of their ancestral Early Sumerians, the founders of the World's Civilization is fully attested. In this regard it is also noteworthy that the Mesopotamian empire, after it was lost to Menes' Gothic dynasty on the downfall of the latter, presumably through the emperors having spent most of their time in the more favoured Egyptian section of their vast unwieldy world-empire, was about 2493 B.C., after a period of semi-anarchy for twenty-six years, " seized by the troops of Guti [or Goth] Land," as the ancient official Kish Chronicle informs us from a contemporary record. These fresh sturdy Goths of Guti Land, a land found to have been located on the S.E. border of Asia Minor within the old homeland of the Sumerians, ruled Mesopotamia for long as a republican confederacy, under princely presidents holding office on an average of three or six years (like presidents in modern democratic times) ; and significantly several of those presidents, already at that early period over four thousand years ago, bore the distinctive Gothic titles of *Iarl* or *Iarla* and *Duk*, that is " Earl " or " Jarl " and " Duke." [1] And under their enlightened rule, misguided Mesopotamia so far recovered and materially prospered and attained such a renaissance in art that the latter part of this Guti or Gothic " dynastic " period is acclaimed by Assyriologists as " The Golden Age " of the Sumerians in Mesopotamia. Even the

[1] WMC. 357 f.

## GOTHS AS HUMANE IMPERIAL RULERS 177

later liberty-loving Goths of Europe, who in their cherished independence had kept aloof from the enervating luxury of the Greco-Romans, their remote kinsmen on the south, and only asserted their strength when their independence was attacked and their besought friendship betrayed by the unscrupulous Romans, have their humane and enlightened rule appreciatively noticed by Sir Flinders Petrie. Speaking of the wreckage of civilization in Europe by the terrific wholesale massacres and destruction by the invading hordes of barbaric Huns, the arch-enemies of the Goths, and by the Saracens and the intervening internecine wars of the nations resulting in the Dark Ages of Europe, he remarks: " Had the Goths been left alone in their humane occupation of Italy there might have been a set-back for two or three centuries ; but by expelling them Civilization was thrown fifteen centuries back." [1] And Freeman, maintaining that there was no set-back under Gothic imperial rule whilst it lasted, writes : " Italy under Theodoric (the Goth) was the most peaceful and flourishing country in the world, more peaceful and flourishing than it had been for a long time before [under the Romans] or than it has ever been since till quite lately. The dominions of Theodoric stretched far beyond Italy to the north, east, and west, and he ruled the West-Gothic kingdom in Gaul and Spain as guardian for his grandson." [2] But let us return to Egyptian Civilization of Gothic origin.

Deprived of some credit as a pioneer and originator, Egypt is compensated for the loss by the new interest which attaches to it as illustrating the manner and causes of the diffusion of civilization. Its history, as now restored, shows us the sudden almost instantaneous rise of a culture displaying a certain uniqueness of creative aptitude as the result of conquest by a powerful civilized neighbour ; and suggests that, as contrasted with the origin, the spread of civilization has little connexion with physique or any high racial quality, but may be achieved in the absence of these by the mere contact of advanced with backward peoples, provided facilities are afforded for the exertion by the former of their full educative possibilities on the latter—facilities for more rapid

[1] *Migrations*, the Huxley Lecture for 1906, *J. Anthrop. Inst.*, xxxvi [32].
[2] *General Sketch of European History*, 109.

spread being not unfrequently afforded by sympathetic imperial colonizing sway by civilized races and nations.

The effects of the Sumerian conquest were in a word the first large-scale demonstration of the truths enforced by so many later incidents of both ancient and modern history that intercourse, not race, is the main cause of the progress of nations. Many of the advances of civilization have resulted from race-mixture, in particular of the Aryan and Mediterranean and so-called "Celtic" types, though the mixing sometimes retarded or delayed progress. The inventiveness which is the basis of civilization and of national advance seems comparable in its evolution to an infection or inoculation rather than to a plant; and it has spread over the earth not so much as the results of special racial physique and inheritance, but by contact and converse of those who already possessed it with those who possessed it not—provided that the latter acquire or have already acquired the mental aptitude for creative progress which is associated with higher brain quality and larger frontal brain-lobes (no matter whether high or broad or long shaped), the deficiency in which brain size and quality admittedly accounts for so many of the dark backward races having remained so far behind the white, brunette and yellow peoples in their reaction to civilization.

And, seeing that it is much easier to control contacts than to change heredities we may derive from the rapid spread of civilization through the Nile Valley after its first discovery by the Sumerians far better auguries for the future of mankind and for their advance in science and the arts than can possibly be entertained by those who look upon certain special physical strains, whether Greek or Hebrew, whether Aryan or Mediterranean or Teutonic, whether white, brunette or yellow, whether short- or long-headed, as indispensable conditions of human progress.

# APPENDICES

## I

### SANSKRIT TEXT OF MAHĀ-BHĀRATA EPIC re MENES & HIS DYNASTY IN EGYPT

THE stanzas of the Sanskrit text of the *Mahā-Bhārata* on Manasyu's genealogy, of which I have given a literal transliteration on p. 4, occur in the text of the great Calcutta edition of that Epic, published in 1834, Vol. I, section 94, slokas 3695 to 3697.

This genealogy of King Puru's dynasty purports to have been recited by the Brahman priest and Vedic teacher Vaishampāyana to the Puru-line king Janamejaya (III), immediately after the Great Bhārata War, that is, as we have seen, about 650 B.C.

I here transliterate the Sanskrit writing of these three slokas into roman letters :—

" Pravīreshvara-raudrāshvastrayah-puttrā mahārathāh |
pūroh paushtyāmajāyanta pravīro vamsha krittatah |
Manasyura bhavatta smācchurasenī-sutah prabhuh |
prithvyāsh-catur-antāyā goptā rājīvalocanah |
Shaktah samhanaanovāgmī sauvīrītanayāstrayah |
manasyorabhavan puttrāh sūrāh sarve mahārattāh | ."

## II

### INDUS VALLEY SEALS OF SARGON & HIS FATHER WITH TITLES " PHARAOH " & " GOTH," AND MENTIONING EGYPT, DECIPHERED

THE great nest of imperial Sumerian seals in the second batch unearthed by the Indian Archæological Survey Department, under Sir J. Marshall, at Mohenjo Daro, which I have shown was the capital of the Edin colony of the Sumerian

## 180  EGYPTIAN CIVILIZATION OF SUMER ORIGIN

emperors of Mesopotamia, was, I found, especially rich in the seals of Sargon and his son Menes and their dynasty, and contained besides these also seals of Sargon's father, the Emperor Bur-Gin or Puru II, as shown in Plate IV. Of Sargon himself I found no fewer than six new seals, as enumerated at p. 30, in addition to the two formerly deciphered. In Seal 8 he seems to call himself "Son of Khamaesshi (or Egypt)," suggesting that his basket-birth incident occurred on the Nile.

In detailing the decipherment of Sargon's new seals and those of his father, I follow the order in which they are figured in Plate IV.

### The Great Bull Signet of Sargon, Nos. 1–2

This exquisitely beautiful seal, with the Indian humped bull as its chief device, and figured as No. 1 in Plate IV, with its impression showing the reversed direction in No. 2, reads as follows:—

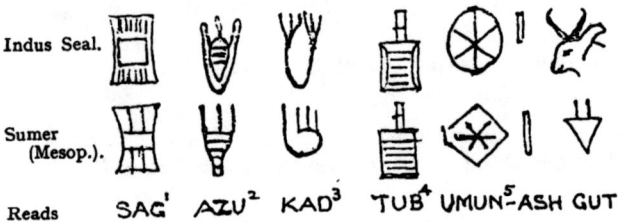

Reads  SAG$^1$  AZU$^2$  KAD$^3$  TUB$^4$  UMUN$^5$-ASH  GUT

Transl.: SAG, the Seer, the *Kad*, the tablet of the One Lord, The Goth.

FIG. 51.—Seal of Sargon as SAG, *The Seer*, The *Kad*, The One Lord, The Goth.

Here the title *Sag* appears to be short for *Sagara*, his title in the Indus seal previously deciphered,[5] and his solar title frequently used in the Indian Epics. And his title of "Seer" (for he was an initiated high-priest)[6] is repeated in the Indus seal of his son Aha-Men, No. 6, App. III.

Of the two following seals which are obviously those of "Sargon's" father, the first three signs are written very diagrammatically; but the evidence for their decipherment is detailed in the footnotes.

[1] B. 291; Br. 6461.    [2] B. 188; Br. 4666.    [3] B. 311; M. 5059.
[4] B. 157; Br. 3935.    [5] WISD. 69.    [6] WMC. 207 f.

# INDUS VALLEY SEALS OF SARGON & FATHER

### No. 3. Seal of Sargon's Father as PURU GINA of Egypt and Magan

This Seal No. 3, Pl. IV, reads:—

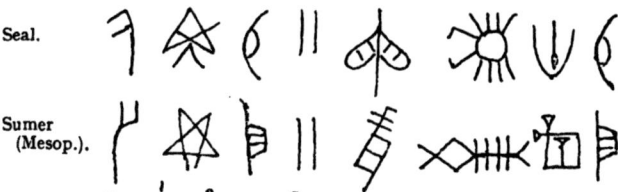

Seal.

Sumer (Mesop.).

Reads: PURU-AR² GAN³A MUSH - SIR   MA-GAN

Transl.: PURU the Ar, GINA of *Mushir* (Egypt) and *Magan*.

FIG. 52.—Seal of Sargon's Father as PURU GINA of Egypt and Magan.

The name in this and in the next seal are in series with those for this king in the archaic prefixed Isin Lists (see Table, p. 151 and WMC. Table opposite p. 140, No. 36, cols. 1 and 2).

### No. 4. Seal of Sargon's Father as PURU (or BU) PAR-GIN of Uridu Land

This seal reads:—

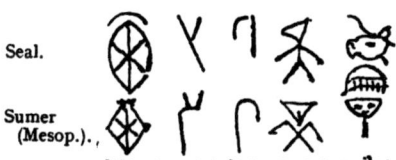

Seal.

Sumer (Mesop.).

Reads:   UMUN PURU PAR GIN URI-DU

Transl.: Lord of Lords PURU⁴ PAR-GIN of *Uridu* (or *Uriki*) Land.

FIG. 53.—Seal of Sargon's Father as PURU Par-Gin of *Uridu* or *Uriki* Land deciphered.

His title in this seal significantly is in series with his usual

---

[1] B. 325; Br. 7502; and cp. 6971 and 11255. It seems clearly this Serpent sign written freely, and identical with the second sign in next seal the identity of which is fully established.

[2] The Plough sign *Ar*. B. 261. With secondary meaning "exalt"= "Aryan" (WSAD. 15).

[3] *Gin* or *Gan*. B. 119; Br. 3171-3. This Indus form of the sign is very diagrammatic. It is clearly this Garden sign (and not the Sun sign *Udu*) as evidenced by its forming the second syllable of Ma-gan, and its recurrence in seals, Figs. 79 and 92, pp. 201 and 208.

[4] This sign is certainly the *Puru* or *Bu* Serpent-sign (see note 1) as evidenced by its repeated use with the *Bu* value in Pharaoh Kib-bu's seals in Figs. 86, 88 and 93, pp. 205-208.

## 182  EGYPTIAN CIVILIZATION OF SUMER ORIGIN

Mesopotamian title of *Urudu Gina* (cp. Br. 506), so-called "Uruka-Gina."

### No. 5. Seal of Sargon as Sharru Gin

This seal reads :—

Seal.

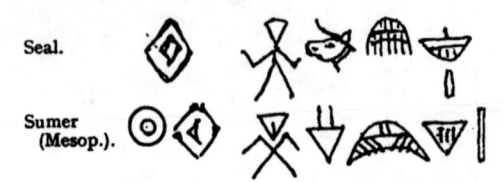

Sumer (Mesop.).

Reads :   SHARU' - GIN  GU- URI$^2$-KI- ASH

Transl. : SHARRU-GIN of *Uriki* Land.

FIG. 54.—Seal of SHARRU-GIN of *Uriki* Land deciphered.

[1] B. 364A ; Br. 6630.    [2] B. 316 (as before).

Here *Uriki* Land is the usual Sumerian name for the Semitic *Akkadu* and Amurru, as we have already repeatedly seen in the foregoing pages with detailed proofs. *Uri-ki* is sometimes read arbitrarily by Assyriologists as "Ur City," and occasionally as Uruk or "Ereah."

### No. 6. Seal of Sargon as Shar-Gin, The Great Khāti

This seal reads :—

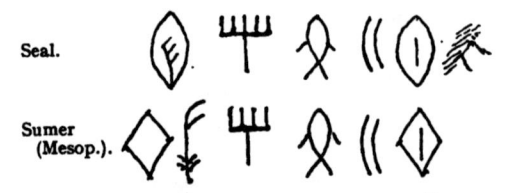

Seal.

Sumer (Mesop.).

Reads :  SHAR' GIN GAL- KHA- A- TI $^2$ GU....

Transl.: SHAR-GIN, The Great *Khāti* of . . . . Land.

FIG. 55.—Seal of SHAR-GIN, The Great *Khāti* of . . . Land deciphered.

The great importance of the use here by Sargon of the title *Khāti* or "Hittite" has been remarked in the text, see p. 30.

[1] B. 353 ; Br. 8221.    [2] Br. 7685.

# PHARAOH MENES' SEALS IN INDUS VALLEY

**No. 7. Seal of Sharum-Gin, The Gut of Agdu Land**
This seal reads :—

Seal.

Sumer (Mesop.).

Reads : SHAR- UM - GIN GUT GU· AG·DU-ASH
Transl. : SHARUM-GIN, The *Gut* of *Agdu* Land.
FIG. 56.—Seal of SHARUM-GIN, The *Gut* of Agdu Land deciphered.
[1] B. 353 ; Br. 8221.

**No. 8. Seal of Gan, The Son of Khamaesshi or Egypt at Agdu Land**
This seal reads :—

Seal.

Sumer (Mesop.).

Reads : GAN-PUR KHA-MA-ES-SHI[2] GU-AG-DU-ASH
Transl. : GAN, The Son[3] of *Khamaesshi* (or Egypt) at *Agdu* Land.
FIG. 57.—Seal of GAN, The Son of *Khamaesshi* Land deciphered.
[1] B. 160 ; Br. 4036.  [2] As before.  [3] *Pur* or *Bur*="Son." Br. 7522.

**No. 9. Seal of Gan, Bur the Piru or Baru (Pharaoh), The Gut of Uri-du Land**
This seal reads :—

Seal.

Sumer (Mesop.).

Reads : GAN-PUR PAR-U GUT GU-URI-DU-AS
Transl. : GAN, PUR, The Son, The *Gut* of Uridu Land.
FIG. 58.—Seal of GAN, PUR, The *Pharaoh*, The Gut of Uridu Land deciphered. (See p. 31 for these titles.)

Seal No. 10 in Plate IV is that of Menes or Aha, the son of *Sa-Gani* or "Sargon-the-Great" as King-Companion, and is included in the Menes' series of Indus Seals deciphered in Appendix III, here following.

## III

### MENES' SUMERIAN SEALS FROM THE INDUS VALLEY DECIPHERED

THE nine seals of Menes or Manis, which I discovered amongst the second batch of seals unearthed at Mohenjo Daro in the Indus Valley by the Indian Archæological Survey Department, under Sir J. Marshall, are figured in Plates IV, No. 10, and V, Nos. 1 to 8; and enumerated at pp. 43 f.

In these Menes, as ruler of the Edin colony, calls himself variously Men, Mānshu, Aha (or Akha), Aha (or Akha)-Men, and Aha-Mena. In three he bears the title of "Under King-Companion," in three the higher title of "Lord-Companion," and in one the imperial title of "The One Lord." In two he is styled "The *Gut* (or 'Goth')"; in one he is "Aha the Overthrower of King Mush" (that is his younger brother in Mesopotamia); in one he is "Under King-Companion in Magan and Mush (-(?) sir), or Egypt; and in three his sonship of Sha-Gani or Gin (that is king "Sargon-the-Great") is recorded.

It is also noteworthy that in the seals of this dynasty we now find for the first time the use of the "Ligature" in Sumerian or Aryan writing, that is the use of signs written by attached strokes to other signs when forming compound words. This especially occurs with the use of the possessive *ge* stroke for "of."

# PHARAOH MENES' SEALS IN INDUS VALLEY 185

### Seal of Aha, son of Shagani, The Pharaoh at Edin Land

This seal, No. 10 in Plate IV, reads :—

Indus Seal.

Sumer (Mesop.).

Reads :   UMUN-MAN A-HA MAR SHA-GA-NI BARA GU-EDIN-AS

Transl. : Over-Lord-Companion AHA, the son of SHA-GANI, The *Pharaoh* in Edin Land.

FIG. 59.—Seal of AHA, son of SHA-GANI, The *Pharaoh*, deciphered.

[1] B. 532 ; *Shakanu* or *Shakunu*, Br. 6821, 12182-5. On *Sha-ga-ni*, Br. 11952, 11942, 11947.
[2] B. 301 ; Br. 6880.

This seal indicates that Aha Menes was joint king with his father Sargon at the Edin colony ; but whether this was before or after his revolt is not evident.

### No. 1. Seal (Pl. V) of Menes as Mānshu, The Pharaoh, at Edin Land

This seal reads :—

Seal.

Sumer (Mesop.).

Reads :   SHAG-MAN MA— ANSHU  BARA GU-AG-DU-AS

Transl. : Under King-Companion MĀNSHU, The *Pharaoh* at Edin (or Agdu) Land.

FIG. 60.—Seal of MĀNSHU, The *Pharaoh* at Edin, deciphered.

[1] On Horse-sign *Anshu*, B. 211 ; Br. 4981, defined as " Mountain ass."

186  EGYPTIAN CIVILIZATION OF SUMER ORIGIN

### No. 2. *Seal of Aha-Men*

This seal reads :—

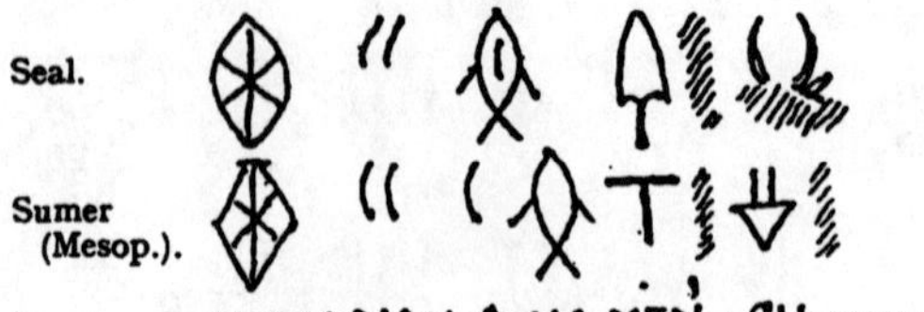

Seal.

Sumer (Mesop.).

Reads : UMUN-MAN A-HA-MEN'-GU·······

Transl. : Lord-Companion AHA MEN . . . . at . . . .

FIG. 61.—Seal of AHA MEN deciphered.

[1] B. 478 ; Br. 10355.

### No. 3. *Seal of Aha-(?)Men the Gut or Goth*

This seal reads :—

Seal.

Sumer (Mesop.).

Reads : UMUN-MAN A-HA-MEN' GUT GU- AG-DU-AS'

Transl. : Under King-Companion AHA-(?)MEN, The *Gut*, at Agdu Land.

FIG. 62.—Seal of Aha-(?)Men, The Gut, deciphered.

[1] B. 240 ; Br. 5510.

### No. 4. *Seal of Aha The One Lord, Son of The Goth Gin*

This seal reads :—

Seal.

Sumer (Mesop.).

Reads : UMUN-AS̀ SU-HA MAR GUT GIN-GE GU-AG-DU-AS̀

Transl. : The One Lord AHA, son of The Goth GIN at Agdu Land.

FIG. 63.—Seal of The One Lord AHA, son of The Goth GIN, deciphered.

# PHARAOH MENES' SEALS IN INDUS VALLEY 187

*No. 5. Seal of Aha-(?)Man, son of The Seer Gin*

This seal reads :—

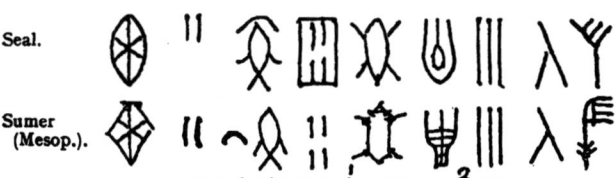

Seal.

Sumer (Mesop.).

Reads :   UMUN-MAN A-HA-MAN MAR AZU²-ES-TAR GIN

Transl. : Lord-Companion Aha-(?)Man,[1] son of the Seer [2] Esh-tar Gin.

FIG. 64.—Seal of Aha-(?)Man, son of Seer Gin, deciphered.

[1] These four strokes may read *Man-Man* as before ; or the whole sign, with its enclosing tabulature, may read, " Of the house of *Sha*," *i.e. Sha-Gani* (see above, Fig. 59).

[2] This sign, although its interior is not cross-lined, is clearly the same sign as in Sargon's seal as " The Seer " (Fig. 51).

*No. 6. Seal of Aha as Overthrower of King Mush*

This seal reads :—

Seal.

Sumer (Mesop.).

Reads :   A-HA   SIG[1]   UKU²- MUSH

Transl. : AHA, The Overthrower of King MUSH.

FIG. 65.—Seal of AHA as Overthrower of King MUSH deciphered.

[1] B. 175 ; Br. 4420.    [2] B. 150 ; Br. 3862.

*No. 7. Seal of Aha of Magan and Mush(-sir)*

This seal reads :—

Seal.

Sumer (Mesop.).

Reads :   SHAG-MAN A-HA MA -ES-GAN-MUS´

Transl. : Under King-Companion AHA of MA(esh)-GAN (and) MUSH(-sir).

FIG. 66.—Seal of AHA of *Ma-gan* and *Mush(-sir)* deciphered.

188    EGYPTIAN CIVILIZATION OF SUMER ORIGIN

*No. 8. Seal of Aha Mena at Uri-ki (Akkadu) Land*

This seal reads :—

Seal.

Sumer (Mesop.).

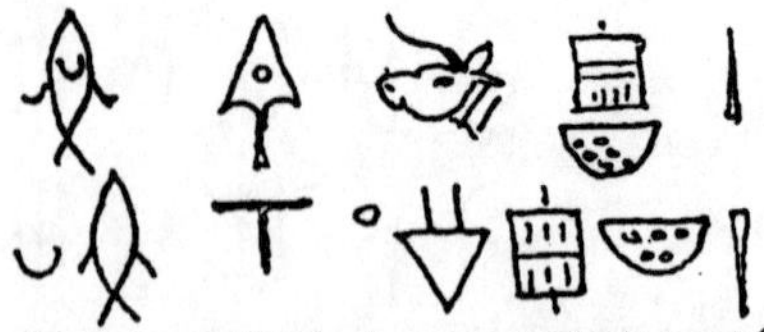

Reads :   A-HA-MEN-A GU-AG-DU-AS'

Transl. : AHA MENA at Uriki (Akkadu) Land.

FIG. 67.—Seal of AHA MENA at *Uriki (Akkadu)* Land deciphered.

## IV

### GREAT EBONY LABEL FROM MENES' "TOMB" AT ABYDOS WITH SUMERIAN INSCRIPTION DECIPHERED

THIS large ebony label figured in Plate VII (in duplicate), which was found in the "tomb" of Menes at Abydos by Sir F. Petrie, as described on pp. 61 f., is of astounding historical importance through its inscription.

In the following pioneer decipherment of this inscription, reference should be made to my careful drawing of the signs in Fig. 13 on p. 62.

The inscription is in four lines, each separated, as is usual in Sumerian writing, by horizontal bars into separate compartments or registers. The direction in which the writing is to be read is indicated by the direction in which faces of the animal signs in the pictographs are turned, the reading being through the face of the animals. Thus the first line is seen to read in the retrograde direction, from right to left; the second line in the reverse direction to that, namely from left to right; and the third line in the same direction as the first; and similarly so the last line. Therefore the inscription is written in "The Ox-plough-furrow" or boustrophedon fashion, as in the ancient Hittite and Early Greek inscriptions. The pictographs are artistically grouped and composed for pictorial effect.

The first hieroglyph of the first line, beginning at the pierced hole for the string of the label (see Fig. 13), has been supposed by Egyptologists to picture "two ships."

# MENES' TOMB EBONY LABEL DECIPHERED

This may be so, but it also resembles a conventional form of the plumed-crown head-sign for " king " in Sumerian, as shown in the annexed decipherment table (Fig. 68). All the other hieroglyphs readily equated with those of the Early Sumerian writing of the Predynastic and First Dynasty Pharaohs, and those of the Indo-Sumerian seals and the standard Sumerian diagrammatic lithic script of Mesopotamia, as seen in the tables below, though several of the signs are drawn in more realistic and naturalistic fashion. And all yielded directly good sense in the Sumerian language when read syllabically.

The language is Sumerian or Early Aryan. Only one Semitic idiom occurs, in the Semitic plural form of *Mushrim* for " The Two Egypts (Upper and Lower) "—the Chaldean and Hebrew *Mizraim*—as the subject aborigines of Egypt were Semitic speakers, and presumably at that time called their united land " Mushrim." The Sumerians, as we have seen, called it *Mushsir*, and the Akkads *Mushri* and *Mushur;* and that land is still called by the Arabs *Misr*.

### First Line of Menes' Great Ebony Label

Let us now take up the lines seriatim for decipherment as in my previous tables, and place the signs in the usual Sumerian or Aryan direction for reading from left to right. Full references are given for the authentication and literal translation of all new signs; but where signs have been identified in previous Tables their references are here mostly omitted.

The first line reads :—

Reads: LUGAL MIN-AŠ BARA MUŠ-ŠIR-MAD-AGA-TAB-GE

Transl.: " King MIN-ASH (or MAN-ASH) (or " Manash of Ships "), the Pharaoh of *Mushsir* (Egypt), the Land of the Two Crowns.

FIG. 68.—Line 1 of Menes' Tomb-Label deciphered.

[1] On *Man* value, Br. 9945; and on *Min*, 9946. The first sign may possibly read *Ma-ma* or " Ships."
[2] B. 325; Br. 7507.   [3] B. 304; Br. 6949. Pictures a plumed crown.

## 190  EGYPTIAN CIVILIZATION OF SUMER ORIGIN

The king's name here spelt *Manash* or *Minash* has been obviously inserted in small signs within the king sign, after the latter was written. Its *Minash* phonetic value is in series with his *Minos* title amongst the Cretans and Greeks. The Fly sign here, drawn naturalistically, with the phonetic value of *Mush* and forming the first syllable of Mush-sir or "Egypt," has hitherto been supposed by Egyptologists to be "the shield and arrows of the goddess Neith," a late goddess, although the sign is seen to be decidedly different from the Neith emblem.

The Sumerian name *Mush* for this winged insect, which is here represented like a winged Scarab beetle, seems to me possibly the source of the later Egyptian name *Mukhrr*[1] for the scarab beetle, the sacred flying beetle of the Egyptians. And this suggests that this ancient name of *Mush-sir* for Egypt, in which the affix *Sir* is pictured by a Serpent (disclosing the source of our modern word "Serpent"); a sacred totem animal of the pre-Sumerian Semitic aborigines in both Egypt and Mesopotamia, probably designated Egypt as "The Land of the Scarab and the Serpent."

The continuation of the First Line of the Label reads :—

Label.

Sumer (Mesop.).

Reads :   KU¹  MIM²  WI³ - ŠU⁴  XU(BAK)⁵  GIR⁶  AHA⁷  MIN-AŠ⁸

Transl. : "the perished dead one in the West, of the (Sun-) Hawk race, AHA-MIN-ASH."

FIG. 69.—Line 1 of Menes' Label continued, decipherment.

[1] *Ku* "perished," B. 481 ; Br. 10526 f.
[2] *Mim* = die, M. 1923, pictures a pole surmounted by the skin of an animal, B. 116.
[3] *Wi* = "West" as before. The *shu* affix is seen on full sign in the duplicate label, 4–8, as before. The pair of long strokes with a shorter medial one inside the square seem probably to be the name *Man* or *Min* duplicated with the intermedial stroke *ash*, thus giving the name *Minash* or *Manash*. Otherwise it is a diagrammatic form of *Bara* or "Pharaoh" as before.  4–8 as before.

---

[1] BD. 295A.

## MENES' TOMB EBONY LABEL DECIPHERED

### Second Line of Menes' Great Ebony Label

The second line of this label I read as follows :—

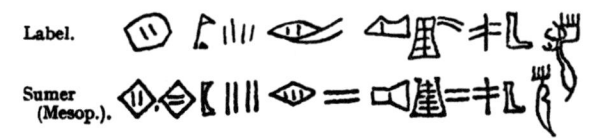

Label.

Sumer (Mesop.).

Reads : SAB ŠU² A-A³ KI⁴-TAB⁵ AB⁶-ZU⁷-TAB⁸ KHAD-DU¹⁰ LUSA¹¹

Transl.: " of the Lower (Sunset or Eastern) and Sunset (Upper or Western) Waters and their Lands and Oceans, the Ruler the King."

FIG. 70.—Line 2 of Menes' Label deciphered in first part.

¹⁻¹¹ As before. The king sign reads *Lu-sa* as well as Lu-gal (see previously).

This imperial title of " King of the Lower or Sunrise Ocean (*i.e.* the Persian Gulf, Indian Ocean or Arabian Sea with Red Sea) and of the Upper or Sunset or Western Ocean (*i.e.* the Mediterranean) and of their Lands," was the regular world-empire title used by Sargon and most of his dynasty on their own monuments in Mesopotamia, and *it is here written by the same Sumerian signs.*

The Sumerian pictographic signs for this imperial title are artistically grouped together to form a whole design, which has suggested to Egyptologists, who were unable to decipher them, " a man making an offering, with two signs above, possibly *uāau*, 'alone.' Behind him is a bull running over wavy ground into a net stretched between two poles. . . . At the end is a crane or stork standing on a shrine. The third line shows three boats in a canal or river passing between places. In the fourth line is a continuous line of hieroglyphs the first of such that is known. . . . On the backs of these tablets are painted signs; a spindle and a *men* sign, with two kinds of gaming pieces."[1] And Prof. Griffith conjectured that the hieroglyphs in the last line read " who takes the throne of Horus."[2] (!)

[1] PRT. ii. 21.   [2] *Ib.* 51.

## 192  EGYPTIAN CIVILIZATION OF SUMER ORIGIN

Proceeding with the decipherment of the rest of this second line, we find it reads as follows:—

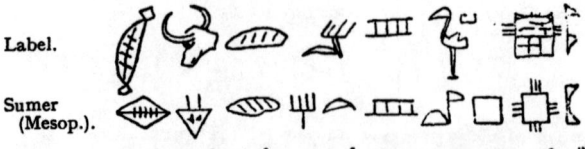

Label.

Sumer (Mesop.).

Reads: MUŠ¹-RIMU² KI(3)³ SA⁴ ŠA⁵ GANA⁶ XU⁷-GIR⁸ BARA⁹-ŠU¹⁰

Transl.: of MUSHRIM Lands, son of Great SHA-GANA (or SHA-GUNU or GIN) of the (Sun-) Hawk race, the Pharaoh, the (pre-)deceased.

FIG. 71.—Line 2 of Menes' Label continued decipherment, recording his sonship of SHAGANA or "Sargon."

1, 3-10 As before.     2 *Rimu* is the Semitic Akkadian for *Am* or Wild Bull.

Here Menes in this Egyptian label is called "The son of the Great Sha-Gana," that is "Sargon." And significantly the second syllable of his father's name is spelt here by the identical Sumerian hieroglyph as in some of the First Egyptian Dynasty inscriptions and in one of his Indus seals.¹ The form *Sha-Gunu* is seen to be in series with the common Indian Epic form of his name as *Sha-Kuni*.

### Third Line of Menes' Great Ebony Label

The third line reads:—

Label.

Sumer (Mesop.).

Reads: MA¹-EŠ² KAD³ NIR⁴ U⁵-URU⁶ RA⁷-DU⁸ MA-EŠ⁹ XU¹⁰-RA¹¹-DU¹²

Transl.: The Commander-in-Chief of Ships. The Commander-in-Chief of Ships, the complete course made to the End of the Sunset Land, going in ships. He completed the inspection of (continued in next line).

FIG. 72.—Line 3 of Menes' Label deciphered.

1-3, 4, 7 As before.

⁵ *Du*=command of a ship, B. 180; M. 3014. The sign resembles somewhat *Nir*, "Lord," B. 282.

⁶ The Š sign here is not *Uru* as figured but *Ushu* "The end of the Sunset" (B. 403) as in Fig. 39, p. 118.

⁸ *Du* or *Shar*=great, complete, Br. 8231.

⁹-¹² Signs as before—the word thus formed *Xura-du*="inspect, behold," Br. 8526.

---

¹ WISD. 64 f.

## MENES' TOMB EBONY LABEL DECIPHERED

The realistic ship-pictographs in this line give us the earliest Sumerian or Egyptian drawings of a multiple-decked ship or galley with cabins and high prow for deep-sea voyaging at this early period. These pictures may be compared with the earlier single-decked masted deep-sea ship carved on the reverse of the ivory dagger handle in Plate V of WMC. (the upper ship). It was doubtless with this multiple-decked class of ship that Menes invaded Upper Egypt by way of the Red Sea. It is noteworthy, however, that the mast appears to have been omitted, presumably for want of space; for in the inscriptions of Manis Tusu and others in Mesopotamia, the diagrammatic Sumerian ship-sign has a mast with a yard near its top, as seen in second line of Fig. 72. Significantly, the ships on the label present a general resemblance to the old Phœnician triremes of the ancient navies of the Mediterranean, which were propelled by oars in three tiers, with cabin at the stern, and which were the regular warships of the Phœnicians and Greeks until about 360 B.C., and which though carrying a mast and sail are usually drawn without them, as they were only used occasionally. The 30 (or 31) strokes on the double bar line below the ships may possibly represent the number of the vessels of Menes' fleet which took part in his voyage to the Far West; or they may be reduplications of the sign for "land," as in lines 1 and 2.

It is also noteworthy that Menes bears here the title of "Commander-in-Chief of Ships," by a name spelt *Kad-du*, which is in series with, and apparently coined on the model of, the Khād or *Khaddu* title borne, as we have seen, by his remote ancestor the Sumerian sea-emperor Uruash, the founder of the First Phœnician Dynasty, some four centuries earlier, and which is the earliest known naval power in history. This title is evidently synonymous with the "Sea-lord" (*Nunna*) title which was borne by Uruash and his descendants. And as King Minos in Greek and Cretan tradition, he was a great admiral, with "swift ships," who sailed the seas to extend and defend his dominions.

## 194 EGYPTIAN CIVILIZATION OF SUMER ORIGIN

*Fourth Line of Menes' Great Ebony Label*

In the fourth and last line of the label is given the very important territorial name of the land in the Far Western Ocean where Menes' "built a holding" and died. The name is artistically formed into a monogram. I have provisionally deciphered this monogram with the aid of a lens as reading " *U-ra-ni-i* Land " as detailed below, and I venture to believe that it will prove correct. It is unfortunately omitted in the rougher duplicate label (Plate VII B) presumably from being too complex ; but a space was left for it, and its associated wedge-sign of " built " is duly graved therein, and gives with its hieroglyph context the same reading, minus the place-name, as in the more complete label.

This fourth line I read :—

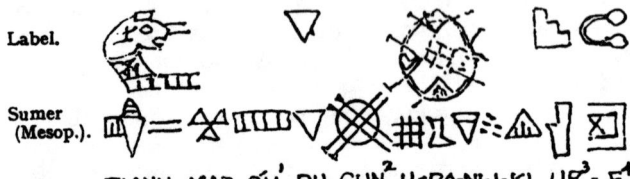

Reads :  TiANU- MAD-SU'-DU GUN$^2$ U-RA-NI-I-KI UR$^3$- E$^4$

Transl. : of the Western Lands. He built a holding (or possession) at Urani Land. At the Lake of the Peak.

FIG. 73.—Line 4 of Menes' Label deciphered.

[1] B. 481 ; Br. 10509.  [2] B. 307 ; Br. 6985.
[3] B. 205 ; M. 3311.  [4] B. 61 and 263 ; Br. 1182, 5841.

The term for " The Western Lands " is here written by the usual Sumerian sign of the head of a lion, doubled by two strokes, but the sign is drawn more realistically. This term designated the Western Lands as " The Lands of Lions," that is the old shaggy alpine lion of Phrygia and the Taurus of Asia Minor, as figured in Pl. I, WMC., and the African lion of the Libyan and Mauretanian or Moroccan border of the Mediterranean. This same sign we have seen used in the same sense in the Egyptian inscriptions of Menes' descendants in his dynasty. The sign has also the phonetic value of *Pirig*, and is defined as " a people," which

# MENES' TOMB EBONY LABEL DECIPHERED

thus appears to give us the Sumerian source of the name "Phrygian." And its Akkad value of *Labu* or "Lion" probably gives us the source of the name "Libya." It was commonly used in later Mesopotamian inscriptions for Amurru or Amorite Land, including Tyana (? *Tiana*) in Cappadocia, N. of the Cilician Gates, an old Hittite capital, which was latterly a prefecture of the Greeks and Romans, and thus implying that "The Western Land" of the Sumerians commenced at Hittite Asia Minor and Syria-Phœnicia, and included the Mediterranean lands west of Egypt. This totemistic title of "The Land of the Lions" would seem to be analogous to that for Egypt as "The Land of the Scarab Beetle and the Serpent" (*Mush-sir*).

The continuation of the last line of the label reads as follows :—

Label.

Sumer (Mesop.).

Reads : NAM$^1$ XAL$^2$ MUŚ LUGAL MA-ANŚU-ŚU$^3$ GAR$^4$ LAĹ$^5$-IŚ$^6$-DU$^7$

Transl.: Fate pierced (him) by a Wasp (or Hornet), The King of the Two Crowns MĀNSHU. This bored tablet set up of hanging wood is dedicated (to his memory).

FIG. 74.—Line 4 of Menes' Great Ebony Label completed decipherment.

[1] *Nam*, "Fate," pictured by a swallow, B. 85 ; Br. 2103.
[2] *Xal*, "pierce," B. 2 ; Br. 78.
[3] "Tablet writing," also "bored," B. 365, 8673, 8688.
[4] "Set up, or place," B. 532 ; Br. 11978.
[5] "Hang," Br. 10081.
[6] "Wood," B. 258 ; Br. 5697.
[7] "*Ru*" present, dedicate, B. 1 ; Br. 24. This sign which I have accidentally omitted in my tracing in Fig. 13, will be seen quite distinct as the last sign in the photograph in Pl. VII.

On the identification of the locality of this "Uranī Land" in the Far Western Ocean, where Menes' met his tragic death, see text, p. 65 f.

## V

**FIRST EGYPTIAN DYNASTY PHARAOHS' SUMERIAN SEALS FROM THE INDUS VALLEY DECIPHERED—COMPRISING KINGS NARAM OR NARMAR, GANERI (KHENT OR KUNTI), BUGIRU (BHAGIRATHA), DUDU OR DAN (DHUNDU), AND SHUDUR KIB OR KING KIBBU OR QA (OR SUHOTRA)**

*With titles of " Governor," " Pharaoh," and " Goth "*

THE seals of the other Pharaohs of the First Dynasty of Egypt, the descendants and successors of Menes, which I discovered amongst the second batch of Sumerian seals unearthed at the old capital of the Edin colony in the Indus Valley, are shown in Plates V, XI and XV, and are enumerated in the text therewith. Here I give my pioneer decipherments of their inscriptions on the same model as the others.

These seals whilst concretely evidencing that the First Dynasty Pharaohs, subsequent to Menes, continued to hold the Indus Valley as a colony of their Egyptian empire along with Mesopotamia, are also of the immense further historical importance in that they give in many instances the genealogies of the Pharaohs back to King Gin or " Sargon," and to his son Aha Menes—the seals of the last two kings Dudu or Dan and Shudur Kib or Qa being especially rich in genealogical details. And significantly King Gin or " Sargon " is again given his title of UKUS, or descendant of the first King of the First Dynasty of the Kish Chronicle, which he uses in his own inscription in Egypt (p. 23), and which is his *Aikshvaki* title in the Indian Chronicles.

### PHARAOH NARMAR OR NARAM'S SEALS FROM THE INDUS VALLEY

We have seen how the son and successor of the Emperor Manis or Menes, namely *Narām Enzu* in his own Mesopotamian inscriptions, wrote his name with the Sumerian pictograph of " The Wild Bull," and used that pictograph freely in his inscriptions in Egypt, where he adopted the form of name of *Nar-mar*.

# PHARAOH NARMAR'S SEALS IN INDUS VALLEY

In his Indus Valley seals we now find that he also calls himself NERĀM, in which *AM* is written by the same Sumerian sign as used by him in his Mesopotamian inscriptions as *Naram*. This title for him, as Nerām, is also repeated on seal, Fig. 91, as *Neramma*. He used therein usually the name of *Ner* and *Maru* and *Mar Nera*. And like his father Menes and his grandfather "Sargon," he as well as his descendants freely call themselves *Gut* or "Goth." This title of *Ner* or *Nera* is written by a Sumerian sign which designates him as "Lord of the Deep Waters." And we have seen that traditionally as "The Wild Bull" or Minotaur son of Minos he ruthlessly dominated Crete and the adjoining isles of the Mediterranean.

In three out of his four seals he bears the viceregal title of "Under King-Companion," with the addition, as in most of the other Indus seals, of the words "at Agdu Land"—that is *Agudu*, or "Agade" in Mesopotamia. In one, however, he is called without any subordinate title "The Gut of The Lower Land," that is the land of the Lower Sea or Indian Ocean. Significantly, in two of these he calls himself "The *son* of the great Lord Gin" (*i.e.* "Sargon"), and not as the grandson of the latter. This is in keeping with the later Babylonian tradition, as we have seen, which calls Naram Enzu the "son" and not the grandson of King Gin or "Sargon."

### No. 1. *Elephant Seal of Narmar as Mar-Nerām*

This seal, with its chief device as the Elephant or "Great Bull," is figured in Plate XI, Nos. 9 and 10, for seal and its impression respectively. The Elephant was an appropriate symbol for this king, whose name was "Wild Bull," as it is generally styled in the East "The Great Wild Bull," and this is also its name in Sumerian as *Am-si*;[1] and our modern word "Elephant" is supposed to be derived from the Semitic *Aleph*, "an ox." But besides the Elephant he is also called *Ama* or *Am* in this seal by the Wild Bull sign.

The name here if reading "Land of Ships" is of

---

[1] Cp. MD. 826; and in Tibetan, as translated from the Sanskrit WBT. 390.

## 198 EGYPTIAN CIVILIZATION OF SUMER ORIGIN

historical interest as identifying Edin presumably with the ancient "Potala" of Indian tradition, the site of which had become lost. Pot-ala, or "Abode of Boats (*Pot*)," was supposed by some to have been possibly on the Indus, and "Patala" was the name given by the Greek historians of Alexander to the last port in the Delta of the Indus, whence the Macedonian on leaving the Indus Valley sailed westwards to the Persian Gulf and Mesopotamia.

As the Tiger seal in Fig. 74, WMC. p. 548, bears the name of *Marru* and is of the same general form as this seal, seems to have two dots within its Ox-head sign besides the large top one, and thus may also read *Am*, it thus seems possible that it also may be a seal of Narmar or Naram, and not that of his earlier namesake, Maru or Madgal.

This seal reads :—

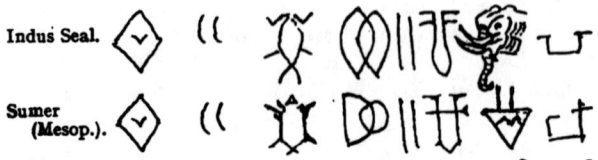

Indus Seal.

Sumer (Mesop.).

Reads :   SHAG- MAN   MAR - NER[1] A GUT   AM$^2$- MA$^3$

Transl. : Under King-Companion MAR-NERAM-MA the Gut, or NERA the Gut AMMA.

FIG. 75.—Seal of NARMAR as MAR-NERAM-MA deciphered.

[1] On this sign and its meaning of "Lord of the Deep Waters" (Anunaki), see before. On the *Am* value of this *Gut* sign when it bears two crescents or dots, see B. 183.

[2] The usual Sumerian word for "elephant" is *Am-si*, and in Akkadian *Pilu* or *Piru*, MD. 826. The sign is here obviously used for "Ox" as a territorial word for "Land" (M. 4038).

[3] *Ma*="ship," as before.

# PHARAOH NARMAR'S SEALS IN INDUS VALLEY

### No. 2. Seal of Narmar as Nera

This seal, No. 11 in Plate V, reads as follows :—

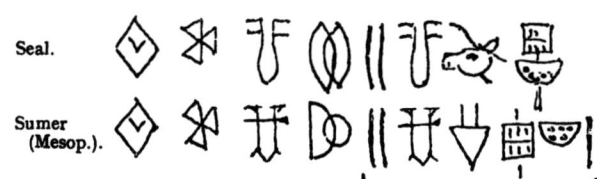

Seal.

Sumer (Mesop.).

Reads : SHAG-MAD GUT NER-A GUTGU-AG-DU-AS

Transl. : Of the Lower (Eastern) Land, the *Gut* NERA, The Gut at Agdu Land.

FIG. 76.—Seal of Narmar as NERA deciphered.

[1] On this *Ner* name, see before. Here the Ox-head signs seem to contain three small dots inside, thus giving the value of *Ama*.

### No. 3. Seal of Narmar as Marru, son of the Lofty Goth Gin

This seal, No. 1 in Plate XI, reads :—

Seal.

Sumer (Mesop.).

Reads : SHAG- MAN MAR-RU-U TUM-U GUT ARA NER-ES GIN

Transl. : Under King-Companion MARRU, the Lord, Son of the *Gut*, the *Ara*, The Lord of Deep Waters GIN.

FIG. 77.—Seal of Nuder, King-Companion MARRU, Son of ARA, The Gut of the Deep Waters.

[1] A Fly, B. 390; Br. 6058. It is significant that the Fly sign *Tum* is used to spell out the Sumerian word Son (*Tumu*), so as to leave no ambiguity as to this designation here.

[2] This seems the Plough sign, which as *Ara* has the meaning of "Lofty," the source of *Ara* or "Aryan."

Here Narmar is called "Son" of the Goth Gin or "Sargon"; and the *Ara* title of the latter appears to designate him as "The Aryan," and is in series with the latter's Indus Valley seal as *Sag-ara*, and his father's seal, Fig. 52, p. 181.

## No. 4. Seal of Narmar as Nerau

This seal, No. 2 of Plate XI, reads :—

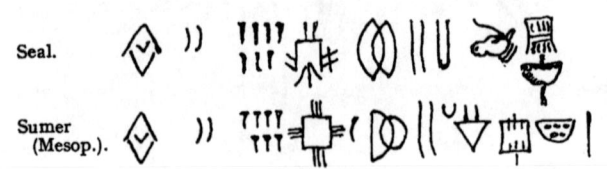

Seal.

Sumer (Mesop.).

Reads : SHA-MAN IMIN-BARA-GE NER-A-U GU-AG-DU-ASH

Transl. : Under King-Companion of The Heavenly Pharaoh, NERAU at Agdu Land.

FIG. 78.—Seal of Narmar as NERAU deciphered.

[1] Br. 12200. On this *Imin* or this *Himin* or " Heaven " of the Goths, see before.

### PHARAOH, SHA-GIN II, GAN-ERI, OR " KHENT'S " SEALS FROM INDUS VALLEY

The Indus Valley seals of this Pharaoh, the third of Menes' Dynasty, and the great-grandson of his namesake, the Great Gin, Gan or Shar-Gin or " Sargon," and the son of Narmar or Naram-Enzu of Mesopotamia, are four in number and are especially interesting as disclosing along with his Egyptian tomb-inscriptions the proper form of his name as written in his Mesopotamian inscriptions as Sumerian emperor, which is now shown to read *Gani-Eri*, and not " Gali-sharri " or " Shar-Gali-sharri," as hitherto read by Assyriologists. And we have seen that in one of the contemporary Egyptian inscriptions he is actually styled " Sha-Gani II." He is the " Khent " of Egyptologists and the *Kunti* of the Indian lists. His title also in the first of these Indus seals now deciphered, namely " Lord Gin of Serpent (*Bu*)-Land," is interesting as a designation of The Land of Egypt ; and it probably implies that his capital was at Buto in the Lower Delta.

These seals are shown in Plate XI, Nos. 3-6. The first seal reads as follows :—

# PHARAOH " KHENT'S " SEALS IN INDUS VALLEY

### No. 1. Seal of Gan-Eri of Bu (Bu-to) Land and Agdu

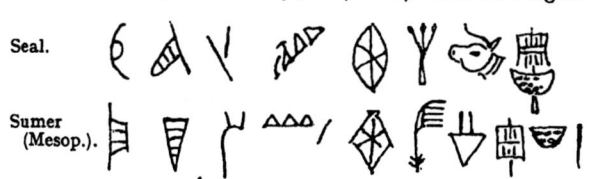

Seal.

Sumer (Mesop.).

Reads: GAN-ERI' BU-MAU-GE UMUN GIN GU-AG-DU-AS'

Transl.: GAN-ERI of *Bu* (*Bu-to*) Land, The Over-Lord GIN at *Agdu* Land.

FIG. 79.—Seal of GAN-ERI of Bu (Bu-to) Land, Lord GIN of *Agdu* Land deciphered.

[1] B. 229; Br. 5377. Pictures a Sling. In the more realistic Indus pictogram the strings of the sling, which are absent in the Mesopotamian diagram, are shown.

### No. 2. Seal as Sha-Gin

This seal, No. 4, Plate XI, reads :—

Seal.

Sumer (Mesop.).

Reads: SAMAN-SA-GIN-AGDU

Transl.: Under King-Companion SHA-GIN at *Agdu* Land.

FIG. 80.—Seal of King SHA-GIN deciphered.

### No. 3. Seal as Lord Gin

This seal, No. 5, Plate XI, reads :—

Seal.

Sumer (Mesop.).

Reads: AS-GIN AG-DU

Transl.: Lord GIN at *Agdu* Land.

FIG. 81.—Seal of Lord GIN at *Agdu* Land deciphered.

[1] B. 534; Br. 12196, and cp. 428 f.

## 202 EGYPTIAN CIVILIZATION OF SUMER ORIGIN

### No. 4. Seal as King Gan, Gin or Dili, the Gut King of Khāmaesh (Land)

This seal, No. 6, Plate XI, reads :—

Seal.

Sumer (Mesop.).

Reads : SAG-MAN GAN GAL-KHA-A-MA-ES UK-DILI TUB GIN GUT

Transl. : Under King-Companion GAN, of the Great *Khāmaesh* (Land) King DILI, the tablet of GIN the *Gut*.

FIG. 82.—Seal of King GAN, GIN or DILI, King of *Khāmaesh* deciphered.

¹ B. 150 ; Br. 3862.          ² B. 1 ; Br. 27.

The title of *Dili* borne by him here is significant, as it is found on his ivory label in Egypt, and is his title in the Indian King-lists of *Dili-pa*.

### PHARAOH BUGIRU OR BAGERI'S (OR BHAGIRATHA'S) SEAL FROM INDUS VALLEY

One seal of the fourth Pharaoh of Menes' Dynasty I found in the Indus Valley second collection. It is somewhat roughly carved and forms No. 7 in Plate XI. It reads as follows :—

Seal.

Sumer (Mesop.).

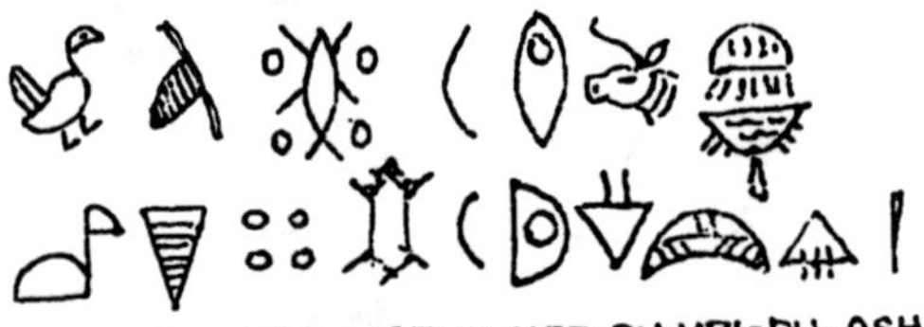

Reads :   BAG-ERI  GAR-MAR-U  NER GU-URI-DU-ASH

Transl. : BAGERI of the House of MARU-NER, The *Gut* of *Uridu* (Akkadu).

FIG. 83.—Seal of BAGERI, the *Gut* at *Uridu* deciphered.

This seal is very important historically as disclosing the short reign of this Pharaoh, the 4th of Menes' dynasty, and his identity with Bugiru, the 4th Egyptian King of that dynasty and with Bhagiratha of the Indian King-lists. He is seen to be obviously the first of the four temporary kings

## PHARAOH DAN'S SEALS IN INDUS VALLEY

who ruled in Mesopotamia only for a total period of three years in the interregnum following the death of King Gani-Eri and the accession of the son of the latter, King Dudu. In the Kish Chronicle and in the Isin lists, those scribes write his name as " Ni-gi-gi " or " I-gi-gi," of which name no inscription has ever been found. It now seems probable that in their corrupted reading they mistook the sign *Bu* for the somewhat similar *Ni* sign ; and it is evident that he held the Indus Valley as well as Mesopotamia and Egypt.

It is noteworthy also that he claims descent from Maru-Ner, that is Narmar, and not from Gan-Eri or Sha-Gin the Second.

### PHARAOH DUDU, DAN OR " DEN'S " SEALS FROM INDUS VALLEY

Two fine large seals of this Pharaoh, the 5th of Menes' Dynasty, and the son of the Emperor Gani-Eri, I find in the second Indus Valley collection. They are shown in Plate XI, Nos. 8 and 9. He also bears in his Mesopotamian inscriptions the same title of Dudu, as well as in the Kish Chronicle (WMC. p. 61).

#### No. 1. *Seal of Dudu or Dan as Son of Gani-Eri*

This very large seal (No. 8 in plate) reads :—

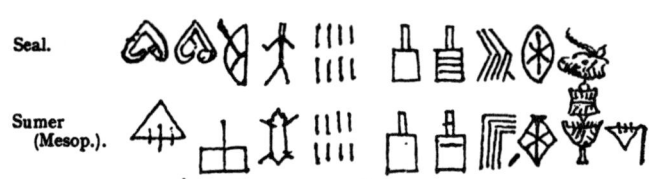

Reads : DU-DU' DAN² MAR GA¦NI³ ERI⁴ TUB TAX-CE-U GUAG-DU

Transl. : DUDU DAN, Son of GANI-ERI, the tablet of the Minister, The Lord at *Agdu* Land.

FIG. 84.—Seal of DUDU DAN, Son of GANI-ERI, The Lord Minister at Agdu deciphered.

[1] This is clearly a conventional form of the Sumerian " Mound " sign *Du* duplicated.
[2] B. 279.
[3] These eight strokes have the Akkadian value of *Shakanu* or *Shukunu*, Br. 11978, 12185. These values are obtained by giving different polyphonous values of the four stroke-sign as *Sha* + ga + ni (cp. Br. 11942 f.). Thus the double four strokes give us *Ga-ni*.
[4] B. 39 ; Br. 889.

Here the spelling of the second element in this king's father's name is by the same sign as the father himself uses in his own inscriptions in Mesopotamia. And he gives the equivalent title of *Dan*.

### No. 2. *Seal of Dudu or Dan, son of Gan-the-Second and of the House of Aha, Ner-Sin and Gin the Ukus*

This second seal (No. 9 in plate) is of immense historical importance as giving his genealogy back to Gin-the-Great or " *Sargon,*" *who is significantly called herein* " *The* UKUS," that is a descendant of the first Sumerian king of the First Sumerian Dynasty and the King *Ukusi* of the Kish Chronicle and King Ikshvaku of the Indian lists, as we have seen. And Sargon calls himself, or is called in his Egyptian tomb inscription, *Ukus* or *Ukussi* (p. 23), thus strikingly confirming the accuracy of my decipherments. We have also seen that " Sargon " in the Indian Chronicles is repeatedly called " a descendant of the first Aryan solar king Ikshvaku." And it is noteworthy that in this seal Dudu or Dan calls himself literally " The Son of GAN-*the-Second.*"

This seal reads :—

Seal.

Sumer (Mesop.).

Reads : DAN MAR GAN-TAB GAR-A-HA U NER-ES GIN-U-KUS GUT

Transl. : DAN, the son of GAN-*the-Second* of the House of AHA and NER-SIN [2] ruler of (line) of UKUS, The *Gut.*

FIG. 85.—Seal of DAN, son of GAN-*the-Second* of the House of AHA and the Lord of Deep Waters GIN-*the*-UKUS, The Gut, deciphered.

[1] B. 251. The only known specimen of this sign recorded is the late Assyrian one figured in this second line ; but it essentially agrees with this ancient Indus Valley form. On the *Kus* value for this sign instead of *Kush*, cp. Br. 5615 and 5024.

[2] *Ner-eš* or " Lord of the Deep Water." It reads *Ner-Sin*, and thus is in series with his Mesopotamian title of Nar-am-Sin.

# PHARAOH KIB OR QA'S SEALS IN INDUS VALLEY

## Pharaoh Shudur Kib, Kibbu or Qa's Seals from Indus Valley

I found no fewer than six signets of Shudur Kib,[1] the last of the Pharaohs of Menes' Dynasty, in the second batch of the Indus Valley seals from Mohenjo Daro or Edin. They, like those of his father Dudu or Dan, are rich in genealogical details, and they show that this Pharaoh ruled the Indus Valley colony of the Sumerian empire as well as Mesopotamia, where some of his records have been found.

### No. 1. *Seal of Shudur Kib as Kibbu Shuha*

This seal, No. 10 in Plate XV, reads :—

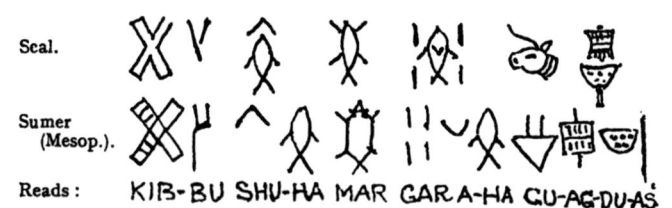

Seal.

Sumer (Mesop.).

Reads :    KIB-BU SHU-HA MAR GAR A-HA GU-AG-DU-AS

Transl. : KIBBU SHUHA, son of the House of AHA at *Agdu* Land.

FIG. 86.—Seal of KIBBU SHUHA of House of AHA deciphered.

### No. 2. *Seal of Shudur Kib as The Pharaoh at Agdu*

This large seal, No. 1 in Plate XV, reads :—

Seal.

Sumer (Mesop.).

Reads :   KIB BARA TUB U GU-AG-DU-AŚ

Transl. : KIB, The Pharaoh, the Seal of the Lord at *Agdu* Land.

FIG. 87.—Seal of KIB, The Pharaoh deciphered.

---

[1] See TDC. 63, where, however, the transcription of the name is hopelessly misread and Semitized.

## 206  EGYPTIAN CIVILIZATION OF SUMER ORIGIN

The Fire-worship of this king, which was an aspect of his Sun-cult is devoutly expressed in his seal No. 3. And significantly he calls himself therein " the Son of Shar Gin II and Dan, the former being the great-grandson of Sar-Gin I or Sargon the Great.

*No. 3. Seal of Shudur Kib as Kib the Gut, Kibbu, son of Dan and Shar-Gin and of House of Ner(-Mar ?)*

This seal, No. 2 in Plate XV, reads in its first line :—

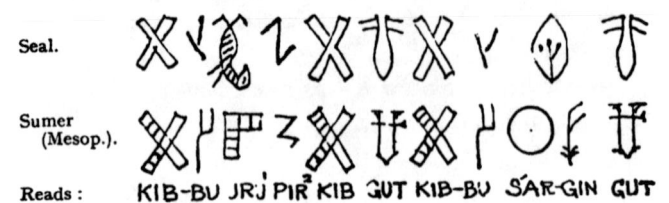

Seal.

Sumer (Mesop.).

Reads :  KIB-BU JRJ PIR KIB GUT KIB-BU SAR-GIN GUT

Transl. : KIBBU, devotee of Fire, KIB the *Gut*, KIBBU of SHAR-GIN *Gut*.

FIG. 88.—Seal of SHUDUR KIB as KIBBU, son of DAN (the son of) SHAR-GIN the *Gut*—1st line deciphered.

[1] B. 516. The pictograph of a Dog and Dog's head respectively, with sense of " devoted," M. 8684 f.
[2] B. 347 ; Br. 8141, 8147. *Pir*=" Fire," and Sumerian source of that English word.

The second line of this seal reads :—

Seal.

Sumer (Mesop.).

Reads :  DAN GE MAR GIN   GAR NER GU- URI-(KI-AS)

Transl. : End of DAN the son, of the House of NER (-MAR ?) at *Uridu* (Akkadu) Land.

FIG. 89.—Seal of SHUDUR KIB or KIBBU, son of DAN, 2nd line deciphered.

This seal inscription thus literally reads : " KIBBU, devotee of Fire, KIB the Gut, KIBBU of SHAR-GIN *Gut* and DAN the son, of the House of NER(-MAR ?) at *Uridu* (Akkadu)."

## PHARAOH KIB OR QA'S SEALS IN INDUS VALLEY 207

This king's title in his seal No. 4 equates with his *Suhotra* title in the Indian king-lists.

### No. 4. Seal of Shudur Kib as Shuhahatura Kibbu, Kib the Gut of House of Sha-Gin and Neramma

This large seal, Nos. 3–4 in Plate XV, is important in containing the name of his ancestors as Shagin (II) and *Neramma*, that is Naram Enzu, reads in its first line :—

Reads: TUM' SU-HA-HA-TUR-A KIB - BU KIB GUT

Transl. : For the life of SHUHAHATURA KIBBU, KIB the *Gut*.

FIG. 90.—Seal of SHUHAHATURA KIBBU, KIB the Gut, 1st line deciphered.

[1] B. 390. Fly sign = " Life," M. 6816.
[2] B. 95 ; B. 2665 ; MD. 181, pictures a Tomb.

The second line, in Fig. 118 is of great historical importance in giving his genealogy back to Nerāmma or Narām or Narmar.

The second line of this seal reads :—

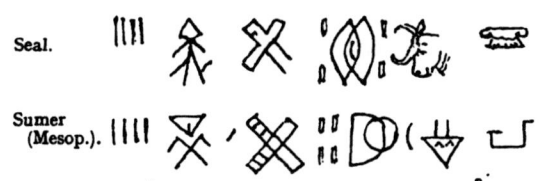

Reads: SHA'-GIN-GE KIB GAR-NER-A-AM-MA

Transl. : of (the House of) SHA-GIN, KIB of the House of NERAMMA.

FIG. 91.—Seal of SHUHAHATURA KIB, 2nd line deciphered.

[1] Br. 11952.   [2] *Gu* = " Land," M. 4038.

The inscription on this large seal thus reads : " For the Life of SHUHAHATURA KIBBU, KIB the *Gut* of (the House of) SHA-GIN, KIB of the House of NERAMMA. Compare with this *Neramma*, the form of that name in seal Fig. 75.

## 208 EGYPTIAN CIVILIZATION OF SUMER ORIGIN

His next seal, No. 5, appears to designate him as the Pharaoh of Magan, in which, however, the *Ma* syllable is not expressed. As *Gan* means " Garden," it may thus read " The Garden," which was, as we have seen, a designation of the Edin colony on the Indus.

*No. 5. Seal of Shuhudur Kib, Pharaoh of (Ma-)Gan at Agdu*

This seal, No. 5, Plate XV, reads :—

Seal.

Sumer (Mesop.).

Reads : SHU-HU-DUR KIB PAR GAN GU-AGDUA'S

Transl. : SHUHUDUR KIB, Pharaoh of (Ma-?) GAN at *Agdu*.

FIG. 92.—Seal of SHUHUDUR KIB Pharaoh deciphered.

[1] B. 160 ; Br. 4035.
[2] On *Dur* value, cp. Br. 8631 and 11319.

In his next seal he bears the title of Sea-emperor (if this *Ner* be not intended for *Ner-a* a contraction, as we have seen, for Narām or Narmar). And he records his descent from Aha Men or Menes.

*No. 5A. Seal of King Kib as* KIBBU *Lord of the Deep and Son of* AHA MEN

This seal, No. 5A in Plate, reads :—

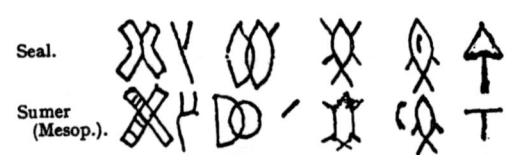

Seal.

Sumer (Mesop.).

Reads : KIB-BU NER-GE MAR A-HA-MEN

Transl. : KIBBU, Lord of the Deep, son of AHA MEN at . . . Land.

FIG. 93.—Seal of KIBBU, Lord of the Deep and son of AHA MEN deciphered.

Here the description " Son " of Aha Men means, as not infrequently, " descendant."

## PHARAOH KIB OR QA'S SEALS IN INDUS VALLEY

### No. 6. Seal of Shudur Kib as King Qa

This small seal, No. 6 in Plate XV, which is noteworthy as being engraved to give an impression which reads in the non-reversed direction, reads:—

Seal.

Sumer (Mesop.).

Reads: QA LUGAL MA-ES-GAN-MUSH

Transl.: QA, King, of MA(-esh)-GAN, MUSH(-sir).

FIG. 94.—Seal of Shudur Kib as King Qa of Magan and (?) Egypt deciphered.

[1] B. 63.

The final *Mush* in this seal is presumably short for Mush-sir or "Egypt."

### SEAL OF SHUDUR KIB'S SON GUT-SHU

This small seal of a son of Shudur Kib, named Gut-Shu, No. 7 in Plate XV, reads:—

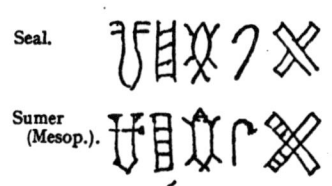

Seal.

Sumer (Mesop.).

Reads: GUT-SU MAR PAR KIB

Transl.: GUT-SHU, son of Pharaoh KIB.

FIG. 95.—Seal of GUT-SHU, son of Pharaoh KIB deciphered.

Nothing is otherwise known of this son of Pharaoh Kib. He did not succeed his father, who ended The First Dynasty of Menes in Egypt and the Dynasty of Sargon-the-Great in Mesopotamia. But he is now seen to have been in the Indus Valley colony, though without any official title.

## SEAL OF KING URIMUSH, YOUNGER SON OF SARGON-THE-GREAT

Here it is convenient to give the seal of King Urimush, the younger son of Sargon-the-Great, who succeeded the latter for nine years on the Mesopotamian throne (see Kish Chronicle, p. 35), who has left several inscriptions as emperor at Agudu, and who was massacred and succeeded by Manis-Tusu or Menes in Mesopotamia, as fully recorded in our text.

This seal, which I found in the second Indus Valley collection, is No. 9 in Plate XV. It reads:—

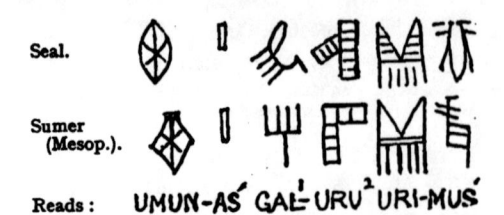

Seal.

Sumer (Mesop.).

Reads: UMUN-AS' GAL-URU² URI-MUS'

Transl.: The One Over-Lord, the Great Hero URI-MUSH.

FIG. 96.—Seal of King URI-MUSH deciphered.

[1] This sign might also read *Pesh*, " The Monster Fish," B. 303, a title of Lord of Deep Waters, *Anunaki*, MD. 553.
[2] B. 516.     [3] B. 316; M. 5311 f.

Here it is seen that King Uri-Mush uses the imperial title; and in his Mesopotamian inscriptions he also calls himself emperor.

# INDEX

A.=Aryan; C.=civilization; dyn.=dynasty; E.=Egyptian; f.=father; G.=Gothic; k.=king; M.=Mesopotamian; n.=name; s.=son; S.=Sumerian; t.=title.

ABYDOS, predyn. tombs at, discovered of Sargon-the-Great and his ancestors, 1, 5, 14 f., 16 f., 19 f., 22 f.; 1st dyn. tombs at, as Sargon's son Menes' dyn., 14, 32 f., 57 f., 63, 68; tomb inscriptions at, in S. deciphered for first time, 14 f., 19 f., 23 f., 25 f., 58, 62 f., 92 f., 104 f., 107 f., 111 f., 123 f., 127 f.

Acchura Seni, queen of Sargon and m. of Menes, 4, 24, 27, 37; E. tomb of, 24 f.; inscription deciphered, 24 f.; and see Lady Ash

Achaians as A. race, x, 168

Admiral, Menes as, 63 f.

Aegean, aborigines as Iberian, x, 35; C. as S., 71 f.

Ægyptus t., 5

Aeria, n. of Egypt and Crete re Aryan colony, 167

Agade, n. of Sargon's and Menes' dyn. M. capital; see Agdu and Akkad

Agdu or Agudu, M. capital of Sargon-the-Great and his dyn. on Indus seals, 30 f., 35, 43 f., 88 f., 96, 183, 186, 197; see Agade

Agriculture, E. as S., 33, 53, 146

Aha, t. of Menes, 3, 9, 43, 44, 57, 69, 109, 125; S. equivalent used by k. Manis, 9, 43; see Tusu; its hieroglyph same as in S., 9, 57

Aha-Man or -Men, t. of Menes, 44

Aha-Manj, 78; and see Manj, Men, Mena, Menes and Tusu

Aha-Man, t. of Menes, 43, 44, 78 tab.

Aikshvāka, t. of solar Aryan k. including Menes and dyn., 21; see Ikshvāku and Ukusi

Akha, variant of Menes' t. Aha, 9; and see Ahu

Akhenaten, k., 163

Akkad or Akkadu, Semitic n. for S. city n. Uri or Ari, 30 f.; n. used by Narmar in E. for M. capital, 95; see Agdu, Ari, Uri

Alexander - the - Great, route of, re Menes, 46, 198

Alexandria, library, 14

Alphabetic (later) use of E. Hieroglyphs, 7, 78

Amarna period, 48

American (Early) C. of Indo-Aryan Origin, 172

Amorite land, 13, 28, 88, 96 f., 120, 127, 129, 195

Amorites, as Aryans and S., x, 35; as sea-merchants, 13, 28, 96 f., 168 f.; in Ancient Britain, 13, 168; Phœnicians as, 168 f.; see Amuru, Marutu, Muru

Amulets, E., of S. origin, 33, 73, 138

Amuru, n. for Amorites, 13, 96 f.

Animals, sacred and symbolic, E. as in S., 163 f.; see Bull, Deer, Goat, Hawk, Goose, Lion, Serpent, Wolf

Ankh, as the S. Sun-Cross, 165, 166

Anshan, 38, 45; see Persia

Ansu-mat, t. of k. Narām *Enzu* or Narmar, 37 f.

Ap, predyn. k., 15, 19 f.; tomb inscriptions deciphered, 19; real n. of, 19 f.; see k. Gin, Kad

Ara, t. of "Sargon," 199; of Menes, 181; of Narmar, 199

Arabia, re Menes, 1, 45 f.; conquered by Menes or Manis, 45 f.; silver mines in, 45

Ari (? "Aryan"), S. n. for Amorite, 167

Aryan as racial term, x, 34 f.

Aryan race of Menes and dyn., viii f., 2 f., 7 f., 31 f., 34, 51, 80 f., 130, 151, 167, 174 f., 179 f.

Aryans, Early, king-lists of, identical with S., viii f., 2 f., 6 f., 80 f., 150 f.

Asa-Manja, t. of k. Menes, 2 f., 6 f., 37 f.

Asar, Asari, E. and S. t. of Osiris, 5; t. of 1st S. k., 5; E. hieroglyph of, identical with S., 5

Aset, goddess of S. origin, 163 f.; see Isis

Ash, lady, n. of Sargon's queen in E. and M., 4 f., 25; E. tomb inscrip-

211

tion of, deciphered, 24 f. ; see Acchura Seni
Athens re k. Narmar, 72
Ati-ensak, t. of k. Naram, 81
Atlantis, 67
Atmu or Atumu, god, in E. as S., 164 f.
Atta, k., 81
Axe, double, in Crete as S., 73
Axes, of 1st E. dyn. of S. form, 33 ; 2-headed in S., 74
Azab Merpaba, k., 78, 123

B, E. hieroglyph sign, originally = R, 137
Babylonia, see Mesopotamia
Bagid or Bagidgiru, 4th k. of 1st E. dyn., 78, 106 f., 202 ; his E. inscriptions, 106 ; his Indus seal, 107, 202 ; E., S. and Indian lists, 107 ; identity, see Bhagiratha
Bahu or Bahuka, as k. "Ro" and f. of Sargon, 16 f. ; as predyn. k. in E., 16 f. ; his E. inscriptions deciphered, 16 f. ; his Indus seals, 17 ; real date of, 151 ; and see Par-Gin, Puru-Gin, Ro
Bahu-Bida, 6th k. of 1st E. dyn., 122 f. ; his n. deciphered, 123 ; identity in S. and Ind. lists, 123
Baku, k., 17 ; see Bahuka, Puru-Gin, Ro
Bal, Bala, t. of Set demon in E., S. and Gothic, 165 ; see Set
Banners of k. Narmar, inscriptions of, deciphered, 94 f. ; see Standards
Baptism rite, non-Semite, in E. as S. and A., 166
Bar, t. for Pharaoh, as S., 4, 13
Bar-Gin, k., n. of f. Sargon, 16 f. ; as predyn. k. "Ro," 15 f. ; his E. inscriptions deciphered, 16 f. ; his Indus seals deciphered, 181 ; his real date, 151 ; see Par-Gin and Ro
Basket-birth legend of Sargon on Nile re Moses, 28, 31, 136, 183
Beads, glazed, of E. affinity at Stonehenge, 168
Beard in S. usage, 40
Beliefs, religious E., of S. origin, 167 f.
Bezau, k., 138
Bhagiratha, 4th k. of 1st E. dyn., 77, 106 f.; his E. inscriptions deciphered, 107 ; seal of, in Indus Valley, 107, 202 ; see Bagid ; date of, 151 ; genealogy of, 203
Bidi, 6th k. of 1st E. dyn., 77, 123 ; see Bahu-Bida, Miebidos
Bird-form vases in E. as S., 33
Bismya, S. amulet button re E., 138
Boats, see Ships

Bowl, stone, of k. Udu, 141, 145, 159
Bowls, stone, E. as S., 33
Brick-walls, recessed, E. as S., 33
Britain, colony of Sargon and Menes in, 13, 66, 70, 81, 115, 119 ; cup-mark inscriptions as E., 57, 70, 116 f., 118 f. ; death of Menes in (?), 67 ; 1st dyn. E. mythology in Early, 115 f.
Bronze Age in Britain, 13 ; in Crete, 71 f.
Bronze chariot of Menes' father, 4
Bull, on k. "Ka's" or Sargon's great signet, 30 ; t. of Narmar, 72 f. ; Cretan, see Minotaur and Wild Bull
Burial, customs, E. like S., 33 ; funerary furniture and offerings, E. like S., 33 f.
Buru-Gin, k., 16 f. ; see Puru-Gin and Puru
Busahap, t. of k. Dudu or "Den," 113
Buto, capital of Ancient Egypt, in delta, in S., 27, 48, 50, 200
Button, amulet, 33, 73, 138 ; seals in Crete as S., 73
Byblos, site of Osiris' coffin, in Syria re Gothic tradition, 164

CALENDAR year reckoning, E. as S., 146
Carchemish re Menes, 49
Cartouche, of S. origin, 114
Catti, n. for Khatti or Hittites and Ancient Britons, 81
Caucasian race, unscientific t., x
Cemeteries at Abydos re S. at Kish and Ur, 33
Charms, see Amulets
Children of the Sun civilized by Indo-Aryans, 170 f.
China C. re Indo-Aryan, 169 f.
Chisels of 1st E. dyn. of S. form, 33
Chronology, conjectural of Egyptologists, 139 f. ; long and short date schools, 156
Chronology, real and dated, of Egypt, predyn. and 1st dyn. recovered, viii f., 56, 60, 139 f., 146 f., 151 f. ; of Menes and his dyn., 56, 60, 151, 155 f.
Civilization, E., of S. origin, 33, 55, 167 f., 174 f. ; date of E. C., 2 f., 139 f., 174 f. ; diffusion of, 133, 167 f., 175 f.
Clay figurines, E. as S., 33
Clay sealings, E. as S., 15 f., 33, 73
Cobra, see Serpent
Coinage introduced to China by India, 169
Colonization of Egypt by Sumerians, 2 f., 13 f., 27 f., 55 f., 167 f.
Constitutional govt. of Menes, 52 f.
Contracts, land, by Menes in M., 53

# INDEX

Copper chisels, E. as S., 33; mines, E., 50; tribute, 88
Coptos, early captivity of Menes, 54 f., earliest E. statues at, 54; see Koptos
Cornwall tin mines re Sargon and Menes, 13, 66
Cosmetics in Ancient Egypt and M., 33, 91
Cow, in M. Moon-cult of Chaldea as in E., 162; see Hathor
Cretan or Minoan C., as S., 71 f., 131; date of, 75, 141, 151, 158, 175
Crete, Aeria n. for, re Aryans, 167; Dorians in, 75; k. Minos of, as Menes, 71 f.; funerary rites in, as E., 73; Minotaur of, as k. Narmar, 72 f.
Cross emblem, of Menes, 50 f., 166; Menes' red Cross (St George's), 51, 166; Ankh as, 165 f.; see Cruciform
Cruciform mon. of Manis or Menes, 46, 50 f.
Cultivation and irrigation, E. as S., 33
Culture of Menes and dyn. identical with S. of Manis' period in M., 33
Cup-mark inscriptions, E. as S., 57, 66, 70; as in Ancient Britain, 57, 66, 70
Cuttle-fish, E. sign, 85
Cylinder-seals, E. as S., 20, 33, 73
Cyprus, k. Narmar's seal in, 72

D, an original value of B hieroglyph Foot-sign, 116 f., 118 f.
D or Du, Mound sign in E., 110 f.
Daedalus, 66
Dan or Dana, n. of 5th k. 1st E. dyn., 78, 108 f., 203 f.; see Den, Dudu and Dundu
Date, fixed, of E. C. found by new synchronisms, E. and S., 139 f., 174 f.; of Cretan C., 75, 141, 151, 158, 175; of Menes' accession, 56, 81, 157 f.; of Menes' death, 157; of Menes' dyn., 151 f., 157 f.; of Menes' invasion of Egypt, 36 f., 157; of predyn. Pharaohs, 157 f.; of rise of World's C. no earlier than c. 3380 B.C., 154 f.; no C. in Egypt before c. 2780 B.C., 14 f.
Dates of early E. history, real v. conjectural, 140 f.; for World's C. earlier than c. 3380 B.C. fictitious, 154 f.
Dating by archæology, fallacies of, 15, 141
Dead, burial of, E. as S., 33; resurrection of, 114 f.
Decipherments, first, of E. predyn. and 1st dyn. inscriptions, 16 f., 19 f., 115 f., 188 f.; of Indus Valley seals of Pharaohs, 17 f., 29 f., 43 f., 88 f., 103 f., 125, 180 f., 184 f., 196 f., 200 f.

Delta, ancient n. for E., in S., 27 f., 48; see Iatu
Den Setui, 5th k. of 1st dyn., 78, 108 f., 112 f., 203; real n. and date of, 151; see Dan, Dudu
Devil-worship of aborigines, 27, 163 f.
Dhundu, Indian form of n., 5th k's. n. Dundu or Dudu
Diffusion of C., by S. colonization, 167 f.; not by Egypt to India and Indonesia and America, 168 f., 173, 177
Dili or Dili-pa, t. of 3rd k. 1st dyn., 102 f., 104 f., 202; date of, 151
Dilmun, Semitic n. for Iatu or Nilemouth, 13, 27, 48; as n. for Lower Egypt, 27, 48
Diorite blocks of M., from Sinai peninsula, 40, 45 f., 47, 73; see Magan
Dorians, A. tribe in Crete, 75
Dudu, Dan or Dundu, 5th k. of 1st E. dyn., 77, 78 f., 80, 108 f.; agreement in S. E. and Indian lists, 78 f., 108 f.; descent from Menes or Manis discovered, 78 tab., 109 f., 114, 204; date of, 108, 151; E. inscriptions of, deciphered for 1st time, 113 f.; invokes resurrecting Sun-angel Tasia or Tascio as in S. and Ancient Britain, 114 f.; name in E. written by same sign as in S. in M., 116 f.; real date of, 151; Seals of from Indus colony deciphered, 109, 203 f.; tomb of in Egypt, 114 f.; t. as Usaphaidos, 113; t. as Ukus or descendant of 1st S. k 108, 204
Duke, t. of Early Sumerians, 176
Dundu, n. for k. Dudu, 110 f.
Dunu, variant of Dudu, 78
Dur city, 88
Dur-Ilu conquered by Sargon as (?) Troy or Ilos, W. M. C., 206
Dynastic Egyptians, of Aryan race, viii f., 2 f., 34 f.; as Sumerians, ix f., 2 f., 34 f.; as Early Aryans, 77 f.
Dynasty I, E., of Menes identical with k. Manis dyn. in M., 2 f., 6 f., 78 f., 130 f.; Aryan origin of, 2 f.; fixed dates for kings of, 139 f.
Dynasty II, E., as (?) S. or Aryan, 132 f.
Dynasty V, predyn. k. list of, 14

EAGLE banners of k. Narmar, 95; inscriptions of deciphered, 97 f.; and see Hawk (Sun-)
Earl, t. of Early Sumerians, 176
Earthenware, decorated, predyn. and 1st dyn., E., like S. of Sargonic period, 33
Eastern C., separation of, from Western and E., 132

Ebony labels of tombs of 1st E. dyn. deciphered, 57 f., 61 f., 188 f.; Menes' grant, 61 f., 188 f.; Menes' lesser, deciphered, 58; Dudu or Dan's, 116; see Ivory labels
Edda epic, mythology of Goths in agreement with early E., 163 f.
Egypt, as a pre-Sargonic colony of Sumerians, 2 f., 167 f.; as diffuser of C., 133, 167 f.; dyn. Pharaohs of, as S., 2 f., 7 f., 31 f., 34, 57 f., 80 f., hieroglyphs, of S. origin, viii, 8 f., 159 f.; independent, rise of, 134; inscriptions of predynastic and 1st dyn., in S. script deciphered, 16 f.; see Decipherments; language of ancient, as radically S., viii, 33; origin of n., 2, 5
Egypt, conquest of, by Menes, route and date, 37 f., 55 f., 76; by Sargon-the-Great and his ancestors, route and dates, 27 f., 77; Indus Valley relations with 1st dyn. of, 41 f., 103, 167; mentioned in Indus Sumerian seals, 31 f.; Phœnicians in Early, 49 f.
Egypt, names of, as Aeria and Heriē (or "Land of Aryas"), 167; as Gopta, 2; as Dilmun, 13, 27, 48; as Iātu mouth, for delta, 13 f., 48; as Ham or Kham, 48 f.; as Khamasi, 49; Khamaessi, 31, 48 f.; as Khemia, 49; as Kimash, 50; as Misr or Mushsir, 48 f.; as Mushrim, 63, 192; as Pu or Bu (Buto), 27, 48, 50, 200
Egyptian Chronology, real, discovered, see Chronology
Egyptian Civilization of S. origin, see Civilization
Egyptian Hieroglyphs derived from S., see Hieroglyphs
Egyptian Inscriptions, predyn. and 1st dyn. in S., deciphered for 1st time, see Decipherments
Egyptian King-lists, disagreements in, 78 f.; monuments agree with S. and A., 78 f., 150 f.
Egyptian Language derived from S., see Language
Egyptian Mythology of S., A. and G. origin, 163 f.
Egyptian Synchronisms with early M. discovered, 2 f.
Egyptologists' translit. of E. names, 7 f., 16 f., 79 f.
Elam, as S. colony of M., 38 f., 52; Menes, formerly governor of, 38; Menes' statue from, 39; Narmar re, 99
Elephant, in Early American Maya art of Indian origin, 72; Narmar's seal of, 89, 197 f.

Embalming, 24, 172 f.
Empire, world-, of Sargon and Menes, re rapid diffusion of C., 175 f.; re unity of C., 175
Enamel and inlaid eyeballs of E. statues, as in S., 33, 39 f.
Erin, as (?) Urani, Land of Menes' death, 67 f.
Europe, S. n. for, 12 f., 96, 120, 129; see Tianu and West
Eye, the royal, t. of Menes, 2, 4; paint for, in E. as in M., 33 f., 91 f.
Eyes, blue, of 1st dyn. and predyn., E., 34 f.; in inlaid statues, as in S., 34, 40

Face painting, E. as in S., 33 f., 91
Faience and coloured glazed beads, E. and S., 33; in Ancient Britain, 168
Falcon, see Hawk
Farming of Menes, 59
Fenkhu or Fankhu, E. n. for Phœnician, 167
Figurines, clay, early E., like S., 33
Fleet, of Menes, in Indian Ocean and Red Sea, 46, 54; in Mediterranean, 62 f.; of Sargon, 12 f.
Food offerings, votive funerary, E. as in S., 33
Foot hieroglyph, value in early E., 116 f., 118 f., 137
Funerary offerings, E. as in S., 33; immolation in 1st E. dyn. as in M., 33
Future life, belief in, E. as in S., 33, 114 f.

Gan, Gana, Gani, n. of k. "Sargon-the-Great," predyn. Pharaoh "Ka" in E. and S., 30, 77, 114; n. of his great grands., Gan II, 3rd k., 1st E. dyn. in E. and S., 30, 109, 114; Gan II, E. t. of latter, 109 f.; see Gin, Kin, "Ka" and "Khent"
Gani, n. for k. Gan, see above; Gani II., n. for Gan II, see above
Gani-Eri (or -Ri, or -Rit), 3rd k. Menes, E. dyn., 35, 77 f., 101 f., 114, 119, 200 f.; identical in n. and person with 3rd k. Manis' dyn. in M., 35 f., 78 f., 101 f.; date of, 151; E. inscriptions of, deciphered, 103 f.; genealogy of, in E., 101 f.; Indus seals of, deciphered, 200 f.; see Shar Gani-Eri
Gani Sag, t. of k. Gani-Eri, 78 f.
Genealogy of k. Menes and his ancestors discovered, viii, 35 f., 150; of Sargon's ancestors, 150 f.; of Menes' descendants, 35 f., 150-1

# INDEX

George's, St, Red Cross *re* Menes, 51
Gibraltar passed, by Menes and his fleet, 62 f. ; by Sargon's fleet, 12 f.
Gin, n. of k. Gani or "Sargon-the-Great" in E., M. and Indus Valley, 23 f., 150, 182 f. ; n. of Gani II in E. and M., 103, 201 ; see Gan, "Ka," "Khent," Kin and "Sargon"
Gin-Eri, n. of 3rd k. 1st E. dyn., 80; see Gani-Eri
Giraffes in Narmar's palette, 72
Gods, chief E., of S. and G. origin, 163 f. ; offerings of stone mace-heads to, in E. as in S., 33
Goose, solar, in E. and S., 34
Gopta, Indian n. for Egypt, 2, 4
Goth, t. of predyn. and 1st dyn. kings in E. and S., 13, 30, 44, 88 f., 103, 108, 125, 180 f., 186 f.
Gothic origin of chief E. gods, 163 f.
Goths as Aryans, x, 34 f. ; as Sumerians, 13 f., 133 f. ; as imperial rulers, 176 f.
Government, constitutional, of Menes, 52 f.
Grail, Holy, with oldest historical inscription of 1st S. k., 141, 145, 159 ; see Udu's Stone-bowl
Grave-amulets, E., as S., 33, 57, 66, 70
Graves, see Tombs
Greece *re* k. Narmar, 72
Greeks, Hellenic, as Aryan and *Non*-Mediterranean race, 35
Guni, n. for k. Gani I and Gani II, 30, 77 : see Gani
Gut-Shu, s. of Pharaoh Qa or Kia, 209 ; seal of, 209

HAM, n. for Egypt, 49 f., 167 ; sons of, t. of Phoenicians, 49, 167 ; see Kham
Ha-Manish, k., 48 f.
Hamite race, as A., x, 35, 167 f. ; as non-Mediterranean, x, 35, 167 f.
Hand, The Hidden, of E. explained by G., 166
Hari tribe, 88
Haryashwa, k., 101 ; see Uruash
Hat, t. for Khatti or Hittite, 81
Hathor, E. goddess, S. and G., 165
Hawk banners of k. Naram, 95 ; inscriptions of, deciphered, 97 f.
Hawk-race, t. of Menes, 63 f.
Hawk, Sun-, in predyn. and dyn. E., derived from S. and A., 16 f., 21 f., 34, 50 f., 52, 164 f. ; frame or cartouche of, in E. derived from S., 21
Hemi form of Hathor in S. and G., 165
Herie (or Arya-land), n. for Egypt, 167

Herodotus on E., vii
Heru, 164 f. ; see Horus
Hierakonpolis (Hawk-city) *re* k. Narmar's mace, 90
Hieroglyphs, E., derived from S., viii, 7 f., 33, 56, 61 f., 85, 113 f., 159 f., and plates II, XVIII-XXI ; alphabetic use of, 7 f., 78, 159 f. ; date of E., 160 ; neo-archaism of E., 56, 160 ; *re* Hittite, 159
Hippopotamus *re* Menes' death, 60, 65
History of predyn. and 1st dyn., E., new keys to, vii f., 1 f.
Hornet *re* Menes' death, 63 f.
Horse-sacrifice, 37
Horus, cult of S. origin, 21, 163 f. ; name of S. origin, 21, 57, 164 ; as E. k. title, 20, 21 ; in G., 165
Hyksos dyn. period exaggerated, 158

IATU, Iatur, n. for Nile and Egypt, 27 f., 48 ; also in S., 27 f.
Iau-au, n. for Nile, 64
Igigi, t. of 4th k. of 1st dyn., 77 f., 106 f., 203 ; date of, 151 ; genealogy of, 203
Ikarian Sea, 96
Ikshvāku, Sanskrit n. for E. and S. eponym *Ukusi*, 1st S. k., 21, 23, 34, 155 ; Sargon and 1st dyn. E. kings claim descent from, 21 f., 34, 155, 204 ; see Ukusi
Immolation, funerary, of slaves in 1st dyn. as at Ur, 33
Immortality, E. belief in, as S., 33, 114
Indian k. lists of Early Aryans uniquely complete, 2 f., 6 f., 144 f., 146 f. ; see King Lists
Indian translit. of S. names, 4 f., 104
Indonesian C. derived from Indo-Aryans, 169 f.
Indus Valley, S. colony, under Menes and dyn., 41 f. ; seals of S. Governors of, 41 f., 179 f. ; E. Pharos, predyn. and 1st dyn., in, 17 f., 29 f., 43 f., 82 f., 103, 125, 179 f., 184 f., 196 f., 200 f.
Inscriptions, early E., predyn. and 1st dyn., deciphered for 1st time, see Decipherments
Ionians, as Aryans and *non*-Mediterranean race, x, 168
Irrigation, E., as in S., 33
Isin, old S. king-lists, 48, 78 tab., 141 f.
Isis (Ase-t), deified queen of Osiris, of S. origin, 164 f.
Isit, n. for Isis, 163 f.
Ismailia, 38
Ivory labels of Menes deciphered, 57 f.

J, letter and sound in E. and Roman alphabets derived from S., 8
Japanese early writing *re* Indo-Aryan, 170
Jars, polished stone E., predyn. and 1st dyn. as in S., 33
Jewellery, 1st dyn. E., as in S., 33

KA, E. hieroglyph sign and value from S., 23; predynastic E. k. n., 19 f., 23 f.; his identity, ancestry and date discovered, 19 f., 23 f.; see Kad
Ka-ap, misreading of n. of k. Kad, 19
Kad, t. of Sargon as predyn. E. king, 23, 30, 51; t. of Menes, 51, 193; t. of Sargon in Indus Colony seal, 30; t. of k. Dudu of 1st E. dyn., 119 f.; t. of Phœnicians, 24; real date of, see "Sargon-the-Great," Qad
Kakau or Kaiekhos, k. 138
Kassi, A. dyn. relations with Egypt, see Amarna
Kebh, last k. 1st E. dyn., 80; see Kib and Qa
Kenkenes, k., 80, 101 f.; real date of, see Gin-Eri
Keshini, queen, 37
Khad or Khat, t. of Phœnicians, 81, 193; and see Kad
Kham or Ham, n. for Egypt, 49 f.; see Ham
Khamaesshi, n. for Egypt, 5, 31, 48 f., 103, 183 f., 202
Khamanish, k., 49; see Ha-Manish, 48 f.
Khamasi land, n. for Egypt, 48 f.
Khan(m), E. corn and wine god in G., 165
Khanu-mu ("Khnumu"), E. god in S. and G., 165
Khatti, Catti, Hatti or "Hittites" as Aryans, x, 29, 81
Kheb, n. of animal which killed Menes, 64
Khemia, n. for Egypt, 49
Khent, 3rd k. of 1st E. dyn., 30, 77 f., 80 f., 101 f.; for real n. see Gan-Eri and Gin Kunti-jit
Kheta or Khata, E. n. for Khatti or Hittite, *q.v.*
Khetm, n. of earliest known hist. predyn. k. of E., 15 f., 18; his real n. deciphered, 18; date of, 151; see Tukh
Khnumu, E. creator god, as S. and G., 165; see Khanu-mu
Khonsu, t. of Horus, as S. and G., 165
Khu or Hu, n. for Sun-Hawk in S., 21

Kia, n. of last k. of 1st E. dyn., 78; date of, 151; see Kib, Qa, Shudur-Kib
Kib, Kibbu or Kibi, n. of last k. of 1st E. dyn., 78, 80, 124 f.; identical n. in E., Indus seals and M. monuments, 78 tab.; his E. inscripts. deciphered for 1st time, 124 f.; his genealogy discovered, 78 f.; his n. written in E. mon. by identical S. signs as in M., 127 f.; see Shudur-Kib, Kia, Qa, Qebhu
Kimash, n. of Egypt, 50, 134
Kin, variant n. of k. Gin or Sargon-the-Great, 35, 77; see Gin
King-lists, Eg. of Manetho and Seti I, etc., 1, 14, 78 tab.; compared with Early Aryan and S., viii f., 2 f., 78 f.; revised reading of names of predyn. and 1st dyn., 79 f.
King-lists of Early Aryans, Indian, identical with S. and Early E., vii f., 2 f., 17 f., 77, 78 f., 101 f.; dated table of, 148 f.
King-lists of Sumerians in Kish Chronicle, 2, 10, 34, 78; in older lists, 48
King-names, E., predyn. and 1st dyn. agree with S., 11 f., 78 tab.
Kings, E., predyn. and 1st dyn. prehistory, genealogy and dates discovered, 11 f.
Kish, S. imperial city cap. in M., 35, 52, 59, 144; chronicle of, see below
Kish Chronicle of Early S. kings in agreement with E., viii f., 2, 10, 35, 36, 77, 141 f., 144 f.
Knock-Many prehist. tomb *re* (?) Menes, 68 f.
Koptos, as Menes' 1st E. cap., 54 f.; oldest E. statues at, bearing Menes' or Mins' n., 55; *re* Menes' annexation of Eg., 54 f.; *re* n. of Egypt, 2, 4; *re* Red Sea traffic, 55; and see Coptos
Kosseir, Red Sea port of Coptos, Upper Egypt, *re* Menes, 54 f.
Kshatra, Sanskrit form of Khatti or Hittite, 52
Kuni, variant n. of, n. of k. Guni or Sargon, 2; see Guni
Kunti-jit, k., 77, 80, 102 f., 200; see Khent
Kur, S. n. for Asia Minor or Syria, 169 f.
Kuru, t. of A. inhabitants of Kur, 169 f.; their preservation of Early Aryan and S. king-lists WMC., 34 f.
Kuru-Panchala, A. conjoint tribe as Syrio-Phœnicians, 169

# INDEX

LAKE MENZALEH *re* Menes' or Manj's invasion of Lower Egypt, 38
Language, Egyptian, of S. origin, viii, 8, 33, 56, 161 f.
Lapis lazuli beads, E., like S., 33; inlaying E., like S., 33; tribute, 88
Law-codes of Menes as S., 52 f.
Letter signs in E. hieroglyphs of S. origin, 9 f., 19 f., 159 f.
Libya *re* E. C., 1; n. in S., 195
Life, after-, E. belief, like S., 114 f.; key of, Cross, as S., see Ankh
Lions, land of, in E. and S., 194 f.
Lydia C. as A. and S., 169 f.

MACE-HEADS, stone, predyn. and 1st dyn., E. as in S., 33, 90
Madgal, k., 39
Magan land as Sinai peninsula, 46, 47 f., 54, 60; conquered by Menes or Manis, 45 f., 47 f., 54; by k. Narmar or Naram, 47 f., 99; Narmar's victory palette on, 99 f.; n. in M. records of Naram, 47, 99; n. in Indus seals, 44; products of, 47 f.
Mahā-Bharata, Indian epic on Menes, 2 f.
Makhi, E. fire-altar god, as S. and G., 165
Makhi-ur, E. harvest-god in S. and G., 165; see Michael, Mukla
Malayan C. not diffused from E., 171
Man, n. for Menes, 72, 78 tab.; n. for E. and S. Sun-god, 55, 72; and see Min
Mana, weight, 53
Mana-ilā, k. of the West, contemporary of Narmar, 88, 99
Manasa, t. of Menes, 51 f.
Manash form of Menes' n., 63, 78 tab., 189
Manasyu, Indian form of n. Menes or Manj, 2 f., 4 f.; its *yu* affix = "uniter," 5
Manetho's list of E. Pharaohs, 1, 14, 78 f., 81, 140 f., 154 f.; dynasties of, overlap, 154 f., 157 f.; regnal years exaggerated in, 59, 81, 158
Manis or *Manis-Tusu* as Menes, ix, 6 f., 32 f., 44 f., 58 f., 130; Aryan race of, viii f., 2 f., 34 f., 35 f., 51 f., 77; son of Sargon-the-Great, 36, 41 f.; E. inscriptions of, deciphered, 57 f., 69 f.; as governor of Indus colony, 41 f.; as governor of Elam S. colony, 38, 46; conquers Arabia to Mayan (Sinai), 45 f.; conquers Egypt *via* Red Sea, 37 f.; culture of, like Menes, 157; date of, 151, 157 f.; deported by his father, 38;
Goth, title of, 44; obelisk of, 40; overthrows k. Mush, 44; portrait of, 39; seals of, in Indus colony, 43 f.; Sun-worship of, 34, 50 f.; see Menes
Manj, k., usual E. n. for Menes, 2 f., 7 f.; in agreement with Indian lists, 2 f., 7 f.; see Manja
Manja, Indian List n. for E. Manj or "Menes" and S. Manis, 2, 7 f.
Manshu, t. of Menes, 43, 64
Manu god, 55
Manu(n)dan or Manum, k. of Magan, 60 f., 99 f.
Mar-Nar, t. of Narmar, 83
Marutu or Martu, 13, 28, 168; see Amorites
Mauretania *re* Egypt, 129, 168, 194
Mayan C. *re* E., 172 f.
Mediterranean race, ambiguous t., x, 35; Sumerians and Aryans not of, x, 34 f., 172; 1st dyn. and predyn. Pharaohs, not of, x, 34 f., 56
Mediterranean Sea, and Menes, 63 f.; and Sargon, 12 f., 66; and see Crete
Megoliths, prehistoric, in Britain, with cup-mark script as in Menes' tomb, 66
Memphis (Minnofiru) *re* Menes, 1, 157
Men, n. for Menes, 43, 44; and see Aha-Man
Mena, n. for Menes or Manj, 8 f.; in Indus seals, 44 f., 186, 188
Menes, Aryan race of, 2 f., 4 f., 6 f., 31 f., 34 f., 51 f., 56 f., 130 f., 151, 167 f., 179 f.; as Manis-Tusu, s. of Sargon, 6 f., 35, 43 f., 58 f., 63 f., 69 f., 130 f.; as Mani-Tusu in E., 58, 69; as Tussi-Mena in E., 58; as admiral, 63 f.; as governor of Elam S. colony, 38 f.; as governor of Indus colony, with seals, 41 f.; 43 f.; as M. emperor at Kish, 35; as k. Minos of Crete, ix, 65 f., 71 f., 75, 141, 193; as Phœnician, 49, 131, 166 f.; as Sun-worshipper, 34, 50 f., 61 f., 190 f.; conquers Egypt, 37 f.; constitutional government of, 53; contracts of, 53; Cross, emblem of, 40, 46, 50 f., 166; culture, date (real) of, 56, 81 f., 151, 155 f.; death, tragic, of, in Western Ocean, 60 f.; dyn. of, identical with Manis, 130 f.; established S. C. in Egypt, 6 f.; farms of, 53; fleet of, 54, 63; founds 1st E. dyn., 1; genealogy of, recovered, 1 f.; name of, proper form, 2 f.; and see Manj; t. of mother of, 4, 25; government of, 53; inscriptions, E., of, deciphered, 57 f.; land-laws of, in M., 52 f.; law-giving of, 74; money of, 53; obelisk

of, in M., 40, 52 f. ; portrait of, Pl. I, 39; reign of, 59; revolts against father, 36 f., 38 f. ; seals of, in Indus Valley, deciphered, 184 f. ; tomb of, at Abydos, a cenotaph, 61 ; tomb ebony labels, deciphered for first time, 57 f., 61 f., 188 f. ; Red Cross (St George's) of, 57, 166; unites two E. crowns, 5, 14 ; world-monarchy of, 4, 38, 40, 45 f., 63 f., 191 f.
Menzaleh Lake *re* Menes' or Manj's invasion of Lower Egypt, 38
Mer-pa-ba, k., 123
Merneit, E. goddess, 190; and see Neith
Meshannipadda, misreading for Ur, k. Pāshi-padda, 142 ; his real date, 151
Meshkalamdug, misreading for Ur, k. Pashunutu, 151 ; his real date, 151
Mesopotamian synchronism with Early Egypt discovered, 2 f.
Michael, St, invoked in 1st E. dyn., 109, 114, 119 f., 165 f. ; see Tasia
Miebidos, k., 78, 123 ; see Bidi
Min, E. n. of dual Sun-god as S., 55, 72 ; as n. of Menes, ix, 55, 72, 189 ; oldest E. statues of, at Koptos *re* Menes and Red Sea, 55
Minash form of Menes' n., 63, 78, 189
Mines, Tin in Cornwall, under predyn. k. Sargon, 13, 66 ; copper diorite in Magan, 45 f. ; silver in Arabia, 45
Minoa, 66, 72
Minoan C. derived from S. through Menes, 73 ; real date of, 75, 141, 158 ; see Crete
Minos, k. of Crete as Menes, ix, 65 f., 71 f., 75, 141, 193 ; date, real, of, 75, 141, 158
Mino-taur Bull, as k. Naram or Narmar, 72 f. ; atrocities of, in Vedas, 89
Mishir or Misir, n. for Egypt, 13, 48
Misri-Keshi, queen, 136
Mizir and Mizvaim, n. for Egypt, 13, 48
Mohenjo Daro, S. capital on Indus, in relation with 1st E. dyn., 29 ; S. seals of, with titles of " Pharaoh " and creation of Egypt, 29 f.
Money coinage diffused to East by Aryan Phœnicians, 169 ; Money of Menes, 53
Moses, basket birth-legend of, *re* predynastic k. Sargon's on Nile, 28, 31 f.
Mummification, 24, 172
Muru, n. for Maruta or Amorite, 13, 28
Mush, n. for k. Uri-Mush, 44, 49, 77, 187
Mush, n. for Mushsir or Egypt, 44
Mushrim, Menes' 2 lands of Eg., 63, 192

Mushsir or Mushsur, n. of Egpyt, 13, 48 f., 117 f., 125, 188 f., 190 f. ; as land of Menes, 63, 188 f. ; as land of Dudu, 117 f. ; as land of Shuhadur Kib, 125
Mythology, E., as S. and Gothic, 163 f.

NABODNIDUS' date for "Sargon-the-Great," 142 f., 147
Names of E. kings, predynastic and 1st dynasty, 16 f., 29 f., 78 f. ; spelling of, 29 f. ; variant forms in restoring, by Egyptologists, 16 f., 78 f. ; solar titles of kings, 21 f. ; solar titles of Early A. kings, 3 ; see Horus and Titles
Naram-Ba, variant n. for k. Naram or Narmar, 77, 84 ; see Naram-Enzu
Narām-Enzu, k., S. n. for Narmar as s. of k. Manis, 5, 35, 73 f., 76 f., 78 f., 83 f., 89 f. ; Aryan race of 35, 77, 83 f., 87 ; and see Narām Sin ; genealogy of, 35, 77 f., 83 f. ; conquest of Magan (Sinai peninsula) by, 87 f. ; date of, 142 f. ; inscriptions of, in E., deciphered, 92 f. ; inscriptions of, in Indus colony, deciphered, 88 f.,196 f. ; portraits of, 84 f. ; s. of k. Minos of Crete, 72, 84 f. ; as Minotaur, 72 f., 84 f., 86 f., 90 ; tomb of, in Egypt, 84 f.
Narām Sin, k., as Narmar, 35, 84, 86 f, 100, 109 ; see Narām Enzu
Narima land, 131
Narmar, 2nd k. of 1st E. dyn., 15, 72 f., 78 f., 83 f. ; as Narām-Enzu (or -Sin) of M., 72 f., 78 f., 83, 109 ; as Narama in E., 78, 197 ; as Ner-Sin, 109 ; as Aryan, 35, 79 f., 83 f. ; as sea-emperor, 72 ; as s. of Menes, 76 f. ; as grand-s. of "Sargon," 197 f., 199 ; as co-regent with Menes, 59 ; date (real) of, discovered, 142 ; E. inscriptions of, deciphered, 93 f. ; palette of, inscriptions of, deciphered, 90 f. ; seals of, in Indus colony, 88 f., 196 f. ; standard inscriptions of, deciphered, 94 f. ; t. as Goth, 88 f. ; t. as k. of Akkad, 88 f. ; t. as Mar-Nera and Nera, 89, 197 f. ; Sin, t. of, 35, 84 f., 109 ; atrocities of, in Crete, 72 f., 197 ; in Egypt, 89, 90 f. ; as Minotaur or Wild Bull, 72. f., 83 f., 90, 197 ; see Maru, Narām and Nera
Narmara, t. of k. Narmar in Vedas, 89
Naru, district of Egypt, 131
Neith goddess, symbol of, 190
Ner-Sin, n. of Narām-Sin, 109

INDEX 219

Nera or Nerra, S. n. for Narmar or Narām, 48, 88 f., 197
Ner-Mar or Mar-Nar, n. for k. Narmar, 83, 197
Nile, ancient n. of, as Iatu in S., 27 f.
Nile, as Nilu in S., 28; mouth or Delta, n. in S., 27 f.; Sargon's basket-birth legend on, 28
Nilu-bani, t. of k. Sargon in S., 28, 31 f.
Nippur Sun-temple, historical, S. archives, 12, 40, 45 f., 87
Nordic t., not a synonym for Aryan Race, x

OBELISK of k. Manis or Menes in M., 40, 52 f.; emblem of Ra in E., 40
Oceania C. derived from Indo-Aryans, 169 f.
Offerings, funerary, E. like S., 33
Oman or Ormuz Straits re Menes, 46
Omen literature, 12, 99
Ormuz re Menes, 46
Osiris or Asar, E. solar Father-god, 5, 164 f.; of S. origin, 163 f.; hieroglyph of, identical in E. and S., 164 f.; Kingdom of, in E. mythology in Syria, as in S. and Gothic tradition, 164 f.; see Asar and Atmu
Ousaphaidos, k., 1st dyn. n. found in E. inscription, 51, 113

PAINTING, cosmetic, of face in E. as in M., 33, 91; see Palettes
Palermo Stone, 14
Palette, Narmar's victory slate, 72, 91 f.; inscriptions of, deciphered, 93f.
Palettes, carved slate, E. or S., 33
Panag, E. form of n. Phœnician, 167
Panch, Panch-ala, as Phœnician, q.v.
Par or Bara, S. n. for Pharaoh, 4, 13, 22 f., 41 f., 45, 97, 183 f.
Parāa, E. n. for Pharaoh, 2, 4, 22; see Par
Patah (or Ptah), E. god as aboriginal father-demon Budu, Bodo, in S. and G., 165
Patala, 198
Pau, t. of 2nd last predyn. E. k., 16 f.
Perab-sen, k., 138
Persia re Menes, 40 f., 45 f., 88; and see Indus colony
Persian Gulf re Menes and dyn., 40 f., 45 f., 193; re Phœnicians, 167 f.; re Sargon, 12 f.; re Sumerians, 3, 43 f.
Pharaoh, t. in Early E., 2, 4; in Indus seals, of Menes and his dyn., 43 f., 89 f., 125, 185 f., 200, 205
Pharaohs, E., in S. Indus colony, viii, 3, 43 f.; and see above; predynastic, as S. kings, viii f., 3, 13 f., 17 f., 24

Phœnician, n., 167; A. form of n., 167 f.; E. forms of n., 167; as Hamite, 35, 49, 167 f.; Kad and Khat, t. of, 24, 29; alphabet derived from S., 159; and see Kad and Qadi
Phœnicians, as A. and S., x, 35, 131, 167 f., 172 f.; as Amorites, 168 f.; as Hamites, 35, 49, 167 f.; as Non-Mediterranean race, x, 34 f.; as Sun-worshippers, 55; as diffusers of C., 167 f.; as sailors, 167 f.; 193 f.; in Ancient Britain, in Egypt, 167 f.; in India, 101, 167 f.; in Mediterranean, 67 f, 167 f.; in Persian Gulf, 167 f.; 1st dyn. of, 167; Menes and 1st dyn. as, 49, 166; Semitic v. Aryan, 168 f.; world-conquest by, 167 f.; and see Atlantis
Phrygia, n. in E. and S., 194 f.
Pictographic writing, S., as source of E. hieroglyphs, 23 f., 159 f.
Pir, S. t. of Sargon-the-Great, 3, 48
Plough, S. and E., 33, 161
Plurality of k. titles, S. and E.
Polynesian C. derived from Indo-Aryans, 169 f.
Portraits of k. Menes or Minos, 39; of Narmar or Naram (Mino-taur), 84 f.; of Dudu, 109
Potala, 198
Potter's wheel, E. as S., 33
Pottery, painted, E. predyn. and 1st dyn. re S., 33, 73; Cretan, in 1st E. dyn., 73; Syrian, in 1st E. dyn., 56; incised decoration, E. as S., 33
Prabhu, Indian n. for Pharaoh, 2 f., 4 f.
Pra-cin-wat, predyn. k., 17, 151; as predyn. Pharaoh "Ro," 15 f.; as f. of Sargon, 15 f.; see Par Gin, Puru-Gin, Puru II and Ro
Pra-Vira, k., as Sargon-the-Great, 3 f.
Predynastic Pharaohs of Egypt, why so-called, 14; as S. and A. kings, viii, 13 f., 151; cylinder seals of S. type, 33; dates (real) of, 139 f., 151; hieroglyph writing of, S., 159 f.; Sargon and f. and grandf. as, 13 f.; see Ka, Ro, Khetm
Ptah, E. god, as aboriginal demon of S. and G., 165; see Patah
Ptolemy Philadelphus, canon of, 14, 147, 149
Pu, n. for Lower Egypt, 27, 48 f.; and see Buto
Punic, n. for Phœnician, 167
Purāna, Indian Epic, with king-lists of Early Aryans, vii, 2 f.
Puru, k., t. of Sargon's f., 4, 16 f.; in E. tomb inscriptions, 16 f.; date of, 151; see Puru-Gin

Puru II, k., 4, 17, 78 tab.
Puru-Gin, k., E. t. of Menes' grandf., 16; E. tomb inscription, 16 f.; date of, 151; see Pra-Cin-wat and Uru-ka-Gina

QA, k., last k. of 1st E. dyn., 78 tab., 80, 124 f.; E. inscriptions of, deciphered, 127 f., 205 f.; date of, 152; seals of, in Indus colony, deciphered, 125, 205 f.; see Kib, Qia, Qibi, Shudur Kib
Qa-Sen, k., 78, 80, 124 f.; see Qa
Qadi, Qadu Qeti, E. t. for Phœnician, 24; see Kad
Qebhu, k., 78, 124 f.; dialecta for Kib, *q.v.*
Qia, k., 126 f.
Qibi, k., 78, 124 f.; see Shudur Kib
Quarries, diorite, in Magan (Sinai peninsula), used by S. and E., 46 f.
Queen, tomb inscription of Sargon's, deciphered, 19 f., 24 f.

R., E. hieroglyph of S. derivation, 16
Ra, E. n. for Sun-god, derived from S., 16, 165 f. and WPOB, 242 f.; goose symbol of, as S., 34; Hawk symbol of, as S., 21 f., 34; Horus as, 20 f., 25 f.
Race and E. Civilization, 174 f.; E. 1st dyn. and predyn. as Aryan and non-Mediterranean, viii, 2 f., 7 f., 31 f., 34 f.; E. 1st dyn. and dyn. and predyn. as Goths, 30 f., 34 f., 44 f.; and see Goth; E. 1st dyn. and predyn. as Aryan Phœnicians, 24 f.; E. 1st dyn. and predyn. as Sumerians, viii f., 2 f.; E. 2nd dyn. as Aryans, 136 f.
Rameses II., k., 14
Rann-t, E. goddess in S. and Gothic, 166
Raudrāshwa, k., brother of Sargon in Egypt, 4
Rebirth, see Resurrection, 114 f.
Red Cross of St George on Menes' tomb-label, 51, 166; see Menes and Cross
Red Sea, route of Menes to Egypt, 45 f., 53 f.; route *re* Indus Colony, Persian Gulf
Regnal years, average of, 158
Religion of 1st E. dyn. as S., 163 f.; see Gods, Sun-worship, Symbols
Resef or Reshpu, E. Corn-Spirit as S. and A., 121, 165 f.; see Tasia
Reshpu, E. war-god as S., Hittite and Gothic, 121, 165 f.; and see Tashup and Tasia

Resurrection in Ancient Egypt, 114 f.
Ri or Rit, k., 102 f.; see Gan-Eri
Ro, predyn. k., real n. of, 15 f., 31; inscriptions of, deciphered, 15 f.; real date of, 151; see Bau, Baku, Puru, Puru-Gin and Uruka-Gina
Romans of A. race, x, 35
Romit, n. for Ancient Egypt in S. and G., 166
Route of Menes' annexation of Egypt, 45 f., 53 f.

SAG, t. of Sargon, 30, 180
Sagani, t. of Sargon, 184
Sagara, t. for k. Sargon-the-Great, 8, 29 f., 37, 151, 180; seals of, 29 f., 180
Sagg or Zagg, t. of 1st S. k., 72, 150; see Ukusi
Sampati, k., 123
Sargon, k., n., Semitic corruption of n. of Aryan k. Gani, Guni or Gin, 2; see Sargon-the-Great
Sargon-the-Great, k., as A. and S., 2 f., 11 f., 30 f., 87 f.; as f. of Menes, 2 f.; annexation of Egypt by, 12 f.; as predyn. Pharaoh, 13 f., 19 f., 23 f.; as Phœnician, 30 f.; basket-birth-legend of, *re* Nile, 28 f.; date of, 142 f., 151 f., 156 f.; E. inscriptions of, in S., deciphered, 13 f., 20 f., 23 f., 25 f.; father and grandf. of, predyn. Pharaohs, 15 f.; his Pharaoh t., 13, 22 f.; his Goth t., 13, 30; his Kad t., 23, 25, 30 f.; his Pharaoh t., 29 f.; his Ukus, Aryan t., 21 f.; Indus Valley conquest by, with seals, 29 f., 180 f.; queen of, and inscriptions deciphered, 19 f., 24 f.; tinland conquests of, 13, 66; tomb of, in Egypt, 13 f., 26; world-empire of, 11 f.; see k. Gani, Gin or Guni, " Ka," Kad, Sha-Gin, Sharu-Gin
"Sargon" II, t. of E. k. Gani Eri, Sargon's greatgrand-s., 109; see Gani II, Gin-Eri
Satan, E. prototype of, see Set
Scarab, beetle of E., 190
Script, see Hieroglyphs and Writing
Sea-emperor, S. title for, 197 f.
Sea-empire, of Menes, 4, 44, 63 f., 66 f., 72 f.; of Narmar, 97; of Sargon or k. Gin, 2, 12 f.; of Aryan Phœnicians, 167 f.; *re* Egypt, 167 f.
Sea-kings of early Egypt, 2, 12 f., 63 f., 66 f., 72, 97 f., 117 f.; see Dudu, Menes, Narmar and Sargon
Seal n. in Early E. as in S., 18, 33, 73

# INDEX

Seals, S. cylinder-, in E., 15 f., 20, 33, 73; of Sargon, 26; Sargon's grandf. and great-grandf., 16 f.
Seals, stamp-, or signets of E. Pharaohs in Indus Valley, 29 f., 180 f., 196 f.; of Bageri, 202; of Dudu, 203 f.; of Gani-Eri or "Khent," 200 f.; of Menes, 184 f.; of Narmar, 196 f.; of (?) Puru II, 183; of Sargon or Gin, Gani, 180 f.; of Shudur Kib or Qa, 205 f.; and see Button-seals
Sealings, E., 15, 26, 85, 103 f., 123
Seas, The Seven, 98
Second E. dyn. of A. origin, 132 f.
Semitic Phœnicians v. Aryan, 168 f.
Semty, supposed n. of S. k. of 1st E. dyn., 110; see Dudu
Sen, k., 126
Seni, n. of Menes' mother, 25
Serek, n. for E. cartouche of Babylonian origin, 21, 22
Serpent cult of prehistoric E. aborigines, 27, 163 f.
Set, E. aborig. demon, n. as in S. and G., 163 f.; -animal=wolf, 163 f.
Setui, k., see Den
Sety I, k., dyn. lists of, 14, 78 tab.; sarcophagus scenes of, interpreted by G., 14, 166
Seven Seas, The, 98
Sha-Gana or -Gani, k., father of Menes, 43, 63; and see Gana, Gani and Sha-Gin
Sha-Gin or -Gina, n. of "Sargon," 2, 10, 23; n. of Sargon's greatgrand-s. of 1st E. dyn., 101 f., 200 f.
Sha-Gunu, variant of n. of Menes' f., 43, 63; see Gunu, Sha-Gana
Sha-Kuni, Indian n. of Sargon, 2, 21, 23, 31, 33; see Kuni
Shar-gali-sharri, Semitic readings for k. Gani-Ero, q.v.
Shar-Gani (or -Guni), n. for Sargon, 43 f.; n. of his greatgrand-s., 38, 78 f., 101 f., 142; identical in E., M. and Indus Valley, 101 f.; and see Sharu-Gin in E.
Shar-Gani Eri, 35, 101 f., 104 f.; date of, 151; E. inscriptions of, deciphered, 103 f.; see Gani-Eri, k.
Shar-Gin, k., 29, 125; variant of n. Sha-Gin and Sharu-Gin, q.v.
Sharu-Gin, k., E. inscription of, deciphered, 26; Indus Valley inscription of, 30, 182
Sharum-Gin, t. of Sargon, 30, 188
Shehtu, E. wind-demon in S. and G., 166
Shenu, E. n. derived from S., 114
Shepherd, t. of Sargon and 1st dyn. E. kings, 23

Ships, of Menes' fleet, 45 f.; 54 f., 62 f., 193 f.; of Sargon's fleet, 12, 28, 36, 38; of 100 oars, 168; of Phœnicians, 193
Shudur Kib, last k. of 1st E. dyn., 77, 78 f., 80, 112 f., 205; identical in E., M. and Indus Valley, 78, 80, 124 f., 205; date of, 152; E. inscriptions of, deciphered for first time, 126 f.; his genealogy in E. inscriptions, 205 f.; Indus Valley seals deciphered, 125, 205 f.; son of, 209
Sicily re Menes, 66, 72
Signet seals, see Seals
Silver mines in Arabia in 1st E. dyn., 45 f.
Silver money of Menes, 53
Silver tribute in 1st dyn., 88
Sinai peninsula conquered by Menes, 45 f.; by Narmar, 47, 99; see Magan
Slate palettes, carved, E. as S., 33, 72, 90 f.
Snefru, k., 54
Soane Museum, sarcophagus of Sety I scenes interpreted by S. and Gothic, 166
Son of the Sun, t., 21
Sothic cycle re S. and E. chronology, 156
Spirals, of S. solar origin, 67; on Menes' tomb, 70
Standards of Narmar, inscriptions of, deciphered, 94 f.
Statues, E. and S., 33
Stone-bowls, E. as S., 33
Stone mace-heads, E. as S., 33, 90
Stone sculptures, E. and S., 33
Stone vases, polished, E. as S., 33
Stonehenge, glazed "E." beads at, 168
Sudan re 1st E. dyn., 1
Suhotra, k., 77, 126
Sumerian, culture in predyn. and 1st dyn. Egypt, 33, 55 f.; inscriptions in predyn. and 1st Egypt, 16 f., 23 f., 188 f.; language as basis of E., 7 f.; origin of E. C., 33 f.; rule over predyn. and 1st dyn. Egypt, 2 f.; sun-worship and mythology in predyn. and 1st dyn. Egypt, 163 f.; and see Sun-worship writing, source of E. hieroglyphs, 7 f., 16, 33 f.; see Writing
Sun, as Goose and Hawk in E., derived from S., 15 f., 21, 34. 50 f., 64 f., 160 f., 165 f., 190 f.; and see Hawk and Horus
Sun, Archangel, S., invoked in E., 1st dyn., 67, 109, 114, 119 f., 121, 165; and see St Michael, Tasia

Sun, Children of the, civilized by Indo-Aryans, 170 f.
Sun, Ra, t. of, derived from S., 16, 165 f.; see Ahura, Asar, Horus, Osiris, Ra
Sun, worship, E., derived from S., 12, 21 f., 33 f., 67 f., 163 f.; Aken-aten's, 162; Manis' or Menes', 21, 34, 50 f.; Sargon's, 21, 27, 50 f.; non-Semitic nature of, 12, 21 f., 163 f.
Sunset Land, S. t. for West, 12 f., 63, 191 f.; the end of the, 192
Sura, n. for sun of S. origin, 164
Susa, cap. of Elam, *re* Menes, 52
Swallow-sign, 65
Symbols, sacred, see Emblem
Synchronism of Ancient Egypt and Mesopotamia discovered, 2 f., 13 f., 77 f., 151 f.
Syria as S. *Kur*, 164; Osiris' kingdom in, as in S., 164
Syrian pottery in 1st E. dyn., 56
Syria-Phœnician land, 97, 164
Syria-Phœnicians as Indo-Aryan Kuru-Panchāla, 164, 168 f.

TA or Zer-Ta, supposed n. of 3rd k. 1st E. dyn., real n. of, see Gin-Eri, Guni or Khent
Tablets, see Clay, Ebony and Ivory
Tann or "Tannen," E. god, as S. and G., 166
Tashup, Hittite n. for E. Reshpu or Tasia, *q.v.*
Tasia, Tax or Tascio, 109, 121, 165; deified 2nd S. k. as Sun-archangel, 121; invoked by 1st dyn. E. k., as in Ancient Britain and S., 109, 114 f., 119 f., 121; see St Michael, Resef or Reshpu and Tashup
Tas-Mikal, Phœnician n. for Tasia, 121, 165
Tax, E. and S. n. for Tasia, 165
Tekhi, predyn. E. k., 18; inscription deciphered, 18; see Khetm
Terra-cotta, drain-pipes, Cretan as S., 73; and see Figurines, E.
Teshub, see Tasia
Teta, k., 81
Thinis or This, dist. in Upper Egypt *re* Menes, 14
Tianu, S. n. for Western and European lands, 96 f., 120, 127, 129, 195; see Tyana
Tidnu, 97
Tiger seal of Narmar, 89, 199
Time-reckoning of Early dyn., E. as S., 145 f.
Tin-land, Western, of Sargon as, Cornwall, 13, 66 f.

Titles, plurality of kings', E. as S., 29 f., 79, 81
Tombs, E. of S. chambered type, 33; of Menes and his dyn., 60 f.; of Sargon and his queen at Abydos, 15 f., 20 f.; inscriptions of Abydos, in S., deciphered for 1st time, 16 f., 20 f., 58 f., 63 f., 92 f., 104 f., 107 f., 113 f., 127 f.
Triad, solar, in E. myth., as in S., 163 f.
Troy or Ilos *re* "Sargon" and Menes' dyn., 119; and see Dur-Ilu
Tuke, predyn. E. k. 15 f., 17 f.; date of, 151; see Tukh
Tukh, predyn. E. k., 15 f., 17 f.; inscription deciphered, 18; date of, 151; see Khetm, Tekhi, Tukh
Tusu, t. of Manis or Menes, 8 f., 69 f.; used in Egypt for Menes, 57, 69, 70
Tyana, 97, 195; see Tianu

UAZ(T), aboriginal E., serpent-goddess in S. and G., 166
Udu, 4th S. k., 141, 150; date of, 150; inscribed stone bowl of, 141, 145, 159
Udymu, k., see Dudu, Semty, Sudyumna
Ukusi, n. of 1st S. k., 21, 23, 34, 50, 150, 159, 196, 204; date of, 150, 154; patronym of Menes and his dyn. of Sargon, 21, 23, 34, 50, 109 f.; Dudu claims descent from, 109 f.; k. Shudur Kib in Qa claims descent from, 127 f.
Unity of World's C., 175
Ur dyn. tombs as in M. *re* E. type, 33; real date of, 142, 151; immolation at, as in E. 1st dyn., 33 f.
Urani land, site of Menes' death, 63 f., 194 f.; its location, 67 f.
Uri land, S. n. for Semitic Akkad, 30, 90, 96
Uriki land, 44, 182; see Uri land
Uri-Mush, k., s. of Sargon, 35 f., 210; overthrown by Menes, 36, 44; seal of, in Indus Valley, 44, 210; see Mush
Urjayanti, fort of k. Narmara, 90
Uru-ka Gina, k., n. of Menes' grandfather, 4, 17; see Ro
Uruash Khad (or Khab), as sea-emperor founds 1st Phœnician dyn., founds Indus colony, 101
Urudu- (or Uruka-) Gina, f. of Sargon, 17, 181; inscripts. as predyn. k. in Egypt deciphered, 16 f.; see Bahu, Bauu, Par-Gin and Puru
Usaphaidos, n. of 1st dyn. k. discovered in E. inscript., 51, 113; date of, 151; see Ousaphaidos

VASES, animal and bird-form, E. as S., 33; polished stone, E. as S., 33; and see Pottery
Viper hieroglyph in E. as S., 161
Vira, t. of Menes' father, 4 f.; see Pir
Vowels, absence of, in E. explained, 7 f.; in E. as in S., 7 f.

WARRIOR, t. of Menes, ix, 3; see Aha and Tusu
Wasp or hornet causing death of Menes, 63 f., 195
Weaving in Ancient Egypt as S., 33
Weights and measures, E., in Britain, 33 f., WMC., 498
West land, the, 12 f., 96 f., 120, 129; see Tianu
Westerning of S. C. *re* Egypt, 132 f., 167 f.
Wild Bull, t. of Narmar, 72 f.
Wodan or Bodo, in E. mythology, see Patah or Ptah
Wolf-demon in E. as Set, 163 f.
Words of E. as S., viii, 8, 33, 56, 161 f.
World-conquest by, 4, 38, 40,' 45 f., 63 f., 191 f.; by Sargon, 11 f.; by Phœnicians, 167 f.
World-empire *re* diffusion of C., 167 f.; *re* unity of C., 175 f.
World-monarch, t. of Sargon, Menes and his dyn., 11 f.
Writing, E. hieroglyphs of S. origin, viii, 7 f., 16 f., 33, 56, 131 f.; see Hieroglyphs; of 1st E. dyn. in S., 16 f., 19 f., 131; S. in Egypt deciphered for first time, 16 f. 19 f.; see individual king's names; solar *v.* lunar direction of, 93

YAVAN, see Ionian
Yayati, k., 52
Year reckoning, calendar, E. as S., 146
Years, regnal of 1st E. dyn., exaggerated by Manetho, 59, 81, 157 f.; average of, 158; real duration of, 77 f., 151 f.

ZAGG, or Ukusi, first S. k., 72, 150; in E., see Ukus
Zaggisi, k. of M., defeats Menes' father, 38
Zer or Zer-Ta, supposed n. of 1st E. dyn. k., 102 f.; real n. and date of, see Gin-Eri
Zet, conjectured n. of 1st E. dyn. k., 106, 202; real n. and date of, see Bagid
Zoroastrian sun-god in E. mythology, 164 f.; n. and function of S. origin, 164 f.; see Hor-mazd and Horus.